Bc

by

John 'Hutch' Hutchinson

www.johnhutchhutchinson.co.uk

From Mum 2014 - Birthday present.

1

Bowie and Hutch

ISBN: 978-1-291-90403-1
Copyright © John 'Hutch' Hutchinson 2014

Back cover photograph by Masayoshi Sukita.
Cover design by Hayley Forrest.

Published By

LODGE BOOKS

25 South Back Lane
Bridlington
www.lodgebooks.co.uk

Contents

Introduction

Bowie & Hutch is an unusual memoir, Bowie a world superstar and Hutch a comparatively little known, semi-retired jazz guitarist living in rural East Yorkshire.

John 'Hutch' Hutchinson was Bowie's musical collaborator, sideman, accompanying musician and friend, and his story should be an essential read for Bowie fans around the world.

The pair first met in 1966 when Hutch turned up by chance at an audition to form a band with 'an up and coming new singer' called David Bowie.

An off and on musical relationship then continued for seven years, from the Marquee Club days to the fall of Ziggy Stardust in 1973.

Hutch's valuable contributions to David's music during the early years are amongst the building blocks of David Bowie's spectacular career.

Looking back with good humour and affection, Hutch is able to give his first-hand account of life on the road with David Bowie. The book also covers Bowie & Hutch's musical lives in parallel from the beginnings, through the rock and roll years and up to the present day.

John 'Hutch' Hutchinson is still playing regular gigs in York, Scarborough and The Yorkshire Wolds area.

Foreword

Since I first met him in Scarborough sometime back in the sixties John 'Hutch' Hutchinson has been entertaining and elating audiences all over the UK and Scandinavia and the Netherlands with his guitar playing and his original songs. To me Hutch's musical talent has always been amazing and I have been surprised that commercial success never came his way.

This may well be partly down to his apparent reticence to cash in on his connection with David Bowie, but Hutch has always controlled his own destiny, opting at least for a large part of his working life for a career in Oil and Gas exploration rather than be a slave to musical commercialism.

The rumour that had gone around Scarborough town in the sixties, that Hutch had been in London playing with a rising star called David Bowie, proved to be true when Hutch re-joined the singer for the Aladdin Sane world tour in 1973.

It was the early days that were important though, Bowie had obviously appreciated Hutch's talent from the start, and they shared their original musical abilities during their days together at the famous Marquee Club and later during the short lifespan of Bowie's first multi-media group 'Feathers'.

I have been involved in the music business for over thirty years and for twenty-five of those my Doctor Rock show on BBC Radio York has been a great success. When Hutch made an appearance on my show in 2013 the audience response was overwhelming and we have repeated some of that show several times.

Hutch's story of his musical life has many surprises: he was a rock star in Sweden when Benny Andersson was still just the piano player with The Hepstars and ABBA had not yet crossed his mind,

5

and Reg Dwight was just the piano player with Long John Baldry – and so on.

I would highly recommend this book to all Bowie fans and to all who wonder what it must have been like to have been there when it all happened.

Doctor Rock
BBC Radio York

aka Charles White, author of one of David Bowie's Top 100 Favourite Books: 'The Life and Times of Little Richard' 1984.

Chapter One - Out of the Sticks

It was January 1966, not many days after my 22nd birthday, when I found myself in what the street sign said was Wardour Street W1. I had spent most of the day wandering around the wild West End of swinging sixties London with only a vague idea that I should try and find a band who needed a guitarist. I was out of work, I had nowhere to live and was staying with friends, living in the big city while I decided what to do with myself.

I couldn't see anything very wild or swinging about the place on that afternoon, rather I saw it as quite a scruffy city, having spent the previous twelve months in the beautiful 'Garden City' of Gothenburg, Sweden. London was supposed to be *the* place, but I couldn't see anything special about it, the streets were even less interesting than Ralph McTell's famous song suggested, and all I had on my agenda that day was to find the famous Marquee Club.

A short distance away from the Marquee I had already found by accident the equally famous Flamingo Club – I had no thoughts of making an enquiry about that gig however, as even a Northern Boy like me knew that the Flamingo was supposed to be a West Indian venue. Of course I was wrong, it was not anything of the sort, it was simply popular with all London music fans who wanted to stay up very late and get smashed and listen to Rhythm & Blues and Ska. I had played some early imported Blue-Beat and Ska music covers (these names by the way preceded 'Reggae' – they were the same thing) with my old band The Tennesseans in Scarborough, my home town, but I couldn't see anybody taking me on in the Flamingo. A mistake perhaps, who knows, I might have joined Georgie Fame & the Blue Flames – Georgie was a long-time Flamingo Club resident – if I'd gone in and asked about a gig there.

The Tennesseans was an unintentionally misleading name for my first real band; I had taken it from the famous Gretsch guitar that I had coveted for years. I thought that a Gretsch Tennessean, if I ever could get hold of one, would make me sound like Chet Atkins. George Harrison had the same idea I think.

When I had decided that I was ready to form The Tennesseans, I realised that I should try and get the best players to join me, and somehow I managed to persuade Dave Pinkney, by far the best drummer in the area, to leave his home village band The Sherburn Panthers. Dave brought with him the Panthers' piano/vox continental player, a keyboard wizard called Derek 'Chow' Boyes. Chow was a great player, he could play piano like Jerry Lee Lewis and though I might have been the band leader and singer it was Chow who was the strongest part of our sound. Chow brought his cousin Danny Darley in to play bass (Danny by the way had been born on the same day as me – dunno why I think you might be interested in that little fact but there you are). So the three guys were all from the tiny village of Sherburn (the one near Scarborough, not the one in its 'Elmet near Leeds) and two of them had deserted The Panthers in order to join me in my new band. I was a little unpopular in the tiny village of Sherburn for a time.

In spite of our country and western band name, The Tennesseans quickly became a very well developed Rhythm & Blues outfit, and this was thanks almost entirely to the input of our frontman, our 'vocalist' Dave Kirby. He was a Londoner – actually from Maidstone in Kent I believe, but that's near enough London for us in the North. Kirby was an old hand in the R&B business who had escaped from London (we never found out who exactly was after him or what for, if anything at all) to Scarborough by way of the Star Club in Hamburg, and had brought with him a full repertoire of funky Americana previously unknown to us out in The Sticks.

It was Dave Kirby who said to me 'we don't need a rhythm guitarist man, just a three-piece is best, and you don't need no echo machine just play it straight'. So I initially formed a basic three-piece band on that basis, I played raw and twangy through a hot Watkins Dominator amp and recruited Phred (Andy) Boyes to play bass and Ricky Ware to play drums. That line-up was good and it stirred up the locals but did not last too long; Ricky had a builders business to inherit and Phred went on to bigger things with his Boyes Stores empire.

I had already learned the trick of replacing the standard wound third string (as supplied with any of the limited choice of guitar string sets in those days, Gibson or Cathedral usually) with a plain string of any gauge – a spare first or second string usually. Hey presto, instant blues guitarist.

The Star Club Hamburg repertoire that Dave Kirby brought to The Tennesseans was groundbreaking in the early sixties, but it was simply made up of a few Ray Charles blues songs, some of Ronnie Hawkins songs, and a few other powerful 'race-records' (as they were called in America) – songs like 'Bonie Maronie' and the likes of 'Twist and Shout' and 'Hippie Hippie Shake'. Many of the songs that we played were to be borrowed and reinterpreted in due course by all the Liverpool groups, many of whom had done their time in The Star Club Hamburg just as Kirby had done. Some Liverpool bands even turned the old songs into million selling hit records. The Tennesseans were playing most of The Beatles' covers repertoire before we had even heard of The Beatles.

In 1962 The Tennesseans were musically keeping abreast of or even a little ahead of the game, but we were simply living on the wrong side of the Pennines. Liverpool was cool, and Manchester was near enough, but Scarborough was in The Sticks and record company men just didn't venture too far into The Sticks in those days. If these 'A&R' men *had* ever come along to some of our regular village gigs they may not have been too impressed anyway, as the acoustics in the village halls were without exception dreadful, and not many bands managed to sound anything like good. The likes of

Kirkbymoorside Village Hall and Pickering Memorial Hall had not been designed with rock and roll bands in mind.

The Saturday night dances in these places were a social gathering alright, and it did not really matter much who was playing or what was being played. The bar would do good business and quite regularly the farmers would fight. In Malton, at the Milton Rooms, they would fight the jockeys, and at Pickering they might fight the motorcycle lads from Scarborough. Teddy Boys had not troubled the Yorkshire coast too much, and those few that still soldiered on in their drapes (jackets) and crepes (boppin' shoes) were tame enough and just wanted to jive on in peace. I remember an old Ted called 'Kate' who was a hell of a solo dancer; no girls would dare go near him. Still, as has been said before, Saturday Night was Alright for Fightin' in the villages during the early sixties, and there would even be the odd occasion when some guy would decide to take on a member of the band. I well remember one time when I had to use my Gibson SG to defend the stage from invaders at a particularly wild village hop.

In London in 1962 a tall and skinny young man called David Jones was just starting out, at first as a saxophonist and then as a singer. David's first band The Kon-rads had not had an equivalent to Dave Kirby in their line-up, and did not have the benefit of a 'hip' repertoire. Their set list, complete with instructions on 'tempo' and 'feel', consequently contained many quite conservative little numbers like 'In the Mood' (twist) and 'China Doll' (swing), as well as some standard rock and roll numbers like 'Sweet Little Sixteen' (fast). The young David Jones was inclined to make up for the band's lack of real musical credibility by attempting to at least make some improvements to their appearance. David wanted the band to dress in leather, buckskin and beads, a sort of 'Buffalo Bill Wild West Show' outfit really, and had considered adopting the full name of Colonel James (Jim) Bowie, a real-life Tennessean hero at the battle of The Alamo at the Alamo Mission near San Antonio, Texas in February and March 1836.

Incidentally David Bowie pronounces his name Bowie as the 'O' in bow tie, not 'ow!' as in owl. Jim Bowie and his Texicans would in those days have pronounced the name as Boowie – as people will in the rural Grampian region of north-east Scotland where the name originates and still exists today.

In Scarborough, coincidentally and amazingly, my band The Tennesseans were already wearing a stage outfit which did include a fringed 'buckskin' waistcoat, and even our business card logo depicted a 'Davy Crockett' coonskin hat! (I don't think that the logo was my idea, that card was not at all cool.) Davy Jones would have approved of our stage gear for sure, and he probably would have loved our classy Hamburg repertoire too. Never for one moment did I think of changing Dave Kirby's name to Davy Crockett, but on reflection perhaps I should have.

The Tennesseans had originally been called The Dave Kirby Five – it was a cool name at the time because of the national popularity of The Dave Clark Five. Our band (in my humble opinion of course) was musically streets ahead of the local competition at the time, but we had nothing very original to offer on a national scale and we were doomed to be forgotten, to the extent that some years later a local sixties anorak was to omit The Tennesseans altogether from his 'Definitive History of 60's Scarborough Bands' book. The writer's extensive research had perhaps taken him to the village of Sherburn.

I shouldn't really complain about not making it into that little Scarborough pop history book, because I made it instead into both the Hull area's sixties music pop music history – a great book by Ray Moody called 'The Sounds of The Cities - Nearly Famous' – and also into the Gothenburg, Sweden version, '60-Talspop' by Hans

Siden. Also, to my relief, I eventually made it for posterity into several of the better researched Bowie biographies. A couple of the early Bowie Story efforts had me down as 'John Hutchinson, a school friend of David's from Hull (or sometimes from Bromley) who played bass'. I was none of those things, I never played bass in my life, never lived in Hull and I never went to school with David Jones – anywhere – so it was good to see myself in the right place in the history books. The likes of Tony Visconti will have most probably omitted any mention of me in their books, because I will have been to them (just as they were to me) a peripheral character in their David Bowie stories. And anyway Visconti and I just didn't get on.

Ray Moody's comprehensive book on the sixties, Hull and the East Riding of Yorkshire bands 'The Sounds of The Cities - Nearly Famous' continues to amaze me – I pick it up sometimes, flip through the black and white photos of long gone musicians, many old friends, holding their prized Hofner guitars, and worse. I read the band histories and line-ups, and it takes me right back in time. They were great days, life was simple then – can it be like that for each generation? How can it be, there has been just one sixties, just one real musical and social revolution – so far.

These days I play now and then with the talented Keith 'Ched' Cheesman from Hull. He plays great slide guitar, harmonica, bass, you name it, but back in 1967 Ched was playing bass with his mates Mick Ronson and John Cambridge. Their band name was initially The Rats and though they changed it to Treacle for a while the name didn't stick and they changed it back to The Rats again. It was the primordial stew from which The Spiders from Mars would emerge in 1972. In the next millennium, the tribute concerts held in both Hull and London in memory of Mick Ronson featured a 'Spiders from Mars' line-up with Keith Cheesman taking Mick's part as lead guitarist. I should have been there on 12-string of course, Mick had been my friend, my tour buddy in 1973, but the organisers, with Trevor and Woody's agreement I imagine, somehow decided to leave me out of the band for the tribute gigs and I'm still puzzled, just a little hurt and angry about it – when I think about it, but more of that later.

In London as the sixties music revolution gained momentum, David Jones left the Kon-Rads behind and formed The King Bees. The new band was to feature David as a singer, not as a saxophone player, and they would play much hipper blues material. The King Bees recorded a single for Decca's 'Vocalion' label, and it was the young David Jones' first studio-recorded vocal performance. When their record 'Liza Jane' failed to make the charts, David quit the semi-pro King Bees and ambitiously 'turned pro' by joining a full-time professional band from Maidstone who were both ambitious and musically progressive. Formerly called The Jazz Gentlemen and then Band Seven, the band had recently adopted the name The Mannish Boys and now they played rhythm and blues.

The Mannish Boys' new young singer, still calling himself David Jones, soon persuaded the band to adopt the new rebellious long hairstyle, and to try to show a more aggressive attitude in both their musical performance and style of dress. By the year 1964 David Jones, aka Bowie, had already developed a flair for redesigning his bands. And he could sing The Blues.

One of the budding local singers in Scarborough at that same time, an ambitious youngster who would come along to the Tennesseans' gigs to watch and learn from the older boys, was a young Scarborough Evening News typesetter apprentice called Alan Palmer. Alan was quite soon to grow into a great singer and songwriter, and a world famous rock star, having along the way changed his name to Robert Palmer. Robert was Alan's middle name. I never got used to his name change; to me he will always be Alan.

Alan (Robert) and I never really got on too well somehow and I think it was perhaps a clash of young musicians' egos. It certainly was not about singing, he had some voice – that was no contest. Maybe I had put him down in some way in the early days; I was a few years older after all, and as arrogant as any young local guitar hero can be. Anyway there was something competitive going on between us and it was never resolved.

Palmer did call at my flat in London once or twice in the later sixties, to visit one of the girls I shared with. I even introduced him to my friend David Bowie at a Feathers gig, several years before either of them achieved any fame.

After Alan became Robert, some time later in the mid-seventies, he was to take his opportunity to give me the cold shoulder when I visited Island Records at their Basin Street studios. I had been invited there for the day to do some demos for an American A&R man who thought he had found some potential in me and in my songs. Palmer was by chance on that same day mixing something for his next hit album in the label's Mobile Studio which was parked in their back yard. My A&R guy wanted to show me the impressive vehicle, unaware that it was occupied, so Alan (Robert) and I were both surprised to meet up like that. I was pleased to see an old chum from Scarborough (I had been impressed with his rapid musical development and his success) but Palmer apparently was not really interested in what I was doing. He was busy, a little offhand I thought, and so we left him to it. I must have really pissed him off in old days; maybe I had been an arrogant twat too – back in the sixties.

Alan (Robert) Palmer always said in the press that he was from Barnsley – I guess he was probably born there, but believe me Palmer was from Scarborough. Funny that, David Bowie does the same thing, says he's 'from Brixton'. In my eyes David is from Bromley. For the record, Palmer was still a teenage apprentice at the Scarborough Evening News when he joined his first decent band, which was called The Mandrakes. Not any kind of Silver or Paddle Steamer sort of Mandrakes as I have seen reported generally, they were just The Mandrakes from Scarborough.

The Mandrakes were a good band, in tune with the times, and were enthusiastically managed by Ron Gillette, a suntanned old rogue who mystified everybody with his talent for pulling young girls (known in those days as birds, chicks, talent – and fanny) and we were permanently amazed that his very pleasant, smiling little wife either didn't seem to notice – or mind at all. Anyway Ron brought the band along nicely and they displaced all others, including my band The Tennesseans, to become the 'Top Band in Scarborough'. Certainly their lead guitarist Rich Hodgson was playing some good stuff, albeit in what I would have described as a more 'widdley' style than my own 'rootsy or bluesy', perhaps more old-fashioned style. At that time Rich, who coincidently had been in the same class at Junior School in Driffield as a young Mick (Woody) Woodmansey (they called him 'Pecker' at school by the way, as the old boys still do in Driffield to this day), was a friend and early admirer of a lad from Hull, a young guitarist called Mick Ronson who played with a band called The Rats. Mick turned out to be a more 'widdley' player than me too – just as Rich and all the younger guys seemed to be – and very much louder; Jimi Hendrix was making waves and big Marshall 4x12 Stacks had suddenly appeared on stages up and down the country. The young Mick Ronson was a very talented and stylish guitarist and he played a bit like Jeff Beck – his own all-time hero.

The Yorkshire and David Bowie connections and coincidences never cease to amaze me; I was certainly the first Yorkshire man to join David, but the Spiders from Mars (they were actually the

Spiders from East Yorkshire) were grown from a separate branch of coincidence, and John Cambridge was the important connecting link.

Drummer John Cambridge from Beverley, a pleasant and historical market town between Scarborough and Hull, joined Alan (Robert) Palmer's first band The Mandrakes in 1970, replacing their original drummer Mick Stephenson for a time. John Cambridge had, like myself and thousands of other young hopeful musicians past and present, left his home town and joined a London band that was playing full-time, committed to their art and determined to succeed. John's first London band had been Junior's Eyes, having joined them in 1969 after receiving an invitation from guitarist Mick Wayne who had been with John in the much-hyped Hull band The Hullaballoos. Junior's Eyes were a talented bunch and by means of that old black magic they call coincidence (Tony Visconti had happened to be producing both David Bowie and Junior's Eyes at the same time and so had decided to put them together) had become a studio backing band for a still very much unknown David Bowie.

In the summer of 1970, John Cambridge had been strolling through central London when he bumped into Rich Hodgson (you know, the lead guitarist from the Mandrakes) in the street. It might be hard to believe, but back in those days somehow we northerners would accidentally meet each other in The Smoke, in the street or on the Tube, on almost every trip to the big city. Of course we would always be around the music shops and the West End agencies – and nowhere else much in the big city. John explained to Rich that he was fed up, having just been fired from a band called David Bowie & The Hype, possibly for making the band laugh too much and for not taking life seriously enough. The real reason for replacing John Cambridge with Woody Woodmansey will have been known only to David Bowie, Tony Visconti and Mick Ronson, but as Visconti was planning to leave the band anyway, it is most likely that Trevor

Bolder (bass) and Woody Woodmansey (drums) just came as a package to replace John Cambridge. Rich invited John to join The Mandrakes back in Scarborough, as their drummer had just quit the band, and John accepted the gig on the spot.

Whilst he had been drumming in London, firstly with Junior's Eyes and then with The Hype, John Cambridge had become another good Yorkshire pal of David Bowie's (John would be 'best man' at David and Angie's wedding ceremony) and he has remained so – though like myself, John is a friend at a distance. I think they have spoken on the phone and exchanged the odd email – it's a bit like my own 'email' kind of friendship with David these days. There was a time when it was said that Coco Schwab (a very nice lady who I knew on the 1973 tours) was acting as a no-bother filter and that David was unreachable by anybody not currently involved with his business. Those days appear to have gone now thank goodness, and these days we do at least stay in touch by means of an email now and then. I do have to remember not to pester David mind you, as we are many years and miles apart now and there are constraints that lifestyle and fame impose upon old friends of stars like David Bowie.

Leaving David Bowie and The Hype would have been a big disappointment for John Cambridge, no matter if he had to quit, or was kicked out. I've been there myself with David, I quit twice and was fired once, but there's little difference between quitting and being fired in band reshuffles. Johnny is a great drummer, so maybe he did make the band laugh too much. Johnny is a joker – I know he made David laugh.

John once told me the story of the time David's old car had been in urgent need of repair and John had persuaded him that driving north to a friendly and inexpensive mechanic in Hull would save a lot of money. The repairs took a couple of days and while they waited John entertained David Bowie with northern hospitality, taking the soon-to-be biggest rock star in the world to play darts and dominoes at John's local Working Men's Club, drinking several pints, then eating fish and chips as they staggered home. You couldn't make this stuff up!

John Cambridge has certainly been better at keeping in touch with David than I have – John attended David's 50th birthday celebration in New York; you could say that he was our Yorkshire Representative at the glitzy do.

It's not easy staying in touch, or staying friends, with a busy rock star and I lost touch with David for several years. Even when we happened to be in the same city I couldn't get to see him – when David was known to be recording in Copenhagen, Denmark in October 2003, I was by coincidence also in the city to play a small acoustic venue (I was on my way to Gothenburg in Sweden to play several more gigs) and I tried in vain to contact him. Again, more later.

Where was I? Oh yes, The Mandrakes and their famous ex-vocalist. Alan (Robert) Palmer had developed a distinctive vocal style based on his attempts to sound like Paul Rodgers (Paul incidentally is originally from Middlesbrough, just up the road from Scarborough) who was the singer with the band Free at the time. The young Alan Palmer was 'spotted' whilst doing a support gig with The Mandrakes somewhere out of town, and was persuaded to 'go professional' with The Alan Bown Set, a full-time travelling band from the south of England somewhere. Near enough to London anyway.

The process of 'going pro' would not have been easy for young Alan, he will have had to convince his middle class mum and dad that his new job had better prospects than his old job as a typesetter at the Scarborough Evening News. They knew he was throwing away his pension, so I don't know how he managed it.

Bandleader Alan Bown was soon to notice that his audiences had the impression that The Alan Bown Set's new singer, 'Alan' Palmer was the leader of *his* band. So came about the transformation from Alan Palmer to Robert Palmer, and somehow it was an altogether more suitable moniker for the very-soon-to-be, very cool and be-suited vocalist.

An excellent up and coming band called Vinegar Joe was to be the next transfer move for Robert Palmer. With a young Elkie Brooks alongside and a fine band of some of England's finest behind him, Robert Palmer quickly made a name for himself and went on to a great career, with a worldwide following. He made many great hit records and he sadly died far too young. He smoked and drank too much maybe, but then many of us did, so it's just the life lottery that decides who will last a little longer. I really hope that Alan (Robert) had been happy with his success and his life, and that it had been great while it lasted. It must have been. It seemed to me in later years that Alan (Robert) had become very intense in his performances when I'd see him on TV, and those tweed suits looked too hot to sing rock and roll in.

As you can imagine, Robert Palmer had made Scarborough proud. They don't get many local heroes up there, Charles Lawton was born there (his brother ran a pub in the town), and Alan Aykbourne moved to live there so he could try out his plays in a quiet and culturally empty backwater. That's it? Oh no, there was until recently one more: the late charity worker and Disk Jockey Sir Jimmy Saville kept an apartment on the South Cliff for many years. I walked up the main street with the posthumously disgraced Sir Jimmy once in the old days as we would often use the same coffee bar, the 'Tisane'.

Another of The Mandrakes was rhythm guitarist Alan Black, and Alan was from the even more faded but relatively unspoilt resort of Bridlington, a few miles south of Scarborough. The town has a great big south beach (you can see Bridlington Bay from space) and I walk my dog there these days, but Bridlington too seems to have been perilously short of talented residents over the years. Mind you, David Hockney, certainly one of the biggest selling artists on the planet, can for at least part of the year be found living very quietly in the little town. One day in 2013 I was driving through the woods up on Woldgate when I encountered a slowly reversing 4x4 with a film crew aboard, filming the road. This would turn out to be a contribution to David's Tate exhibition of his paintings of the Yorkshire Wolds.

Hockney's series of Wolds paintings are all over this area in the form of postcards; I actually like them a lot though generally my taste in paintings is not at all 'modern' – I like proper pictures. My dog Ruby the Labradoodle and I walk past Hockney's sister's house a couple of times each week as we go to and from the big beach, and I have spotted Hockney a couple of times in the driveway, coffee cup in hand. David is perfectly hidden in Bridlington as many people, locals and summer visitors alike, don't even know who David Hockney is, never mind recognise and bother him. I consult the tide tables and drive down to Bridlington's South Beach when the tide is out; Ruby likes to run after a rubber ball and socialise with the other beach dogs, and to sit in the sea when she gets too hot.

The Mandrakes were proud of Robert Palmer's fame; the other band members had each made a life outside of music with careers, wives, kids and mortgages, but they were all talented musicians and had joined and formed other bands, mostly around the Scarborough area, playing with friends, as we do. I had more or less kept in touch with guitarist Rich Hodgson, and it was he who phoned me in the spring of 2004 to ask me if I wanted to play support to The Mandrakes at their forthcoming 'Tribute to Robert Palmer' gig at the Scarborough Spa Ballroom on Friday 9th April 2004.

I had been flattered and delighted to accept the gig and the proceeds were to go to a heart charity. I took my mates John Precious (electric upright bass) and Dave Cook (drums) with me, and we set up on the very same stage I had seen Johnny Kidd & the Pirates rock and roll on more than forty years earlier. The old ballroom had not changed a bit and was packed with Scarborough people from all of our yesterdays. Some remembered more than others about 'the old days' as is the way with reunions, but we were all united in our determination to pay tribute to the memory of our home town's own Alan (Robert) Palmer.

My trio played our jazzy-bluesy originals set to a pretty good reception from an audience who mostly sat on the ballroom floor, not dancing. Most Scarborough folk had not seen me play for many years so it was good to get a home town, up to date reaction to my music. I enjoyed the gig and the opportunity to pay my own tribute. I think I mumbled something in the way of tribute into the microphone, very conscious that Alan's mum and dad were in the audience and also that Alan and I had not been particularly good friends. We may have had some small-town rivalry going, or maybe it was something else, but we had certainly known each other well enough. Who knows maybe I was not alone in admiring Alan's (Robert's) creative talent as a performer whilst not finding him easy to get along with.

Never mind that my music might have been a little out of place at the event, as we were after all only a support to the main event The Mandrakes, who had advertised that Alan's younger brother Mark Palmer would be making an appearance onstage with them. I hadn't known that Alan had a brother, but apparently the lad was an officer in the RAF and he played bass in a band of guys from his squadron.

I had come offstage at the Spa gig in that hot and elated state that only players know about and was slumped backstage joking with

Pete Liley, another talented Mandrake guitarist (they had a lot of guitarists, a rotating squad it seemed) when a ghost walked in and all my hairs stood on end. The ghost of Alan Palmer had walked into the Spa Ballroom dressing room dressed in the tweed suit and was smiling at me. It said, "Hi Hutch nice set, good to see you again," and I almost fainted. It was Alan's RAF bass-playing brother Mark Palmer of course, and it turned out that he used to come and watch me play almost every week, years before when he was still at school, and I had spoken to him in the past several times without knowing that he was Alan's brother. Mark is a lovely guy, and I never let on that I thought I'd seen his brother's ghost. He might have wondered why I was so pale though.

Mark went on-stage and sang several of his brother's hits, electrifying the Spa Ballroom that night. The audience saw what I had just seen in the dressing room, the return of Alan Robert Palmer for one night only, an unforgettable spine-tingling experience. I then saw the gig for what it really was, a wake for Alan Robert Palmer, a reminder of his talent, and I was as sad and filled with respect and regrets as any other one of the Scarborians privileged to have been there that evening.

The Tennesseans made several forays into The South during the early sixties. Having been recommended to the organisers by a northern fan, on the 19th June 1964 we played at the annual Queens College (Oxford University) Ball. The Tennesseans played in the Taberdars Room and we supported top 'trad' jazzers The Humphrey Littleton Band (who played in The Hall) and folk singer Alex Campbell, who was with us in the smaller room. Alex was splendidly drunk; he was dressed in torn jeans with a piece of rope for a belt, and he carried a whisky bottle in his back pocket. There was a marquee in the Fellows Garden and The Frank Rogers Band and The All Star Steel Band were in there. The Queens College Ball was, in those days, a 'Toffs Do'.

On this trip we somehow (a four-piece band and guitars) all fitted into Cyril Pinkney's little black car. Cyril was Dave's dad, and he would have been one of the few people in our world who had a car. As with other trips to London, after the gig we would try to sleep for a couple of hours in the Arrivals Lounge at Heathrow Airport and have a cup of something hot before returning north.

During one of these (always exciting) trips to The South, and some years before I ever contemplated living in London, The Tennesseans had by chance met and accosted the newly famous and instantly recognisable Jagger and Richards in The Giaconda, the famous West End café. In those early days the young 'Stones' didn't seem to mind the intrusion at all ('yea sure sit down and join us man') and anyway we were just like them weren't we? No different except that we were not famous yet. Actually we never would be famous – that was the difference.

Mick and Keith were nice people, it was early days and their fame had not affected them at all. Mick had drawled at me with his very large mouth, in his broadest Sarf-Landon accent, "Tennesseans? Is it a country band then? Me and Keith are really into Country man." In fact I had already noticed that, I mean just listen to 'It's All Over Now' and several of their other songs. The Stones just never made the fatal mistake of *calling* it 'Country Music' and somehow all of their music, which was very original but certainly not really 'Blues', was passed off and accepted by the general public, jazz, blues and rock fans alike, as 'R&B'.

I was to meet up with ol' rubber-lips again on at least two future occasions when I was with David Bowie, but I don't think Jagger noticed or remembered me, and I didn't go over and say, "Hello again Mick." That certainly would not have been cool. Somehow I was never comfortable talking to rock stars anyway, unless there was something genuine, I mean about music, to talk about, and I didn't think Keith Richards really had anything I didn't already have myself, I mean in terms of musical 'chops' – that is guitar riffs, licks and tricks of the trade, ability, enthusiasm, talent. I did encounter several other top rockers in those early days however, and some of these experiences proved to be of more practical use to me in terms of my musical development.

Over the years in the early sixties The Tennesseans were to play lots of support gigs with top rock 'n' roll acts including Little Richard at the Spa Royal Hall in Harrogate. Some say now that Jimi Hendrix was in Little Richard's band for that tour and was there that evening, but I'm pretty sure he was not – the musicians were good, but unremarkable in the company of Little Richard. I do remember that some of the band wore 'Mrs Mop' headscarves off-stage in the afternoon, and a couple of them were very 'camp'. If Jimi was there he had been keeping very quiet. Little Richard was not quiet; he was very loud and very gay. He watched my band from the wings and we had our photo taken with The Man.

The Tennesseans also supported The Kinks among others, and very memorably the amazing Gene Vincent, who to our disbelief appeared to have purchased and taken some kind of dangerous drugs backstage at Bridlington Spa. Gene was visited by two very heavy looking gentlemen who went into the star's dressing room and locked the door for a good fifteen minutes. Gene came out stoned, we could not smell marijuana, and one of his backing musicians confirmed our suspicions to me.

I don't know whether or not David Bowie's apprenticeship included a support gig with Gene Vincent, but I know that David did see him perform, and did take considerable inspiration from the sinister character that Gene portrayed on-stage. Even Ziggy Stardust was to adopt Gene Vincent's on-stage crouch, one leg stretched out behind him whilst he sang to the ceiling, eyes rolling.

Some years later, in February of 1971, the formative year for his Ziggy Stardust character and a couple of years before his ascent to stardom, David Bowie was to meet Gene Vincent in Los Angeles. The pair got along very well by all accounts, there was mutual respect and it is reported that David persuaded Gene to record 'Hang On To Yourself', a song of appropriate sentiment for Gene Vincent who was by then in rapid decline. Years of drink, drugs and rock and roll had taken their toll on Gene, and before he could book into a studio and record David's song, Gene Vincent died in October 1971, aged just thirty-six.

Gene Vincent had been a gothic black-leathered rebel with a sweetly intense vocal delivery, he always had a great band and was a much greater influence on the developing British 1960's rock and roll bands than he has ever really been given credit for. I think the remaining Beatles might agree with me, certainly John Lennon would have. Gene Vincent, Eddie Cochran, Chuck Berry and Little Richard, who else would you need? Okay, Jerry Lee Lewis maybe. Oh and the Everly Brothers for those harmonies. It is sad to say, but although Elvis was so really great when he started out, he quite soon became soft and irrelevant to us, the UK Rock and Roll Pioneers.

The Tennesseans also played alongside the legendary Johnny Kidd & the Pirates at Scarborough Spa. There were lots of 'Spa' venues around in those days – to us it simply meant any large cold ballroom on the seafront in the north-east, as it was in Scarborough. In Harrogate their inland Spa was naturally a posh theatre with central heating, and there is no seafront up there on the edge of the Yorkshire Dales. At the time, there, alive and in person, loud and proud, eye-patched in pirate boots, Johnny Kidd & the Pirates impressed me even more than all of the Americans. These guys were English, they were just like us and they had found their own way to do it right.

No band in England travelled more miles and played more gigs around the United Kingdom than Johnny Kidd and his band.

Certainly the young David Bowie, still Davy Jones at the time, played support gigs with Johnny and his Pirates. David became slightly piratical himself a little later, and thigh-length leather boots made an appearance, as for that matter did an eyepatch (albeit a sort of pink polka dot one), both certainly down to Johnny Kidd's influence. At different ends of the country, during the early sixties, David Bowie and I both admired Johnny Kidd and his excellent three-piece backing band The Pirates. They were the best band in the land.

Dave Kirby knew Johnny Kidd of course, as they were both 'from London' or near enough, so our band hung out with his band backstage at gigs and met for a cup of coffee at sound checks and the like. And so it was that I found my first and possibly only guitar hero in Mick Green, The Pirates' extraordinary lead guitarist.

I should mention that in those early days only three rock guitarists really impressed me. One was Mick Green, the other two were Brian Griffiths who played in The Big Three in Liverpool (a band with a great drummer who shared my name – in years to come we somehow were to become morphed together on Wikipedia for a while), and the wonderful Cliff Ballard in the USA who briefly made records with Gene Vincent and the Blue Caps.

Brian Griffiths played some horrible European (possibly German) made guitar, probably through some home-made amplifier and speaker, whilst Cliff Ballard played a solid-body Gretsch with thumb and fingerpicks through a Fender amp. Both sounded great.

Mick was the one I got to watch at close quarters though, and to meet and talk to, and he played an old-style Les Paul Junior through a 4x10 Fender Bassman that made the most amazing sound. I would ask Mick all the naive questions that young musicians want to ask older musicians, including I remember well, "Who pays your wages?" and "What will you do when you get too old to play Rock 'n' Roll? Will you get a pension?" I also asked him about guitars and amps and most importantly, "How do you *do* that?" There was a lot of country as well as blues in Mick's style, but it was also LOUD (30 watts at least…) and it was the best thing I had ever heard. I stood and watched, listened and learned from Mick Green, and the Tennesseans were eventually to become a three-piece band like the Pirates. That was after we had taken a democratic vote and kicked Dave Kirby out of the band.

Dave Kirby was a great singer but he always leaned towards excess and mayhem, and it eventually became very tiresome. Years later I was told that Dave had settled down in Gothenburg, Sweden for a while, and was making records with Bob Landers, one of The Spotniks. I found an album of theirs, called appropriately 'Bob and Dave', in a record shop sale bin in Gothenburg, but for some strange reason I did not buy it. A Swedish version of The Shadows (or The Ventures in the USA), The Spotnicks were an otherwise unremarkable Swedish, three guitars and drums, instrumental group who dressed in apparently genuine spacesuits – complete with full-face helmets. They were however, as they still are to this day, legendary in Sweden, and in 2009 I was to meet up with the old boys at their 50th Anniversary 'Spot-fest' in Gothenburg – a twang-band bonanza of '3 guitars and drums', instrumentals-only bands from all over Europe and Scandinavia. It was a time warp; I must have heard 'Sleepwalk' a dozen times. It was great.

I don't know for sure why Dave Kirby had gone to Sweden as it happened some years after I had moved on from Gothenburg, and so our paths did not cross, but it probably had something to do with the blonde girls. Sweden simply did not have ugly girls. During my visit to the 'Spot-fest' gig in Gothenburg in 2009, Mrs Bob Landers, wife of one of the original Spotnicks, told me that Dave Kirby had gone to Copenhagen – and that he never came back. She told me that Dave had sadly passed away in Copenhagen.

In Liverpool a band called The Beatles, and in Kent a band called David Jones and the Lower Third were among many others who supported, watched and admired Johnny Kidd & the Pirates. David Bowie (formerly David Jones) finally adopted the name Bowie because there were just too many singers around called Davy Jones, including one famous one in The Monkees, and also a rather less famous (though no less talented), black Davy who had sung with The Apaches in Gothenburg, just a year or so before I joined them there.

David Bowie and I were to meet up with the late Johnny Kidd (Johnny's real name by the way was Fred Heath) and his Pirates yet again when we made our David Bowie and The Buzz Tour of Scotland in 1966. Tour of Scotland! What a laugh, more of that later.

Two other legendary performers, both also now sadly deceased and both of them called Alex, were also to appear and reappear during my early rock and roll years. In 1965 Alexis Corner was booked to play at a Scarborough sixties smoothies nightspot called The Candlelight Club, which was located above an amusement arcade down near the south bay beach on Bland's Cliff. 'The Tennesseans - Top Beat Group' had been booked as the support band as we would play a regular weekend slot at the club as a kind of novelty addition to the Geoff Laycock Quartet, a wonderfully authentic sounding George Shearing Quartet style band. We were there to play some of the 'beat group' hits of the day and to help pull The Candlelight Club out of the smooth jazz era and into the swingin' sixties.

Geoff Laycock, the owner of The Candlelight, was a brilliant piano player with a great little band which included guitarist Kenny Richards. Kenny had been with The John Barry Seven (John Barry Prendergast was another local lad, from the nearby city of York) until he was displaced by session guitarist Vic Flick – a guy who could sight read music scores backwards and so was a more cost effective musician, considering that The John Barry Seven mostly worked in the recording studio. Besides, Kenny had a day job, in insurance I think, and of course he knew that only one of the Seven was going to make any money anyway.

Kenny Rich (his stage name) generously took the time to play me some of his jazz guitarist albums, and to show me how he played those funny jazz chords. I went out and bought one of the albums, 'Jazz Winds from a New Direction', which was a classic album by country session guitarist Hank Garland, and which featured a precociously talented seventeen-year-old called Gary Burton on vibraphone. Not long after recording 'Jazz Winds' Hank was to have a bad car crash and tragically he was never to be the same again; he never made another album and the jazz world lost one of it's greatest guitarists, just as he was getting started.

I also bought, as Kenny Rich directed, 'The Book'. As many older guitar players will understand, this (in my case at least) means a book called 'Mickey Baker's Jazz Guitar'. This amazing publication apparently first came out in 1955, and incredibly may still be available from Music Sales Limited in Frith Street, London W1. It should be called the Guitarist's Bible, but okay I will call it The Book. If anyone were ever able to read, finish and perfect all of the exercises in that book, they are all but guaranteed fame and fortune as a jazz guitarist.

John McLaughlin *must* have finished The Book. It is also obvious to me that the wonderful Albert Lee also bought The Book, but I would guess that he only made it halfway through; maybe he got bored and anyway Albert had learned all he needed in order to become a spectacular country-style guitarist. Halfway through is more than I managed myself, but The Book is still on my bookshelf and I have not finished with it yet.

The Geoff Laycock Quartet was, strangely I thought, a five-piece. The band was comprised of pianist Geoff, guitarist Kenny, singer

Dennis Williamson, drummer Ken Golder and the bass player whose name I forget now (though he became quite famous when he went to jail for an attempted football pools scam involving his day job at the Post Office). They were all (with the possible exception of the bass player) excellent role models for a young rock band. They were good players, had quick brains, dark humour, drank a lot, stayed up late and screwed around.

It was a magic night in 1965 at The Candlelight Club on Bland's Cliff in Scarborough and The Alexis Corner Band that night was a trio which included a bass player called 'Binky' and the renowned drummer Hughie Flint. Alexis's playing made me realise that you don't have to be a technically gifted player to be a powerful guitarist and entertainer. Alexis played with an intensity that cried out for more technique with which to execute his ideas, but we all got the point he was making anyway.

Alexis was a really nice guy and I was to meet him again in the late seventies in The Silius Club in Kristiansand, Norway. Jim Hornsby (a superb country-style guitarist from Newcastle and one of the funniest men I know) and I were doing five, forty-five minute sets upstairs in the bar – an 8pm till 2am, seven nights a week for a month sort of bar gig. Alexis Korner, this time with the ubiquitous Colin Hodgekinson on bass and 'Various Slapping Sounds', was in town for one night only, to play the proper students' gig downstairs.

I told Colin that I had seen him play regularly with the wonderful jazz trio Back Door up on the North Yorkshire Moors at The Lion pub at Blakey Ridge, and I told Alexis that we had met at The Candlelight Club more than ten years previously. Alexis said, "Oh yeah, I was with Binky and Hughie, you guys were wearing suede Davy Crockett waistcoats and Roy Hudd came in that night." As I said, Alexis was a nice guy, with some memory.

Jim and I arranged to meet up with Alexis and Colin later that night after finishing our gig at 2am, and only after wandering around Kristiansand for more than an hour, looking for the 'party' address they had given us, did we give up and go home to bed. It was a shame, and I never saw Alexis again.

The Tennesseans' encounter with the other Alex was at Bridlington Spa in the early sixties, when we played support to The Alex Harvey Soul Band. Alex was sensational even then, though he was much smaller and quieter in those days. He had an all-star band with him, including Hughie Flint again, and when Alex told me he couldn't always afford those guys, I offered him a gig with us anytime he wanted (a joke maybe, but genuine too – why not?)

I was to meet Alex again in 1973 during my Ziggy Stardust days at a 'Sensational Alex Harvey Band' gig at Earl's Court, where they supported Slade in their heyday. Mick Ronson and I, accompanied by two stunning model-type girls, attended the gig in some style, having blagged two free tickets from Mel Bush, the promoter of simultaneous Bowie and Slade tours.

I can't for the life of me remember how it came about, but Mick and I were dating the model-type girls who were two of a trio of flat mates, each of whom apparently worked at a different, though somehow progressive, level of involvement in the West End Skin Trade (not the leather industry as such by the way). My model-girl was the youngest of the trio and she told me that she worked as an 'exotic dancer'. Mick's girl was a stripper-cum-lap-dancer you could say, and the oldest girl in the trio at their flat was making specialist movies and lots of money.

After the gig we all trooped backstage, and whilst Mick and the others mixed with the other liggers (including Jagger and Richards again), I went and reminded Alex about our gig at Bridlington Spa, and we joked about the offer to join The Tennesseans. Alex Harvey was a nice guy and a great performer too.

Many years later my eldest son Christian told me that his best mate at college in London had a dad called Alex Harvey, a Scottish rock singer who had died, did I know of him? I spoke to Alex's widow on the phone a couple of times in those days and she sounded very nice too. How many times can we say 'it's a small world' eh?

The first half-decade of the sixties had been great fun, music was the way to go, and whether or not it was a proper job or a career with prospects or not, I was hooked and I had to go with it. The Dave Kirby Five, The Tennesseans, and both my musical and engineering apprenticeships were all over. No more engineering for me, I would go to Paris and learn to play jazz. Or maybe I'd go to Sweden first with Bjorn Roswald and just catch a train to Paris later.

Bowie and Hutch

Hutch & Chow at the Condor Club © Brian Cooke

The Tenneseans (Mk1) © Brian Cooke

Chow, Hutch, Little Richard, Danny & Dave

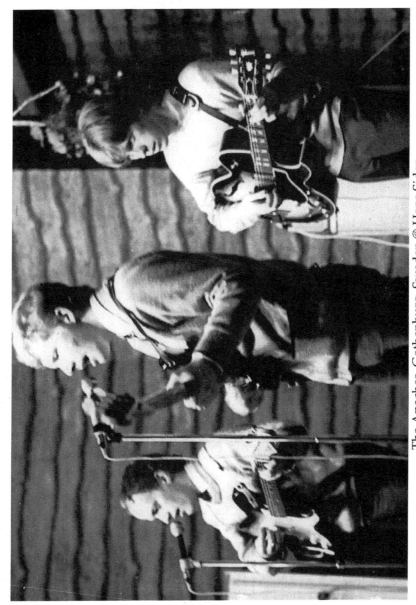

The Apaches, Gothenburg, Sweden © Hans Siden

Chapter Two - Aha, Gothenburg

The Marquee Club looked closed, as I might have expected it to be on a weekday afternoon, but I pushed the door open and went into the darkened entrance corridor where a man in a suit and spectacles was fiddling about at the cash desk. The suited man (his name turned out to be Jack Barrie and he was the manager of the legendary place) told me very politely that they were closed, but I asked anyway if he knew of anyone who needed a guitarist. Jack said yes he did and gave me a phone number, together with the advice that I should not delay in calling the number as auditions were to be held on the coming Saturday morning – on the famous Marquee stage.

Thanking the manager for his help, I went out, found a phone box (no mobiles in those days young reader) and asked the Operator to please connect me with 'Ravensbourne 6489' or something very like that. I pressed button 'A' (older folks remember that – or press button 'B' and get your money back!) and the friendly voice of Spike Palmer introduced himself as Road Manager for 'David Bowie' – a singer, said Spike, with a potential hit record and lots of club and tour dates pending, and who was putting together a new backing group.

I realized that I had in fact spotted this new singer before; the inside back page of the *New Musical Express* had for some months carried a 'band available' advert, with a photo of David in cross-legged pose, for 'David Jones and the Lower Third' (he has always crossed his legs for photos hasn't he?) So this David Bowie had recently changed his name, well that was fine, there were certainly too many Davy Jones's around. I think the advert had been running for several weeks – lots of London bands did that in order to get gigs, and even my heroes Johnny Kidd & the Pirates ran a regular advertisement. The ads were usually just a band name and a phone number but it was a good idea, in those days it was the easiest way for bookers out in The Sticks to get in touch with a band – and it avoided paying any agency commission.

Spike told me I should please be back at The Marquee on the coming Saturday at 10.30am with my guitar, and not to worry that I did not have an amplifier, there would be a 'back line' on stage. I didn't have a guitar amplifier with me in London because I was travelling light, in fact all I had in the world was my guitar, a suitcase and my girlfriend, all three having been with me on my recent adventure in Gothenburg.

I had gone to Sweden a year earlier and in Gothenburg (it was a little known Scandinavian city back in those days and in 1965 many Yorkshire folk that I spoke to didn't even know their Sweden from their Switzerland) I had quickly attained the status of minor local pop music celebrity by means of being the only English rock guitarist in town. I was in fact the first young English guitarist to become resident in Gothenburg, and by lucky chance it had been my destiny to join a ready-made local band that had lost their lead guitarist. In addition to my guitar, suitcase and girlfriend I also carried with me a canny repertoire of Bob Dylan songs – as well as all the blues stuff.

I had taken the ferry to Gothenburg as a foot passenger, with suitcase and guitar in hand, at the insistence of Bjorn Roswald, a Swedish friend who had persuaded me that once I had got myself 'off the rock', that is off the island we all called England (we never talked about 'Britain' or 'the UK' in those days), I could catch a train to anywhere, including to Paris which was my intended destination in order to become a jazz guitarist. I would have taken on anything, any journey, in order to escape the life, for life, of a draughtsman in Scarborough, the Faded Queen of the Yorkshire Coast.

I had become bored with everything about Scarborough and with The Tennesseans. We could play our repertoire backwards, blindfolded. We had been together too long, as with a worn out marriage. The other two members of the band at that stage were Roy Piper, the bass player who has remained a lifelong friend, and Dave Pinkney the drummer. Strangely I didn't see Dave Pinkney again (we had been good pals too, we had started out together) until thirty years later, when The Tennesseans played a Millennium Day charity reunion gig at the Scarborough Spa Theatre (as opposed to the Spa Ballroom). We turned up without rehearsal as Dave had been too busy, and despite the thirty years and more since we had been on stage together, I just wrote a short set list of blues stuff, counted in, 'Memphis Tennessee - one two three four', and we were off again; we didn't miss a beat or forget a chord. Okay I might have missed a few verses out. Sadly we saw just a dozen or so old 'fans' turn up to celebrate the new Millennium with us. It was Rich Hodgson, my old mate and Mandrakes guitarist, who had dreamed that gig up, and it had seemed like a great idea to me too, at the time. It was a disappointment, a reminder that times do change, that people move on and that the glory days are over. We can still look back and enjoy the memories though, can't we?

Roy and Dave were, and still are of course, both very talented musicians, but both had more commitments in their lives in Scarborough than I did at that time, and they were never going to leave the town anyway. I was able to ease my conscience about leaving them when I persuaded Paul Downing to leave The Tycoons behind in Hull, move out of that city and out to the seaside to take my place in the band. Paul is a talented upside-down lefty (just as Jimi Hendrix was) and he played a Gibson 335 very well indeed. Paul was said to be the best guitarist in Hull, and he may well have been the best guitarist in the East Yorkshire area at that time. Certainly the young Mick Ronson used to go and watch Paul play. The thing about upside-down lefties is that you can't figure out what they are up to and it sounds even better for that.

Paul Downing was ambitious too and eventually he became restless just like me, and was later to emigrate to California where he played with The Grassroots and The Standells, both very successful west coast bands in the sixties, playing support gigs to The Doors, The Rolling Stones and the like. Paul also played with Scott McKenzie who had a big hit with 'San Francisco (Be Sure to Wear Flowers in Your Hair)' and in more recent times, as well as making revival tours with The Standells, he played as a 'dep' (a stand-in on lead guitar) with Herman's Hermits on tour in the USA and with surviving members of The Crickets (Buddy Holly's band) together with Maria-Elena Holly, Buddy's widow.

Paul Downing's mark III trio version of The Tennesseans was in due course to follow me to Gothenburg, just as Dave Kirby was to do a little later, and the band's brief visit is still fondly remembered there by old rock fans I have met in recent times in that city.

I had felt for some time that I was missing out on something more exciting than life in Scarborough, and that I had to go in search of whatever it might be. I eventually came to realize that this was just part of my character, for many years I had the feeling that I really ought to be somewhere else. These days, thankfully, that feeling has gone away. Most of the time anyway.

Bjorn Roswald was a regular visitor to Scarborough, every summer he brought his tape recorder with him from Gothenburg in order to record for the folks back home the Scarborough 'Beat Groups' playing live in the pubs and halls in the area. Bjorn eventually was to marry a local Scarborough girl, and naturally opened a successful Swedish Clogs business in the town before deciding to devote himself to the rehabilitation of alcoholics. Bjorn opened a retreat called The Ark, and he is successful to this day in his worthy pursuit.

I had decided that at the end of that long summer in 1964 I would go to Paris and play my guitar there. And learn about jazz perhaps. I had also previously considered but then rejected a suggestion by Dave, a young, long-haired, double bass player (from Wolverhampton I think) that we go to Birmingham (or was it Coventry, anyway The Midlands somewhere), and form a rock and roll band together. Dave was currently playing his first ever summer season on double bass (as opposed to bass guitar, on which instrument he was already brilliant) with the resident band at The Scarborough Spa. I think they were called the Robert Anthony Band – or something very similar. Dave and I had jammed together on The Tennesseans' pub gig at The Cricketers Arms, located just over the road from the cricket ground in Scarborough, and we got along very well, both musically and personally. The bass player's name was Dave Holland and it turned out that young Dave liked jazz too, and when the summer ended and I decided to go to Sweden, Dave went to college to study music in London. He did okay; just a few years later Dave Holland joined Miles Davis in New York and went on to be the number one jazz bass player in the USA and one of the major stars of the jazz world.

Dave Holland and I were to come very close to crossing paths again in 1973 when he was gigging with Stan Getz in Chicago and I was touring America with Ziggy Stardust and the Spiders from Mars – but more of that story later.

I had picked Paris at random, I thought they must have jazz in all the cafés, but I had no game plan, so when Bjorn Roswald suggested that we could have a look at Sweden en route to Paris, I agreed that we should travel across the North Sea together. I thought at least I'd be 'off the rock' and then all I would need was a train ticket to get to Paris when I was ready.

The Roswald's family apartment in Gothenburg was to be a little overcrowded until I found my own place. I did however grab the opportunity to take some interesting (though possibly fruitless) classical guitar lessons with Bjorn's father who was a well respected teacher and player in the city. My problem with those 'lessons' was that I had been playing by ear for too long – I would as instructed 'read' a phrase from a sheet of music but then I would naturally commit it to memory. When asked to play just part of the phrase, starting in the middle somewhere, I was found out. It was too late for me to go straight.

I had been officially informed by the Utlandings-Policen (that is the Foreign Police – in the hotel kitchens they called them the Gestapo) that washing-up was the only kind of work permitted to newly arrived Utlanders (foreigners) like myself. The Gestapo gave me my washer-up's work permit and I quickly found work at Hotel Opalen, quite a posh place which is located almost in the centre of Gothenburg. My workmates were a happy bunch of Spaniards, two of whom were medical school graduates looking for their opportunity to make a life for themselves in wealthy and socialist Sweden, rather than stay in Franco's desperately poor and fascist Spain. They had made their escape in order to avoid compulsory national service in Franco's army.

Given that the Swedes had a very successful brand of socialism in those days it came as a surprise to me that their immigration department were a bit funny about letting people in. My new Spanish pals had done very well to get a foot in the door; the Gestapo must have given them a hard time too. Times change, and these days many of the Swedes that I know believe that their immigration rules have been far too slack over recent years, and that they may have a potential problem with the disenfranchised immigrant minorities in their country. I hope that they don't, Sweden is a wonderful country and it should not change too much.

I did learn a bit of Spanish on the job at Hotel Opalen in 1965, which has proven quite useful over the years, and we did have a laugh in the kitchen – even though it was mostly very boring and very hard work for not very much money. Still it was a start, I had to eat and pay rent.

Following several more quite scary interviews, the 'Foreign Police' eventually issued me a new work permit which enabled me to move a couple of rungs up the employment ladder, to leave my dishwashing career behind and go to work at the 'Levin' guitar factory in Gothenburg – it was a job that had been lined up for me by Bjorn Roswald's father. As a highly respected guitarist and teacher in the city, of course the senior Mr Roswald knew the senior Mr Levin personally. My new job was on the assembly benches for fairly inexpensive 'student model' guitars where I would fit the machine-heads (tuners), bridge saddle, nut and scratch-plate. Just behind me sat the man who put on the strings, tuned them up and 'tested' the guitars for playability and sound. This lucky man's name was Kalle-Andreas and he was great fun. Kalle, just like the rest of the factory apart from the one sales guy and the younger Mr Levin, spoke no English, so I quickly learned quite a lot of Swedish. There was a lot of playing going on, they had a mandolin band that sometimes struck up at lunchtimes, and it was a happy place to work.

The one time the Levin factory was an unhappy place was the day we returned from our summer break. The pretty blonde girl from the workshop downstairs was not at her workbench, because during the holiday she had killed herself. I never learned why she did it; suicide was apparently more common in Sweden than in England and the explanation, the given reason if there was one, was lost in translation. That tragedy has stayed with me ever since.

Through my job at the factory I soon heard that a Gothenburg band called The Apaches wanted to talk to me about maybe deputising for their lead guitarist who had to go and do his compulsory Swedish national service. This kind of military conscription was a concept that I was familiar with, having missed it by only a couple of years myself in England. I hit it off straight away with the band's leader, Jan-Ake Ahlkvist (always known as 'Lillen', meaning Little 'un) and I agreed to join the band on the understanding that I would play some solo gigs too, and that we would share both lead guitar and lead vocal duties between us. Jan-Ake was very much the band leader however; he held the spirit of the band and had very definite ideas about what to play and how it should be played. He was in fact a cousin of Kalle-Andreas, my pal at the Levin factory, though nobody explained that to me at the time. Maybe my Swedish was not that good after all, but in any case I only learned of the family link some thirty years later when Jan-Ake and Gothenburg and I had a grand reunion concert.

The Apaches were my second band in a row with a quite inappropriate name, as they too played Rhythm and Blues, or real Rock and Roll, which were the same thing in the sixties. It's funny, both names are misappropriated these days and reapplied to other music sub-sections or genres – another word that gets a lot of abuse.

The Apaches' bass player Hans Hagstrom (we called him Hasse) was a particularly strong musician and the band rocked with a great intensity, a groove that was something of a surprise to me. I had the natural arrogance that English rock and roll musicians seem to carry around the world with them, even these days, and I thought that only the English and the Americans could play Rock music. I was young and I was English and these Scandinavians were just beginning to learn to play Rock and Roll. I was dead wrong, they were learning very fast.

Jan-Ake told me that they had been working recently with a singer from London called Davy Jones. No it was not that one, or the Monkees one from Manchester, this one had been a black American Davy Jones. Neither I nor Jan-Ake had yet heard anything of a young Davy Jones from Bromley who was working his way round the gigs and learning his trade in London. Nobody had heard much of that one yet.

My initial contribution to the young Swedish rock and roll scene in general, and to The Apaches in particular, was to sort out the lyrics to some of the songs they had imported. I couldn't help but notice immediately that the bands were all singing mostly nonsense that was supposed to be English, and that the audiences didn't seem to notice or mind anyway (things don't change do they). The lyrics on the old Chuck Berry or Little Richard records were often quite unintelligible to most people in the UK, and they were even more so to the Swedes, so they just made up sort-of-words that sounded similar to the English song lyrics but were in fact gobbledegook. 'Murble murble voovy. Comma rotten bail, commalong a see me, in a rotten jail, Bop - Too much Monkey Business, Too much Monkey Business…' – you get the picture.

There were just a handful of young English or American people around in Sweden in 1965. The streets and avenues of Gothenburg were green and spacious and quite empty by today's standards, so when I happened to bump into Hank Marvin and Bruce Welch in the street on the day that The Shadows were to play at the Liseberg Concerthal in Gothenburg, it was quite natural that they should stop and have a chat when they heard my accent. The famous Geordies seemed quite pleased with my Swedish band's name – 'Apache' was their first big hit after all. They also told me that they liked Rhythm and Blues. Of course I had been a fan of the Shadows, especially Hank Marvin – every young guitarist in the UK had been. Funnily enough, ten years later I was to find myself living in a street next to the one in the west end of Newcastle where Hank had been born and had lived as a boy.

Other UK acts passed through Gothenburg, including The Honeycombs who were having breakfast one morning whilst I performed my early shift, washing-up duties at the Hotel Opalen.

One of the Spanish guys said, "Quick come see – pop stars," and we peeped at them through the round window in the kitchen to restaurant door. You know, the window that is supposed to stop those spectacular collisions between waiters running backwards in opposite directions through swinging doors whilst carrying silver trays full of jugs and plates full of steaming food, but they still happen every week.

One night Donovan came to one of my solo club gigs in Gothenburg. He was starring that evening at one of the big gigs, maybe at the big outdoor leisure park, Liseberg, or at Ulevie the football stadium, and quite possibly he came down to my little gig to check me out as I was being feted in the local papers as 'Sweden's Donovan'. This was due entirely to my use of a harmonica harness and my handful of Bob Dylan songs. I would have been happier with 'Sweden's Bob Dylan' and didn't really like the comparison with the comparatively camp Donovan and I'm afraid I said so into the microphone for Donovan's benefit (just my youthful arrogance again I'm afraid). I don't know if he heard me or not, but Donovan didn't stay very long.

The club where Donovan and I almost met was called Villan (The Villa) and it was located in the surviving part of a burned-out old building on a prime site near Liseberg amusement park. There was no bar and it was generally the pre-cannabis era, in Sweden anyway, so the local kids would drink plenty of alcohol before arriving at the club. The local bands had perfected an ingenious and more or less foolproof system of mixing any available liquor (quite often it was the powerful local home-distilled variety – you couldn't call it Vodka) with Coca Cola and carrying the distinctive bottle around with them at all times at the venues.

Some of the other Gothenburg bands were very good and there were some outstanding players, like piano player Goran 'Sam' Samuelsson, guitarist Bengan Karlsson and powerful drummer

Claes 'Frostis' Pettersson, to name but three that spring to mind. One band was more popular than all the rest, they were The Tages and they were certainly the Swedish Beatles, albeit on a purely Swedish scale. They were not the best players, not actually the best band in town, but they possessed the vital energy and charisma and had become the biggest pop stars in Scandinavia. The Tages did go to London to make a record and even anglicized their names for the promo – my pal Goran became Gordon, Anders became Andy – in an attempt to seem to be more like English guys for 'The Market'. I couldn't see the point in that.

I heard that their lead singer Tommy Blom had years later become a prominent Scientologist in Sweden, and I couldn't see the likelihood or the point in that either. The story could be wrong, although over the years I have known some great musicians, including the likes of Mike Garson, Ziggy Stardust's wonderful piano player, who have seen some point in L. Ron Hubbard's ingenious quasi-religious invention. I do know for certain though that Tommy Blom became a successful Swedish Radio DJ and presenter, because he told me so when we met again, after a gap of thirty-nine years, at the 'Cue Club Reunion Gala' held in Gothenburg in 2005.

In the sixties The Cue Club had been one of the best gigs to play in Gothenburg, and The Apaches had many great nights there. The club's young owner was Styrbjorn Colliander, a really nice guy who brought many UK and US rock acts over to Sweden to appear in Gothenburg. Some bands played at the club, and some played on Styrbjorn's various promotions at much bigger venues in the city, like Lorensbergs Cirkus or Liseberg. Among the bands that Styrbjorn brought to Sweden during the sixties were The Spencer Davis Group, The Hollies, Cream, The Who, John Mayall and the Bluesbreakers and The Jimi Hendrix Experience. Styrbjorn Colliander did so much for Gothenburg's musical life, for the city's cultural development, that he should have had a knighthood, or whatever equivalent they might have in Sweden. The reality was a tragically different story. On Sunday 1st February 1976 Styrbjorn had occasion to refuse entry to The Cue Club to a drunk called Gustavus Adolphus. It happens all the time; every weekend at every gig around the western world, guys who have drunk too much have to be turned away at the door, and I know that Styrbjorn would have been polite as well as firm in his decision on that evening. This time however, the percentages came up with a psychopathic drunk and Adolphus went home, then returned to the club with a loaded firearm and shot Styrbjorn Colliander at point-blank range. The man murdered Styrbjorn in cold blood at the door of The Cue Club because he had been refused entry. I had been out of touch with Sweden since 1966 and I knew nothing of this tragedy until the Cue Club Gala was arranged, in Styrbjorn Colliander's memory, in 2005.

My old mate Jan-Ake had been a good friend of Styrbjorn's and he was one of the committee who organised the Gala. Jan-Ake and I were back in touch after thirty-nine years, and I was invited to play with The Apaches again at the grand reunion. It was fabulous, I met up again with many great players and friends from the sixties, and it was as if only a couple of months had passed since the old days. Reunions can be like that – if you are very lucky. I met a group of guys and their wives at the Gala who had attracted my attention by waving a poster at me while I was playing on the stage. The poster seemed to say 'Hutch' on it, but when I came off-stage and saw the poster it was in fact advertising a forthcoming gig by 'The Hutches'.

These guys had been young kids when I had played in 1965 in their home town of Kungsbacka, a nice little place a few miles south of Gothenburg. They told me they had sneaked into the gig while The Apaches had been sound-checking and they heard this English guitarist called 'Hutch' playing. They told me that I was the first one of my kind that they had heard, and they were impressed, so they had named their band after me! The guys were now all middle-aged pillars of society in their area, they were a managing director, a lawyer and the like, but The Hutches were still gigging occasionally and they had been playing gigs for more than thirty years around the Kungsbacka area. What knocked me out even more was the discovery that to this day they all ride Harley Davidsons in a motorcycle group that carries my name too! On their leathers they wear a badge in green and gold that says: 'The Hutches Rock and Ride'. If I had never, ever, returned to Sweden I would never have known that I had sort of given birth to a band name many years before. They were like my unknown Swedish love child... Fantastic.

The Hep Stars were another band around the Gothenburg scene in the sixties; they were good players although they did sing a lot of the gobbledegook song lyrics. We played the same venues and we supported them from time to time. The Hep Stars' leader was their piano player, an unassuming young guy by the name of Benny Andersson. A few years later Benny was to form another kind of band, a vocal pop quartet who had decided to call themselves by all of the band's christian name initials – ABBA. They sold a few records around the world.

I made two records myself whilst in Sweden, both of them were singles on the Platina record label. One was with The Apaches where I sang the B-side 'Walk on By' (the Burt Bacharach song) in my best Bob Dylan voice, and the other one as 'Hutch' (the Swedish Donovan) which featured two Bob Dylan songs, 'It ain't me babe' and 'She belongs to me'. I had been asked by the record company to record 'Hide your love away' by Lennon & McCartney, and I had agreed to that, but I changed my mind in the studio because I knew I could sing the Dylan songs better – my Dylan voice was better than my 'folky' Lennon impersonation. Nobody seemed to mind, so Bob Dylan got the royalties – I must have done wonders for Bob's bank balance over there.

The people at the Levin Guitar Factory had been very good to me (I still had my day job there), they had given me the time off work to go to Stockholm and also the loan of a big Levin 12-string guitar to record with. The Apaches and I had driven all the way to Stockholm to record as there were not yet any proper studios in Gothenburg. All four tracks were put down more or less live, in the same day, and any minor faults (like Jan-Ake's slightly out of time tambourine on one of my tracks – for which Jan was still apologizing in 2005) were shrugged off. I was told later that both singles were said to have become 'hits' in Sweden. I never saw any money though, and I believe it was a pretend thing, based on a 'juke box jury' sort of radio show, as they had so few shops selling rock or pop records, or people to buy them, in those days in Sweden.

The recording trip was the only time I went to Stockholm, we just had no contacts for gigs there, and it was a very long way to drive. I was told that I had an equivalent in that city though, they said, 'Another English guitarist, or he might be an American, is living here, just like you, playing solo and singing with a Swedish band'. This guy was known as 'Boz' in Stockholm (just as I was known as 'Hutch' in Gothenburg) and I saw posters around the south of Sweden with his name on them. I never got to see this 'Boz', our gigs just never coincided, but thirty years later I found out that he had in fact been an American, and that he had returned to the USA and within just a few years had become a world famous recording star. He was Boz Scaggs.

I loved the Swedes and their beautiful garden city of Gothenburg. Their music scene was vibrant, I had learned enough of their language to get by, and I had even taken to wearing clogs and eating fresh yoghurt for breakfast. It may be hard to believe these days, but neither clogs nor yoghurt were in common supply in England in 1965 – not in my part of England anyway. I might well have happily stayed in Sweden forever, but as Christmas approached I did become a little homesick for England and I decided that I should at least go home to see my parents.

I certainly intended to return to Gothenburg; The Apaches had plenty of gigs in the book, and they included a gig in the rock and roll city of Hamburg as part of a tour of Germany. Of course in the back of my mind I knew that Swinging Sixties London was really the place to be for any rock and roll musician, so maybe I'd visit our capital city on the way back to Sweden in the New Year, just to have look.

1966 was almost here, and it was going to be an eventful year.

Chapter Three - An Audition With David Bowie

I turned up as instructed at The Marquee on Saturday at 10.30am with my guitar, dressed in my best outfit comprised of a natural suede leather 'battledress' jacket, matching suede jeans and blue clogs. Now these clothes were more or less standard issue in Gothenburg, but I quickly realised that I had inadvertently moved well ahead in the fashion stakes in London, in fact I think the gear probably got me the gig.

Walking into The Marquee Club was in itself a real buzz for me. I had grown up reading the *Melody Maker* in the days when they liked to write mostly about jazz. Ronnie Scott's was of course the number one jazz gig, but The Marquee was in the picture too. We had nothing like them in the provinces, and I envied the Londoners for that, they could get to see the best of the visiting Americans at close quarters. In the provinces we had to make do with the odd album and with photos and gig reviews in the *Melody Maker*. We might as well have been living in another country; London's West End had a sleazy but somehow glamorous night life with enough scary gangsters and dodgy politicians to rival New York, and it was the home of jazz – at least on this side of the Atlantic. To a young musician living in The Sticks in 1966, London and its jazz clubs were well out of reach.

Then things began to change, as the *Melody Maker* began to increase its coverage of a minority sport called 'The Blues'. It had always been around, we had learned to play the riffs from John Lee Hooker and Howlin' Wolf's records, but now The Blues becoming the thing, something to write about, and people in the UK were buying the music. American blues artistes were coming over now that the Musicians Union had given up on its work permit embargo, and British blues bands were playing the London gigs, often backing the Americans on tour over here. The top London gig, that once had been a jazz gig but was now the place to listen to The Blues and all its popular-music variations, was The Marquee Club.

My first impression was that The Marquee Club was much smaller than I had expected, and it was very dark, apart from the stage where I could see that a band was getting ready to do their audition. Spike Palmer came over to me and introduced himself. Spike was an enthusiastic, capable and experienced roadie, having previously worked for The Rolling Stones, and I took to him immediately. He pointed out 'David Bowie' to me; David was talking to a prim chap in a very tight suit – apparently he was David's manager and his name was Ralph Horton.

The band on stage were ready and they started their audition as Spike gave me my instructions, "When it's your turn up there, just play some Rhythm and Blues licks."

As I listened to Spike a group of people walked into the club, one of them carrying a guitar case. Spike told me that this guy was the guitarist from Van Morrison's original Irish band Them and that he had come to audition for David. I decided that I would have no chance in company like this, but as I was here with a Telecaster round my neck I thought I had better give it my best shot, and anyway get it over with. I had hardly noticed what the auditioning band had done or that they had finished their short set. I took to the stage alone and, feeling not a little strange, did as Spike had instructed. I played a bit, and then a voice from the darkness shouted, "Play some Bo Diddley."

My 'Bo Diddley' was pretty good as I had been doing it for some time with Dave Kirby, and with The Apaches in Sweden, but without bass and drums I thought it sounded a bit weak in the empty Marquee Club. My R&B licks had seemed even more exposed in the otherwise silent club so I was relieved to hear another shout from the darkness, between riffs: "Okay, that's fine, thank you."

I left the stage and put my Telecaster in its case and it was to my amazement that Spike walked over, with his grin on full, and told me, "David says you're in." Spike also said that David and his manager were considering the band that had preceded me, and would I consider joining the ready-made band if they agreed? I said that I would, so Spike went off to consult the band. They apparently said 'no thanks' to the suggestion and were told that in that case 'thanks for coming and good afternoon'. I was even more amazed at this turn of events and when I asked why the famous Them guitarist was not auditioning I was told, "David wants you in." I had to settle for a permanent state of gobsmacked for the rest of that day. It was not until years later that I was told that it was Jimmy Page who played the great guitar licks on the early Them records.

Spike took me over and introduced me to David, and to Ralph Horton. I liked David right away, his enthusiasm was infectious and he was obviously experienced in the hard world of Rock and Roll in London. This was what I had come for, no more Mickey Mouse provincial stuff for me, I had it made – I was in a London band, maybe even heading for the big time.

I wasn't so sure about Ralph Horton and I felt he wasn't sure about me, so I decided that David must have dug his heels in a bit in choosing me for his new band. I felt better about Ralph when Spike told me he had previously managed The Moody Blues. This was to turn out to be an exaggeration, as Ralph had been a roadie, or to be fairer maybe, a 'Road Manager' or even 'Tour Manager' for the Moodies, who after all commanded much respect in those days before Denny Laine left and they became corny. And very rich.

I knew that to survive in the rock and roll business I would have to continue to be tolerant of the apparently standard requirement that managers be 'queer' – as homosexuality was called in those days. Ralph was.

Back in Scarborough, The Tennesseans had been managed by the fragrant Peter Pitts, the proprietor of an established and capable Entertainments Agency in the town. This relationship had been an education and though I had become used to Peter's mannerisms and orientation I remained constantly irritated by the general stereotype of 'The Puff'. Or as it turned out, 'The Poof' – we didn't know how to spell it, none of those slang, common usage, real words were ever in the newspapers in those days. The Larry Parnes School of Starmakers had been the model for some time, ever since Larry's creation of the Fury, Wilde, Power and Gentle kind of pop star had run its course, and it was accepted that the involvement of this kind of queer Svengali character was as necessary to success in the pop music business as were Gibson guitars and Fender amplifiers.

My reservations about Ralph Horton had more to do with his uptight manner and uptight trousers, and his overuse of stinky hair lacquer, than with his fairly obvious sexual orientation. I did hope though that David Bowie was not required to take any part in that sort of funny business – I know it sounds ridiculous these days but we Northern Boys had all heard the rumour that Paul McCartney was obliged to service Brian Epstein in some way. We didn't really believe it.

Homophobia was firmly established in 1960's northern England, regardless of swingin' London, and homosexuality might as well have still been illegal in those days. It had taken me some years to figure out that 'Poofs' came in several varieties and I didn't need to concern myself with all the detail of who does what, with what, and to whom. This approach was to prove invaluable during my rock and roll years and in particular with regard to my relationship with the world famous sexpot David Bowie.

I was told that rehearsals would have to start that very week as several prestige gigs were coming up, not least the first gig of a Marquee Club residency which was to be called 'The Bowie

Showboat'. The new Bowie band was needed quite urgently, but it turned out that David, Ralph and Spike had already decided upon a drummer they had seen during the audition morning session, and they just had to choose a bass guitarist during that afternoon in order to call it a band.

As we chatted during a break in the audition, David Bowie told me that he would have liked to include a Hammond organist in his new band (Georgie Fame, Graham Bond and many others were using them) but none had come to the audition and there wasn't a spare Hammond player to be found in the whole of London. I immediately thought of Chow, my old mate from The Tennesseans, so I told David that I knew a Hammond player who lived in the small village of Sherburn near Scarborough in North Yorkshire, who might well by now be sick enough of his day job as a steel erector for Wards of Sherburn, and who just might jump at the chance of joining a sure thing in The Smoke.

Derek 'Chow' Boyes had started playing rock and roll piano in the Jerry Lee Lewis style at a very young age and had already had several years experience playing the village hall dances for the Teddy Boy generation with The Sherburn Panthers and The Tennesseans. Chow had graduated to a Vox Continental electronic organ in order to play 'Telstar' and the like, but also as a means of avoiding the old pianos that the village hall cleaning ladies lovingly polished but could not tune.

Chow had joined the original line-up of The Dave Kirby Five with me, before the band changed its name to The Tennesseans then kicked Kirby out and eventually became a three-piece. In due course Chow formed his own band and called it Chow's Men and they played the East Yorkshire coastal area successfully for several years. Upon joining the Kirby band Chow had made the bold move of buying a Hammond B3 Organ and a Leslie rotating-speaker cabinet on 'the never-never' or 'on tick'. These were the names for hire purchase and it was new to all of us – it was a risky commitment for any young musician but it was the only way we could get the instrument that we needed. We all bought our guitars and amps 'on tick'; nobody's parents handed out money for guitars in the 1960s. Parents did not in those days dream that their kids could one day possibly become rich rock stars, and parents in those days did not have any money to spare for trivial pursuits anyway.

A Hammond B3 Organ had to be 'split' so that it was transportable. This meant it was sawn horizontally in half, an alarming procedure on such an expensive piece of equipment. The result was that any band that wanted to have an organist had, including the rotating Leslie speaker so essential to the 'Jimmy Smith' sound, three very large, very heavy and highly polished pieces of instrument to carry around and set up – before they even started on the PA system and back-line guitar amps. We were to heave Chow's shiny furniture in and out of vans and up and down city hall and town ballroom staircases all over Great Britain, and at all hours of the night and morning. What a sound though.

David said, "Let's call him." Chow lived at home with his mum who didn't have a phone – not that unusual amongst the working classes in the sixties remember, my mum and dad didn't have one either – so we decided on a Telegram. Younger folks please just Google it or ask your granddad.

In due course Chow responded with a phone call to Ralph and David, he accepted their promises of fame and fortune and somehow transported himself and his split Hammond B3 and Leslie speaker by train to London, via Kings Cross, to Ralph's flat at 79 Warwick Square in Victoria, not too far from where I had found a barely affordable bedsit. That is, a bit of kitchen, a bed, a TV and some things to sit on, all in one little room. I learnt that a bass player and a drummer had been selected and we would start rehearsals immediately at the flat which Ralph shared with an entertainments agent called Kenny Bell. I also learnt that the new band would be called 'David Bowie and The Buzz'.

The Buzz had become necessary when Ralph decided he had to fire David's long-time friends, his former backing band The Lower Third. They had been a talented and powerful three-piece band and had, David told me, been developing in parallel with Pete Townsend's model for The Who – in terms of 'open' chords, use of feedback and 'attitude' if not actual guitar smashing. That must have been Pete's own idea.

I think the Jones-to-Bowie transformation came along around the same time as the dismissal of The Lower Third, possibly as part of a grand plan to 'go solo'. Another variant of this story has it that The Lower Third quit because they were broke and due to starve to death. I can believe this version of events, I have my own experiences to go on, and it was Ralph who told us that they were sacked of course. In any event, if your Svengali says sack your mates, you sack your mates.

It was great to have Chow with us, he was a small piece of Yorkshire which helped me a lot personally, and his powerful Hammond B3 compensated for what seemed to me to be an otherwise fairly bland sounding little band. I had after all just come out of The Apaches in Gothenburg, and those guys had rocked hard and loud.

It might well have appeared to any observer that The Buzz had been hand picked with two main criteria (apart from being able to play) in the minds of David Bowie and Ralph Horton. Firstly the musician must not be too good looking or 'trendy' (with the possible exception in my case because of my Swedish clothes and clogs, not in spite of them) and secondly he must be prepared to adopt a nickname – that is if he did not already have one.

These thoughts crossed my mind when I walked into Ralph's basement flat and David introduced me to John 'Ego' Eager, the drummer who looked like a department manager at Harrods, and was possibly to eventually become one – I must remember to ask Kevin Cann about that, he knows where everybody ended up. Then I met Derek 'Dek' Fearnley, the bass player, who had worked as a portraits and weddings photographer, wore glasses (but not on-stage) and looked kind of geeky before it became the fashion. Both were really nice middle class lads and could play no problem, but somehow I didn't think they were really Rock and Roll, you know? They would probably have agreed with me, they were far too nice.

Still, there we were in Ralph's basement flat, Chow, Ego, Dek and Hutch, now collectively known as The Buzz and ready to rehearse (if not perhaps to rock too much) with this new singer David Bowie, who was, we were assured by Ralph, about to become very famous.

Chapter Four - David Bowie and the Buzz

I was reassured to see a Vox AC 30 guitar amplifier on the floor of Ralph's rehearsal-room living room. Spike had borrowed it from Mal Evans, an old mate of his and the chief roadie for The Beatles who had more amplifiers than they needed. Enough so they would not miss one for a few weeks anyway.

So it was that I started work with David Bowie playing through one of John Lennon's amplifiers, and connected to my guitar with one or two of Keith Richard's guitar leads. The resourceful Spike had borrowed a couple of leads from another old mate, the Stones' roadie Iain Stewart.

Spike was impressively very well connected on the London scene due to his time with The Rolling Stones. I did ask him why he had left them and the story, though not made totally clear to me at the time, concerned some sort of unsavoury incident which had resulted in someone being stabbed. The case had gone to court and had made some newspapers, and in order to minimise any risk of bad publicity for The Rolling Stones, Spike had played the role of scapegoat and resigned his position with them even though he had simply been an innocent bystander. Those were early Stones days, times soon changed and any kind of publicity became good publicity for The Rolling Stones.

Our first rehearsal with David Bowie began with the introduction of some unexpectedly different songs. It was immediately obvious to all of us that David, although he was a great singer, was primarily a songwriter and a very original one at that. He had written a lot of songs, they were not Rock and Roll but they were very good, very musical and they had unusual shapes, nothing like the current Top 20 stuff. We recognised that they were a cut above the rest and we were determined to do them justice, no matter that the songs would be breaking new ground in the rock venues of the day.

Chow, who had landed on his feet and found lodgings upstairs from Ralph's flat, sharing with three young nurses, and Dek who lived somewhere outside London in the green belt and travelled in every day, got right down to it in the basement flat rehearsal room and set to work producing little arrangements to suit David's original songs and ideas. John Eager was also very keen, very eager in fact, to rehearse and to get it right. Ego lived in comfort in Harrow with his parents who, strangely I thought, were not called Mum and Dad; they were called Margery and Harold. I believe that Ego would have been upper-middle class.

I didn't have too much to do creatively on most of David's songs, they were not particularly guitar-based things, except for one on which David 'scatted' in jazz-style to my guitar riff – he could see that my guitar style would suit that idea and he arranged the song 'Good Morning Girl' to accommodate that solo.

David was a natural like that, he had absorbed everything he had ever heard, jazz or rock or musical comedy and the rest, and all of those influences were in his songs. We also rehearsed several covers, just crowd pleasing 'fillers' really, just as every unknown gigging band in the country would have done. The repertoire included some Motown hits like 'Knock on Wood' and other sixties favourites like 'Monday Monday'.

I was asked to play a few instrumentals so that The Buzz could play a short introductory set before the 'Star of the Show' came on, and somehow I managed to sneak a couple that I could sing myself past Ralph Horton's guard. David didn't mind, he knew that I liked to sing a bit. One of my songs was a version of 'Life is Just a Slow Train' that I had taken from a John Mayall and the Bluesbreakers record. We also had to listen to a record called 'Can't help thinking about me' by David Bowie and the Lower Third and then more or less reproduce it note for note so that we were ready to start work on promotion.

We started gigging, ready or not, on the wild and windy winter's night of Thursday 10th February 1966 at the Mecca Ballroom in Leicester. We were to be support act to The Graham Bond Organisation, and Jimmy James and the Vagabonds were also on the bill. As we dragged Chow's musical furniture through the foyer of the ballroom, the doors burst open and a wild-eyed roadie with even wilder long red hair demanded in loud Cockney, "Where the f**k do we bring the gear in, ain't ya got a stage door?" They did, and it was in fact the better way in, the wild roadie knew his stuff; Graham Bond had a Hammond B3 and a Leslie cabinet too. When The Graham Bond Organisation appeared on-stage, Graham got behind the B3, Jack Bruce walked on with his Gibson bass, and the wild-eyed roadie got behind the drum kit. He was Ginger Baker. The Graham Bond Organisation blew The Buzz away that night. It's the only way to learn the trade, watching older, more experienced and more accomplished musicians go about their business, and we wouldn't have had it any other way.

We played every night for a fortnight and reached The Corn Exchange in Chelmsford on February 26th 1966. The gig was unremarkable except for a 'nervous exhaustion' collapse on-stage by our frontman David Bowie at the very end of the last song in the last set. This was followed later backstage by a kind of crying and cuddling clinch involving David and Ralph, and for the new band it was an uncomfortable introduction to the existence of some deep-running emotional currents in our talented singer's life. It was plain to see that David had been wound up as tight as a drum, and he had quite possibly collapsed with relief that he had managed to form a new band that could do the gigs – the way that he wanted to do them. We never thought any less of David for his small breakdowns during that period – they happened a few times and we all took them in our stride. I did have a lot of sympathy, I could see that there was something very wrong, but also that it was something that

David would not or could not discuss with his band. It was then that I realised that I could never commit so much of myself to anything, never mind commit so much to the possibly futile pursuit of success in the music business. David was different; it was more than just music to him.

We were all reassured and very impressed with Ralph Horton's management capabilities when we learnt that our TV debut was to be the 'live' BBC TV show Ready Steady Go! in just a few days time, on March 3rd 1966. The prestigious TV engagement had been made possible by the recent (and not a little surprising) appearance of David's single 'Can't Help Thinking About Me' in the lower reaches of 'The Melody Maker Pop 50'.

The Svengali Ralph had been busy with other people's money. I learned many years later that a successful businessman called Ray Cooke had been persuaded by Ralph to put up the money for some strategic record buying at shops around the country. They would be the shops that were known (by those few 'in the know') to be checked for sales when whoever-it-was compiled the 'Charts' each week. Of course that kind of thing could never happen these days. Could it?

Cathy McGowan the show's presenter was as glamorous and famous as any pop star, as was the show's producer Vicky Whickham, at least within the music business, though I never understood why - it was something to do with being one of Dusty Springfield's friends I believe. Cathy was very professional, smiley and nice to everybody, even to me and The Buzz - we were just a backing group after all.

The other acts on the show that day were The Small Faces, The Yardbirds and Dave Dee, Dozy, Beaky, Mick and Tich - now there was another band with a real thing for nicknames. Although the show was described as being 'live' this meant that we were to record our 'live' sound in the morning, and then mime to ourselves in order for the cameras to shoot the show in the afternoon – the show went out that evening. The introduction to 'Can't Help Thinking About Me' was a distinctive guitar riff that I had copied from The Lower Third's recording and it was also the main 'hook' on the record. I played it on an acoustic 12-string guitar that David lent me, and the morning recording session went off without a hitch from Dave B, Hutchie, Ego, Dek and Chow's point of view.

The afternoon was much more fun, I had decided that I would mime using my Telecaster (to the sound of David's old 12-string on the backing track) and wondered if anyone would notice and tick me off. I got away with it; David noticed but didn't mind and we both enjoyed the joke. The Yardbirds kept pretty much to themselves, but Steve Marriott of The Small Faces was quite the opposite. While David was miming, Steve leapt about behind the cameraman exhorting David to 'come on mate, perform!' Apparently David and Steve had known each other for some time – maybe even since their schooldays I think. Anyway they were both London Boys weren't they?

We all enjoyed our TV debut, it had been great fun, it was certainly the first time on the telly for me and for Ego, Dek and Chow too, and it felt like we had joined some kind of exclusive club – even that we had 'made it' in some smallish way. After we left the TV studios we drove out to Chislehurst Caves for a gig that same evening. The place was damp and horrible, but it was a prestigious gig, all the top acts would appear there, and among the other bands playing that evening was The Herd. They were a great band; they also played The Marquee Club on a regular basis, which was a sure sign of real quality assurance. The Herd included a very young Peter Frampton on lead guitar, and Peter was yet another mate of David's – and Peter's dad Owen Frampton had been David's art teacher at school in Bromley. The Herd were to become one of the Marquee Club's favourite bands and they seemed likely to be heading for national success, but then Peter Frampton left them and went on to bigger things, and the band went nowhere without him.

I was to have my belief that most London musicians knew each other reinforced many times during those days. David and I would often be walking in the West End, maybe to and from The Marquee or one of the studios, when we would bump into Roger Daltrey or another member of The Who, or Ray or Dave Davies of The Kinks or any of the other successful contemporaries of the day in London. The familiar and famous faces were always friendly, they would say 'Hi David' and stop and chat for a minute, and they seemed to be genuinely interested in how things were going for him. Of course David Bowie's career would eventually become much bigger, more spectacular and probably longer lasting than most of his contemporaries from the sixties. David was of course very young in 1966 but still he was perceived as something of a late starter; he is after all a Capricorn – like me.

We had been playing a song of David's called 'Do Anything You Say' at our gigs, and on February 22nd 1966 we went into Regent Sound Studios in Denmark Street to record a demo of the song. Though I didn't see him there, apparently Tony Hatch, the famous songwriter, producer and cheesy celebrity, had been invited along to the demo session and had agreed on the spot that he would produce David's song as the first single by David Bowie and The Buzz for Pye Records. We were to give it our best efforts on March 7th 1966 at Pye Studios with Tony Hatch in the control room. Tony seemed to be a pleasant enough chap, viewed through the control room glass, but he somehow managed the whole production job without a single word to the band, and he barely glanced in the direction of Chow, Dek, Ego and myself.

Before we left the studio the members of The Buzz were individually presented by Ralph with a session fee receipt sheet for £9 0s 0d each, which we all duly signed and handed back to Ralph as he requested. We never saw the money. Ralph always kept us busy, we often worked almost every night of the week, but that did not mean that we always got paid. We were young enough not to care too much about money, so that meant that Ralph got away with it most of the time.

The Ready Steady Go! experience, and the recording session, lifted the spirits of everybody in the Bowie and The Buzz camp and we set about a regular round of gigs in the south of England in the spring of 1966. We travelled around in an old ambulance that Ralph Horton had bought, with borrowed money of course – that was the only kind of money that Ralph had. We knew that he was almost broke but we, the guys in the band, didn't really worry about it, although I'm sure that David did. In reality Chow, Dek, Ego and I were living on borrowed time as the money was running out, but we were all enjoying life, we were professional musicians in a London band that was going places.

We went to lots of places in that old ambulance. It has been referred to as a 'converted' ambulance, but the only changes that had been made to the old bus had been to take the medical equipment out. It even still said 'Ambulance' on the front, although the whole thing had faded and started to rust. We could stand up in our ambulance, so if necessary we could use it as our band room when parked outside many a gig that barely had a toilet let alone a dressing room. Ralph had supplied the four of us (the backing musicians) with a kind of 'Mod' band uniform, smart trousers and checked shirts – no big deal, but in our uniform we more or less looked like a backing band. Chow and I always had plenty of hair on top, so we didn't look like members of a dance orchestra anyway, young Ego always looked as though he was management, and Dec's geeky image had been corrected just a little by Ralph and David by means of a change of hairstyle and some sound clothes advice.

David Bowie and The Buzz by now looked right for the job and we sounded pretty good too, if a little soft and jazzy perhaps.

On the road we encountered several of the 'soon to be famous' as well as some of the already famous big names in Rock and Roll. We played support to a band called The Warriors who had shown, by having their hair dyed platinum blond, that they were really trying. There is no doubt that this would have been a Warriors' management decision rather than the band's idea. The Warriors' lead vocalist had good performance skills and a distinctive though rather squeaky voice. I was to become aware of this chap again a few years later when I discovered that his name was Jon Anderson and I noticed that his new band, called Yes, was putting the squeaky voice to very profitable use.

At the beginning of April 1966 we bravely set off northward up the A1, the 'Great North Road', in a Ford Transit van that Ralph Horton had presumably rented, having decided that the ambulance would probably not survive the trip. It was to be the first Scottish Tour by David Bowie and The Buzz. Other accounts of this trip vary somewhat, some say we played Carlisle, Dundee and Hawick but I'm not sure that's correct; Carlisle sounds unlikely to me as I remember that we went up the East Coast route. I suggest that my memories of the Scottish Tour ought to be as reliable as those of any other, but I wouldn't swear on oath that I have not dreamed up the odd 'memory'. I do know that it was a bloody long journey though, Ralph sharing driving duties with Dek Fearnley, with the rest of us alternately crashed out or semi-hysterical in the back of the van.

I remember that we stayed in a hotel in Edinburgh very close to the top of Princes Street, and that our first gig, wherever it should have been, had been cancelled. At a shop in Princes Street I bought a mohair Scottish travel rug as a souvenir of the tour, and I remember well that the tartan-wallpapered hotel bar was the first I had ever seen with a full complement of real single malt whiskies on view.

I also know that we played support with Johnny Kidd & the Pirates again in Scotland, and although I have been assured that the gig was on Sunday 3rd April 1966 at The Top 10 Club in Dundee, my recollection involves David and I chatting with our mutual old chum Johnny Kidd at Greens Playhouse in Glasgow, where Johnny had with him that evening a 'dep' on lead guitar – and he was a young guy called John McLaughlin. Some memories are made of what – dreams?

I can certainly believe that Ralph managed to blag us a gig in Hawick on the way back south; it would have been necessary in order that we would have some money to buy petrol for our homeward journey, but I remember nothing at all of it. That was the full extent of 'The Scottish Tour', everybody lost money and we returned to London dejected. We never talked about it thereafter and possibly this explains the improvisational nature of the various accounts of the farcical Scottish Tour. I have absolute sympathy with pop history researchers, and nothing but admiration for Kevin Cann, the number one expert on all things Bowie, whose amazing chronicle 'Any Day Now' has so many Bowie facts, figures and dates in it that there just *has* to be a 1% chance of a small error here and there...?

In addition to the usual club, dance hall and the occasional theatre type of gigs, we also played a couple of quite unforgettable ones. One of these was played outdoors in sunny daytime at the Brands Hatch racing circuit on 19th June 1966. The special occasion was a Radio London Trophy meeting and it included an awards show that featured some famous acts that were making their award-acceptance appearances, though they were not necessarily performing live. The Walker Brothers, The Kinks, The Small Faces and Paul & Barry Ryan were among the stellar cast who appeared that day but did not sing.

There had certainly been some motor racing going on, we could hear it but we saw nothing of it, and when we started to set up on the small outdoor stage, another band was sound checking and they grabbed our attention. They were called Tom Jones and the Squires and we had heard of them, Tom Jones in particular, and they were from Wales. Their singer Tom was blessed with both muscular voice and body though he did look a bit of a prat with that large white bow in his hair; obviously it was intended to tie in somehow with the current hit film of the famous book, a comedy period piece which used Tom's name as its title and starred Albert Finney. This bow-in-the-hair business had been played out already by PJ Proby, and I wished that Tom had left it out. It was probably a management idea again; anyway I would guess that Tom Jones changed his management shortly after Brands Hatch, at the same time that he dispensed with the services of The Squires. It's not unusual – and Tom's career took off like a rocket.

The Brands Hatch gig finished in the late afternoon, and as Dek drove our ambulance away through the crowd we had a small but disconcerting taste of just one of the disadvantages that might come with pop music 'fame'. A crowd of exited young people surrounded our vehicle, chased along with us and banged hard on the sides of the ambulance. It is possible that the word had got around that The Walker Brothers were sneaking away from Brands Hatch in this old ambulance, or it could have been a stunt engineered by Ralph, but either way it was a bit scary and they stopped our progress more than once on the way out. I know it sounds like nothing, but we felt trapped in the old ambulance and we were slightly spooked by the time we reached the main road. This kind of stuff was going to happen to David Bowie (and whoever was around him) regularly during the years to come so I imagine he must have eventually got used to it.

The other memorable gig had come our way a couple of weeks earlier, on Sunday May 29th 1966 on the end of the South Pier in Blackpool. The small theatre at the end of the spindly pier regularly put on rock concerts throughout the summer and on this particular week the star attraction was Crispian St. Peters. He was having huge success with 'The Pied Piper' and 'You were on my mind' and Crispian looked set to become an established star. The others on the bill supporting Crispian St. Peters that afternoon were Dave Anthony's Moods and The Mark Leeman Five, both bands being experienced Marquee Club regulars, both much more hip and much less successful than Crispian.

Crispian St. Peters' rapid success was to be very short-lived, which was hard to understand as he was a talented songwriter and performer. Anyway on that Sunday at the 'Summer Beat Spectacular' (or something very similar) Crispian packed them in, and David Bowie and The Buzz bathed on the pier in sunshine and reflected glory.

The hump (getting the equipment in) at Blackpool Pier involved Dek driving the ambulance along the pier in order to park as near as possible to the theatre stage entrance. Getting the ambulance on to the pier went off without major problems as people generally, wherever we were, would get out of our way as quickly as possible. This may have had something to do with the 'Ambulance' sign – Ralph never got around to removing it. On leaving the pier however, high as kites on adrenaline and a couple of beers (no drugs in that band), we played one of our favourite tricks to great effect. Our ambulance had one-way darkened windows (as they all do, for obvious reasons) with a narrow opening ventilation window along the top. The joke was that we would hang an arm or leg out through the small window, at the same time making moaning or screaming noises, and we watched the reactions of the general public through our window. The range of reactions ran through disbelief to horror – and laughter if they got the joke.

We had a guest travelling with us on the trip back from Blackpool. We had seen him before at a couple of gigs, Ralph had introduced him as 'Ken Pitt' and we took him to be an agent, as Ralph was David's Manager. Ken didn't say too much and he seemed pleasant enough. We understood that he had something to do with Crispian St. Peters' management.

We were delighted when Ralph announced that David had been awarded a weekly residency at The Marquee Club. This was to be called 'The Bowie Showboat' and I had a feeling that Ralph and David might have discussed 'all round entertainment' with the Marquee Club management. Just to be playing regularly at the famous Marquee was enough for The Buzz though and we soon felt very relaxed about the venue. We had played a couple of midweek gigs to a smallish crowd when the management decided to move 'The Bowie Showboat' to Sunday afternoons. This was a disappointment to us but anyway, we still had the Marquee residency.

The Marquee gig had several advantages. We could try out new material in relaxed surroundings, we had visits from musical celebrities like Long John Baldry who came to check us out, and we had free admission to the club on any evening of the week.

David, Chow and I took full advantage of this unexpected bonus, and went into the West End as often as possible to see The Spencer Davis Group, Long John Baldry and Bluesology, The Herd and many others at The Marquee. Dek and Ego would generally disappear back into their leafy suburbia when not required by Ralph or David during that time. Dek eventually moved into the flat above Ralph's basement flat, along with Chow and his very nice nurses, but John Eager resisted and was to sensibly remain with Harold and

Marjorie in Harrow. Ego was a sensible lad and he had turned out to be a decent drummer to boot.

One evening I went to see Patti LaBelle and her 'LaBelles' girl group, when I heard somebody near me say, "John Lennon's standing behind us." I swear I did not turn around, that would not have been cool.

Two members of Long John Baldry's excellent band Bluesology (it is the name of a Charlie Parker blues) looked very alike, both being quite short and dumpy in their grey band suits, and they looked nothing at all like pop stars. They were just backing musicians like Dec, Chow, Ego and myself so it didn't matter, however when I saw the two dumpy ones leaving the Marquee club together holding hands I realised that Baldry was not the only one in his band who was batting for the opposition – as some people do still say in the North. The short and slightly dumpy piano player with Baldry in that band was a good player (though not, I thought, as good as Chow on the rock and roll stuff) and many years later I learned that the guy's name had been Reg Dwight – before he changed it to Elton John and decided to make his own records.

Unusually for a sixties backing group, The Buzz were not required to wear suits on stage. This was a relief for all of us as many bands at the time had no choice but to wear them, and The Marquee had high standards. We did of course have the uniform of button-down collared checked shirts and neat trousers, all provided by Ralph who had most likely got them on 'tick' from Mr Gee's of Carnaby Street. The Buzz also had a specially arranged discount price for haircuts at a trendy 'salon' not far from Ralph's flat. The hairdressers was called 'A Cut Above The Rest' (it may have been the first one) and the owner was a man from Manchester who also cut The Hollies' hair – apart from drummer Bobby Elliot's because he didn't have any, just a toupee. This arrangement ensured that we kept our early 'mod' appearance in good shape, even if we were all permanently broke.

David dressed in those days as he has always dressed, to suit himself. Particularly, he wore *those* trousers. The trousers, which David wore at most of our gigs, were made from a red 'travel blanket' tartan and were a very tight fit. This did not restrict our frontman at all in his cavorting at centre front of the stage, and though all we saw was the rear view, all of the band would watch the girls' and boys' faces as they watched David – the bit of him below the belt mostly. The trousers were a great success and congratulations were due to Ralph, I reckoned he'd designed them.

One afternoon I had called into The Marquee to meet David. I can't remember why we were meeting, but we did treat the place very much as our home base and in any case it was preferable to Ralph's flat. A very confident looking band, apparently down from Birmingham to audition for a gig at The Marquee, was setting up and getting ready to play. We sat down to watch them, and so it was that Bowie and I saw The Move (later to become the component parts of both Roy Wood's Wizard and the ELO) in action for the first time in London. They were very dynamic, a true pop group and they deserved the success that was to come to them. Not really my cup of tea, but all credit to them.

During that early summer of 1966 my girlfriend Denise and I got married at Caxton Hall Registry Office in Westminster, directly opposite the Houses of Parliament. Caxton Hall was at that time the Registry Office for the area of Victoria where we were renting our bedsit (one roomed flat). When making the booking I had entered my occupation as 'musician' and I was asked by the clerk, "Do you require that we keep it out of the press?" They had regular experience of 'famous show business people' he said. I said it didn't matter in my case but thanks for asking.

Chow brought one of the nurses along and so they were respectively best man and witness. Nobody else came, David had declined to attend and had gone so far as to suggest to me the night before, while we playing The California Ballroom at Dunstable, that maybe I shouldn't go through with it in the morning. "Why don't we just take those two girls over there home instead?" he said. It could have been Ralph's idea to talk me out of the ceremony, to save him the inconvenience of finding another guitarist to replace me. Everyone knew the way things were going, and I certainly didn't like playing gigs and not being paid when I had a family to support. I prefer to think that maybe David had my best interests at heart; we were good friends after all, though I would say we were not yet close friends during those early 'Buzz' days.

Financially things were getting very tight for The Buzz. Even when we had good gigs we didn't always get paid and we all knew by now that Ralph had big money problems. A businessman from Wimbledon called Ray Cook had been persuaded of David's talent and potential, and had provided Ralph with finance. Cars and vans hired by Ralph from Godfrey Davis ran up a huge bill which Mr Cook had to eventually pay in order to keep Ralph out of jail. The hire company had to come and repossess 'our van' – the one that had superseded the ambulance when it died – from which Ralph had removed the 'Godfrey Davis' logo.

Kenny Bell, the entertainments agent with whom Ralph shared the Warwick Grove flat, has confirmed that much of Ray Cook's investment was squandered by Ralph on extravagant eating and drinking in the West End. Ralph and Kenny also threw parties at the flat. I never went to one, but Chow and Dek went once and discovered that no 'birds' had been invited. They did not stay long apparently, but they told me that it had been a gay old do.

The band's afternoon rehearsals at Ralph's basement flat were regularly interrupted by the doorbell, and Chow or Dek would go and tell the creditor's representative on the doorstep that Ralph was away visiting his sick grandmother, or that he no longer lived at this address. The bill for the flat's electricity supply was among the growing pile of 'unpaid items' of course, but when inevitably the supply was cut off, Ralph demonstrated a surprising ability and admirable resourcefulness, when he reconnected the supply himself via a manhole in the pavement outside the flat. The electricity company eventually discovered the reconnection, filled in the hole and paved it over.

One day it was made known to The Buzz that the mysterious Ken Pitt was (and in fact had been for some time) now co-managing David Bowie. The Buzz, it seemed to me, did not have a manager and were simply being used by these people as a backing band for the time being. I could see the band going the way of Tom Jones' old band The Squires.

My new wife was pregnant, and though I had enjoyed my first taste of London's rock and roll world and I did still have faith that David Bowie would eventually succeed, I was broke and a little homesick and so I decided to return to Scarborough and get a proper job once again. A job that paid.

I knew that in my home town I should stand a reasonable chance of making a living and finding an affordable place to live, and so in June 1966 I said goodbye to David, Ralph, Chow, Dek and Ego. Very sadly I would never see four of these five old band mates again and three of the guys, Ralph Horton, Dek Fearnley and Chow Boyes have since passed on. We had a great time together, great days that I will never forget.

David Bowie and The Buzz were to soldier on without me for the remainder of 1966. My replacement for a short time was a Scot called Billy Grey, who the management of course duly nicknamed 'Haggis'. Dek Fearnley continued to be David's main collaborator, the two of them writing all the arrangements for David's first album, 'David Bowie' (Deram ML1007).

It has been said that some of the brass section arrangements for the album were difficult to read, and that the session musicians had to rewrite some parts right there in the studio during the recordings, but in any case when I eventually heard the album I was very impressed with David and Dek's work. Dek could be proud of the album, and I heard that he was to say many years later that 'this album is my epitaph'. I had lived with those songs myself and I do remember doing some recording on the tracks before I left the band, though my name did not appear on the back of the record sleeve.

The album was eventually released on June 1st 1967, a full year after my departure, and by then I was in Montreal, Canada. I was looking for a new life, again.

Chapter Five - A Bit About Ken Pitt

Ken Pitt's entrance into David's life and career seemed to me to have been very gradual, maybe a little shadowy even, but eventually, more than a year after my departure from The Buzz, Pitt formally became David's manager, Ralph Horton having been persuaded to leave his boy to the care of another. Another what? You may well ask.

Ken Pitt continues to this day to be a slightly mysterious though immensely important figure in the true story of David Bowie's early days and the beginnings of his inexorable rise to fame. This is due largely perhaps to Ken's old-school style and the low profile that Ken had adopted throughout his little known, though very successful show business career in publicity, promotions and management (I think that's it) before he had ever heard of David Bowie.

Kenneth Pitt was from a prosperous family in Southall, the money had been hard earned in the grocery business, but young Ken had wanted to become an artist, not a grocer, and he duly commenced his studies at the best place for that, the Slade School of Fine Art, in Gower Street, London WC1E.

The Second World War had come along and interrupted the best of plans however, and instead of becoming an artist Ken had become a Communications Officer in The Royal Signals Regiment. The young Ken must have been good at his job, for he was given an assignment in a forthcoming very secret, nationally important military operation, and that turned out to be the recapture of mainland Europe from the Germans. Ken landed on the beach in northern France on D-Day 1944, and whilst fighting through France and into Germany, he picked up enough German to become an army interpreter. At the end of the Second World War, Ken was sent to Palestine and spent time in those crucial years in that region during the rebirth of Israel at the end of the war , eventually to be demobbed in October 1946.

That Ken Pitt had worked for the British Intelligence Service in Palestine cannot be confirmed, but I suggest that it is entirely possible that Ken was an agent for the good guys. He would certainly have looked the part, and could have played a sophisticated Bond. Ken was more the Roger Moore than the Sean Connery type mind you.

After the war, still with ambitions to become an artist, Ken went to work in the design department of the leading post-war British film company, J. Arthur Rank. Soon transferred to the publicity department, Ken was given the job of escorting J. Arthur's top stars around the West End. Nice work if you can get it and Ken got it because he tried.

In 1951 Ken was to accompany Alan Dean, the leading British recording star of the day (I had never heard of him either, fame can be so temporary can't it?) on a visit to Hollywood. Ken took this opportunity to introduce himself to every star he could find in California and then offered to handle their publicity when they came over to the UK. The result was that when Ken left J. Arthur Rank, appropriately enough to go it alone, he was to work with the biggest of the big stars, including Frankie Laine, Louis Armstrong, Duke Ellington and Frank Sinatra among others. The first major US client that Ken was to take on as a manager was the wonderful jazz ballad singer and piano player Mel Torme. Ken's other management successes later in the sixties were to include Scandinavian duo Nina and Frederik (I was to dance with the very beautiful Princess Nina at the Café Royal in 1973, the evening of the fall of Ziggy Stardust – more about that later), also the legendary and extremely stylish Rod McEwen, and the equally so Greek singer Nana Mouscouri.

I believe that Ken had the self belief which I like to think of as 'The Svengali Syndrome'. It is a quite common trait with natural managers. During the 1950s Ken took a gypsy busker called Danny Purches from nowhere on the streets of the West End of London to huge, though very short-lived, national fame and possibly even a little fortune – minus Ken's percentage no doubt. Lack of any film or recorded evidence ensures we will have to presume that Gypsy Danny either sang or played violin or guitar. I would guess that he probably did all three, and quite possibly Danny could dance if necessary.

In March 1963, Ken saw a band called the Mann-Hugg Blues Brothers play a gig. Impressed with the band, especially with their charismatic singer, the young Paul Jones, Ken became their manager.

Ken suggested that the band should record a song called 'Doo Wah Diddy Diddy', and following a name change to Manfred Mann (he was the piano player and the band leader, and man-hug just had to go didn't it? – although Mike Hugg did stay in the band) the band had their first massive hit in the summer of 1964.

I think Ken Pitt probably believes, as would all showbiz Svengalis, that classic management was responsible for Manfred Mann's success. As I see it, a great singer with a good band and a daft name released a stupid song that Joe Public fell for. The manager just pulls things together doesn't he? Okay I'm just a guitarist, and I'm no manager, what do I know?

I observed Ken to be a quiet man with a good sense of humour, I quite liked him and he impressed me. He had retained a certain ex-military style (sports jackets, tight suits and the like) and he had a reassuring and professional manner, as you would expect from a man who had worked successfully with Frank Sinatra, and more recently with Bob Dylan on his notorious first 'electric' tour of the UK.

Ken also seemed to have the 'good taste' that working class lads (whether they be from Yorkshire or Kent) could recognise but not understand. David wanted to learn how to acquire 'good taste' and saw that he could learn something of it from Ken Pitt. So Ken introduced David to the writings of Oscar Wilde and Lord Alfred Douglas, and took him to the theatre to see, among other things, Joe Orton's controversial play 'Loot'. Some specialised education, I would say.

To promoters, press, clients and musicians alike, Ken gave little of himself away – a very discreet and private man indeed.

The exception to this was to come along when Ken became active in the Campaign for Homosexual Equality during the 1980s, well after his working association with David was over. Prior to that, Ken had not deemed it necessary to broadcast his own sexuality to the world. Ken perhaps dropped his guard just a little however in his excellent book 'The Pitt Report' with a reference to David's 'big dick swaying from side to side' as he walked through Ken's apartment, and of David's almost totally hairless body – 'apart from a smudging of pubic hair'. These observations do not of course mean that Ken had any kind of homosexual relationship with David Bowie. He was though, I believe, Mad about the Boy.

Ken Pitt had been impressed by an American survey which had 'conservatively estimated' that one in twenty 'US males' are 'exclusively homosexual' and that an 'incalculable number' are bi-sexual. Ken seems to have deduced that this huge (though incalculable) gay population would be sure to purchase millions of records by a suitably presented, apparently bisexual, male recording artist and I think he may have mentioned this to David Bowie.

I have to admit that for me some passages in Ken's book make uncomfortable reading. Ken was plainly in love with his boy David, and though Ken had other male friends at the same time, including a couple of other aspiring singers, it has been said that Ken could be obsessively jealous of David's other friendships, sexual or otherwise. Ken did not seem to have any problem with my own friendship and musical association with David, but I'm pretty sure he told David that he saw no real potential in our 'duo' of Bowie & Hutch, and that he regarded me as a dispensable backing musician who would disappear in due course. Ken was right about the last bit, for when the gigs and the money ran out, I disappeared – for the second time in David's career.

The question, 'Is Bowie gay?' does perhaps hover around all the biographies, and Joe Public has almost always asked me that question, but certainly in those days I did not understand or even care what the options might be, so I was never sure what David's relationship with Ken Pitt was. I just knew that certainly some managers, and probably some musicians, were gay. I know that principle should have been applied to bus drivers and milkmen too, but somehow they all kept it quiet in the sixties didn't they?

I have read an excellent biography 'The Life and Times of Little Richard' (1984) written by an old friend of mine, Charlie White, the Scarborough based Irish author, chiropodist, presenter and DJ known to Radio York listeners as 'Doctor Rock'.

Charlie's amazing book, described by *Time* magazine as 'The Wooliest, Funniest, Funkiest Rock Memoir Ever', appeared in the 2013 'Bowie Is' exhibition's informative list of 'David Bowie's Top 100 Books'. David knows a good book when he reads it.

In the book Little Richard maintains that homosexuals are not born that way, but are, as in his own case, created by seduction at an early age. Richard says, 'Homosexuality is contagious. It's not something you are born with. It's contagious'.

It's a bit like vampires then?

Chapter Six - Oh, Canada

By the time David's first album 'David Bowie' was released in 1967, I had been through a few changes myself. I now had my young son Christian to consider, as well as my wife Denise, and so after a short time back in my home town, good old Scarborough, getting nowhere, the three of us officially emigrated to Canada on a Canadian government subsidised ticket. I had qualified for this lucky break by virtue of a job offer from Air Canada at Dorval Airport in Montreal. The job had been arranged for me, sort of on the old-boy network, by a wartime friend of my Mum and Dad's, a Canadian ex-airman called Burns Agnew. Burns and his wife Doreen had been a part of my childhood, they would come and visit whenever they could and every Christmas throughout the lean post-war years a parcel would arrive from Canada, and it would be filled with Canadian things that were only seen in the movies of the day. Burns was a strong character, a real North American working man, a wonderful bloke who made me want to become a Canadian too. The trouble was, it turned out that there weren't actually too many Canadians like Burns Agnew.

Canada was the new frontier; I got the haircut and bought the sports jacket and the Hush Puppies again, and the shirt and the tie – the straight uniform that straight jobs in those days (proper, engineering type jobs anyway) demanded that everyone must wear. It will still be the same today I imagine, even if the fashions change a bit.

Upon landing in Montreal, Canada my wife Denise didn't like the place, felt homesick and wanted to go back home. It was to take me about a year to save up the air fares back to England and pay back the Canadian government subsidy. There were no credit cards for everybody in those days, and I had no credit or financial help available to me – there was nothing like the 'Bank of Mum and Dad' to pay for return tickets to England and I had to look after myself and my wife and baby son.

I had a job lined up and a room at Burns Agnew's house for my family to stay in while I looked for an apartment, and so I resolved to make the best of things and get on with it. The year in Canada was to be interesting enough. It was not so bad for me really, as I worked with some good guys in the maintenance hangars at Montreal's Dorval Airport where the workplace patter was good and multi-national too. My new workmates were mostly New Canadians, émigrés from every part of Europe, all determined to succeed in the new world. I found an affordable basement apartment on Decarie Boulevard, an inexpensive part of Montreal in those days; I furnished it in some style by UK standards with some solid second-hand Canadian stuff and settled into a routine of working night shifts at the airport and sleeping through the mornings.

A Hungarian New Canadian called Marion would very kindly pick me up in his car every evening. I had no car, couldn't drive anyway. I would wait outside my apartment block in all weathers throughout that cold winter so I would wear two pairs of trousers for the journey to and from work. It was to be years before affordable proper cold weather clothing, the expedition standard stuff that we all have nowadays, would become available to the man in the street in England, and in any case working class guys like me had no idea about cold weather clothing, snow boots and all that. Most of us didn't ski.

Marion had told me he would certainly not wait if I was not in position when he got to my place; there was that limit to his kindness, so I was never late. Most of the time I worked on small mechanical modification or repair jobs with Freddie Dzumkopf (spelt something like that anyway), a Polish New Canadian, and Freddie showed me the ropes and generally kept me out of trouble with the managers. I carried the toolbox and kept the notes while Freddie tinkered with bits of jet aircraft. One night we went aboard a huge Russian Ilyushin jet airliner which was, most unusually, in the hangars for a maintenance check. The Cold War was raging in 1967 and Montreal, Canada was the only place on the North American continent that the Russians were permitted to land an aircraft.

"We'll just have a look around," Freddie said. He had spoken in apparently fluent Russian to the guard who was posted, holding a sub-machine gun, at the foot of the passenger staircase – and the guy let us aboard. It was all very grey inside the plane, as it was on the outside, and its passenger comforts looked to be basic. Freddie took a couple of snapshots inside the cabin – who knows perhaps Freddie Dzumkopf had a watching brief at the airport, he could even have been a CIA stringer.

The night shift at the airport was hard going but the pay was good, and in spite of my wife's insistence that we should return to England as soon as possible I still sort of wanted to become a New Canadian. My job with Air Canada, if I had been able to stick with it, would have given me free air travel all around the world, as well as a real Canadian life. I could see a log cabin and a boat on a lake in my alternative parallel future in Canada. David Northcliffe and his wife, who had also emigrated from Scarborough before us, had coincidentally settled in the Montreal area. David was an art teacher – I would bet that they stayed and became Canadians, got the boat and the cabin too.

I had to forget about London, and the music making part of my life just had to go on hold, at least for twelve months or so, but I had a Harmony Sovereign acoustic guitar with me (the same one that I later used with Feathers and Bowie & Hutch) and so I did get together with a local singer/guitar player called Bruce (there were quite a lot of Bruce's over there at that time) and we somehow fitted in the odd little gig – an amateur schoolroom concert in an afternoon or in a little bar on my occasional weekend off the night shift.

Some of Bruce's friends were young French Canadians and they were nice people, very friendly, and their attitudes were quite at odds with the separatist propaganda in the newspapers that was endorsed by the political pop star French Canadian President Pierre Trudeau in his infamous 'Vive Le Quebec Libre' speech – not to mention the alarming stories of parcel bombs being posted through the letterboxes of Anglo Canadians like me. There was a lot of talk at work of relocating Air Canada to Toronto, and generally a feeling that the French Canadians should in the long run be left to run their separate Quebec province. It didn't matter too much to me, I knew that whether I liked it or not, I had to go back to England.

During my year in Montreal I had naturally absorbed the Canadian acoustic music thing, improving my finger-style picking technique, and some excellent Canadian acoustic singer-songwriters would always be on the radio. Ian and Sylvia were very big, as was Gordon Lightfoot. Around my time in Montreal Neil Young would have been getting ready to leave nearby Toronto for California, but Leonard Cohen must have been around downtown Montreal somewhere in those days. No use to me of course, I was 'going straight' again, working night shifts at the airport, not wandering around the late night music venues. Maybe Canada had been a mistake after all, but I had been dreaming of new frontiers with cabins, boats and lakes – and we should all follow our dreams shouldn't we?

While I did my time in Montreal, back on the streets of London my old bandmaster David Bowie still followed his dream. Following my departure from The Buzz, the band had struggled on with David and played any gigs that came along, whether they were paid or not. The lads were loyal, and could have starved to death had they not had the support of their families – I know Dek and Ego would have managed by living at home with their parents. Chow quite possibly would have had some support from his lovely nurses, but I know he would have gone hungry before accepting what he would have seen as defeat. Their loyalty had made no difference, The Buzz had inevitably been 'dismissed' by Ralph Horton who then very shortly afterwards sensibly disappeared altogether from the London scene – that is, from both the London gay scene and the London music scene. David Bowie was now, by default, managed exclusively by Ken Pitt and so they both set about the task of clearing up the mess that Ralph had left behind.

David's dad Howard Jones (everyone called him John) had kept abreast of developments and was obviously concerned about the demise of The Buzz and David's lack of progress. John Jones, who by the way held down a successful job with the Dr. Barnardo's charity organisation in London, was glad to see the back of Ralph Horton and he, like David, looked to Ken Pitt for salvation.

During my time in The Buzz, David and I never spoke very much about family stuff. As with most bands, there was more banter than conversation, so David never said very much to me about his mum and dad or about Jones family life, and that was, and probably of course still is, not at all unusual among young guys in rock and roll bands. I was never aware during either The Buzz days, or even later the Feathers days, that David had a half-brother called Terry Jones away at sea. Even though David and I later became good friends during the lifespan of Feathers and our Bowie and Hutch duo, the existence of David's absent half-brother never came up – it was just part of David's family stuff after all. I had seen a photograph above the fireplace of a handsome man in a navy uniform but I thought nothing of it, my Uncle Cliff was an oil tanker captain and his photo in uniform had always been around at my own parents' house.

It is obvious that David had loved and very much looked up to the older step-brother who had introduced him to the world of jazz and popular music in the nightclubs in the West End of London in the early sixties. Terry Jones had been a talented amateur boxer and a successful officer in the Merchant Navy before becoming victim to a devastating illness, and Terry's deterioration and premature death will have been incredibly hard for the young David to take as he struggled to find a foothold in the business of making a living in music. David would not have needed my opinion or observations on his private family tragedy.

On the few occasions I did go with David 'home' to Bromley, I found no. 4 Plaistow Grove, Bromley to be a warm family house, much like my own parents' semi-detached in Scarborough, Yorkshire. David's dad was always out at work, or just leaving the house as David and I arrived – I can recall bumping into him on just one occasion and only briefly at that, but John Jones seemed to me to be a nice bloke. It would have been the same had David ever come round to my parents' house in Scarborough, my dad the breadwinner was almost always out of the house, at work or travelling to and from work, in raincoat and trilby, carrying briefcase with sandwiches.

David's mum Peggy Jones was a caring and loving mum who fussed over David when we turned up, just as my own mum would have over me. Peggy very kindly knitted a red jumper for my baby son Christian, and although she never actually met my wife Denise or my son as they were always left behind, waiting in Finchley for me to come home from my own breadwinning (in engineering drawing if not in music – there was not much bread in music at that point), Peggy would never fail to ask after them.

John Jones was an intelligent man and obviously wanted to help David in his quest for fame and fortune in the music business. Personally I doubt that David's dad was fooled by Ken Pitt's exterior veneer of manliness and respectable professionalism, I believe that John would have known that homosexuality was woven into the fabric of show business management, but he also would have known that David's ambition would not allow for any change of lifestyle or career path at that stage in his life. John would not necessarily have suspected Ken Pitt of any untoward homosexual intentions towards his son, he would have just known and very much appreciated that Ken was going to try to get David's career back on track. Let's face it, John Jones could well have had some misgivings about Ken but would have sensibly kept them to himself as there were no other immediate options open.

On June 11th 1967 David Bowie moved into the spare room at Ken Pitt's flat in Manchester Street, London. John Jones somehow packed David's suitcase, a couple of cardboard boxes and an acoustic guitar into his tiny Fiat 500 and drove David away from his terraced family home in Plaistow Grove, Bromley and into the big bad city of London.

Ken had offered to help out with a rent-free room because it had become a little difficult for David at home. Of course it was the usual young musician thing, David was used to keeping late hours and it was disturbing John Jones' routine, as John lived in the real world and had to be up well before 7am to set off for work at Dr Barnardo's offices. To make matters worse at Plaistow Grove, David's half-brother Terry had unexpectedly returned to the nest after spending several years away at sea, and his surprise return home had made the family house a little overcrowded.

It is Ken Pitt's recollection that after John Jones had dropped David and his belongings off, he had said goodbye and told his son that Ken's apartment was 'very nice', and that it was 'very masculine'. David, then just twenty years old, stayed for a year at the Manchester Street flat, while Ken worked hard at the business of promoting his talented protégé.

David's debut album, although not a 'hit' as such, did receive a very favourable response from the music industry in general, and the connection between the Decca label and their USA subsidiary London Records resulted in David meeting up with the already successful young American record producer Tony Visconti. It was one of the most significant of meetings in David's career, as between the sixties and the eighties, Visconti would go on to produce no less than nine successful David Bowie albums, and still more to come.

Another important character to walk into David Bowie's London life whilst I was working the night shift in the maintenance hangars of Montreal's Dorval Airport was the dancer Lindsay Kemp. Lindsay, born in South Shields on 3rd May 1938 and educated at Bradford Art College, was an experienced performer having among many other things studied mime with Marcel Marceau and appeared with Marlene Dietrich in cabaret in Brussels.

In the mid-sixties Lindsay was still struggling for recognition when he formed a dance company at the Little Theatre in Covent Garden. David Bowie, who was still persevering with Ken Pitt's cultural education course, went to see a performance by Lindsay Kemp and was captivated. Kemp duly took over as David's tutor (and according to Lindsay, his lover) and composed a new piece, for three male dancers, called 'Pierrot in Turquoise'.

In addition to David and Lindsay, the third dancer was Jack Birkett, and the small company included Natasha Kornilov, the costume and set designer who also drove the van, she being the only one with a driving licence and Jack being almost blind. David learned his moves in mime, and a few other tricks for sure, with Lindsay and company, before Lindsay discovered that David, when he wasn't looking, was shagging Natasha. She was probably amazed to come across a heterosexual in the company; David must have been a first.

The little dance company broke up after Lindsay slashed his wrists prior to a performance in Whitehaven (with Lindsay eventually taking to the stage with heavy elastoplasts on his wrists) and Natasha responded by taking a handful of sleeping pills later that same evening. Both were to claim later that 'it was just a gesture'. The poor loves had made it hard on our David though.

Ken Pitt had continued to do his best and made steady progress for the continually developing David Bowie, having negotiated a (albeit somewhat less than lucrative) publishing contract with Essex Music, and securing for David a German TV appearance in Hamburg, as well as continuing to edge David towards the dreaded, though ill-defined, arena of 'all round entertainment'. (It was to be while I was around at the end of Feathers that it was proposed that I might become Musical Director for David, the all round entertainer.) David had no band and no gigs, so when Ken eventually ran out of ideas he proposed that David should 'go into cabaret' in the West End where he could expect to earn £100 a week.

David did consider Ken's idea, and in fact, always the professional, he practised and prepared to audition a suitable set of covers; smooth songs for the 'sophisticated', the Nouveau Riche, the cabaret punters, the scampi in a basket crowd. Fortunately, David decided instead to take his new record producer Tony Visconti's sound and timely advice that he should 'stick to his guns' and continue to write and perform his own songs. Ken was the manager, not a musician, and was thinking of the money, while Visconti the musician was thinking of David the musician. And that's what works, breaks new ground and makes money in the long run – sometimes.

David was also by now an aspiring dancer and had, whilst attending Lindsay Kemp's dance centre, met and fallen in love with a tall and elegant red-haired dancer, a girl who both on and off stage called herself Hermione Farthingale.

By August 1968 I was halfway through a summer season with Ron Snaith's Hawaiian Serenaders at Butlins Holiday Camp at Filey in Yorkshire. After a year of incarceration in 1967 I had made my escape from the night shift in Montreal, Canada and had taken the first gig offered to me upon my return to England. The gig came my way, as gigs often do for musicians, because I was hanging around in a guitar shop, the only one in Scarborough in those days, the now sadly departed 'Bernard Dean's Music Shop'. Twelve weeks residency through the summer playing rhythm guitar to Ron Snaith's lap-steel for pretty good money sounded like heaven to me when compared with the ten-hour night shift I had left behind in freezing Montreal.

I was at the same time still disappointed that I'd had to leave my 'new frontier' dreams behind in Canada, and so I suppose I drowned my sorrows nightly at our gig in the Beachcomber Bar. It wasn't hard going, we took our little bottles of something very strong on-stage with us – I remember that it was usually a barley wine called Kings Ale – as we steadily worked our way through four sets of Hawaiian hits from whenever it was that the stuff had been cool, sometime in the 1940s I think.

The Hawaiian Serenaders were a trio of lap-steel, rhythm guitar and bass guitar, and were comprised of Ron Snaith, who I had played with before in a dance band at some army barracks hop (I had been impressed by Ron's old-school Django Reinhardt style flamboyance on electric guitar, as well as his immaculate control of the Hawaiian lap-steel), myself on rhythm and Pete Mensel who had been a good big band trumpet player until his 'lip had gone' and he had taken up the bass.

Ron Snaith was from the Yorkshire Wolds market town of Driffield, not far from Scarborough; it was the same quiet little backwater that would also produce drummer Woody Woodmansey for David Bowie. Many years later Driffield, being the nearest town to our tiny village, would become my postcode, and Dennis Woodmansey, my plumber, electrician and drinking buddy in the village, would turn out to be Woody the drummer's cousin.

Pete Mensel was a professional band musician who had somehow beached at Scarborough, married a dancer from the summer show, settled down and all that. Ron and Pete were good fun; we had the band camaraderie that keeps any decent band going no matter what the gig is like. A sense of humour is essential for proper pro musicians (the non pop star kind I mean) and in our case our stage gear demanded it. Ron supplied his Serenaders with bright and flowery Hawaiian shirts (of the kind that Ry Cooder made cool many years later but were certainly not cool in 1968) and a plastic garland that I think they called a 'lai'. Or maybe, appropriately for the holiday camp, a 'lay'.

Our Butlins gig in The Beachcomber Bar was at times hilarious; kids falling into the mountain stream, and husband and wife disputes and the like, but the best bit was The Thunderstorm. At regular intervals throughout the afternoon and evening sessions Dave the bar manager, an ex-jockey from the nearby Yorkshire racing town of Malton who occasionally supplied us with the odd sure thing (a tip for the day's horse racing I mean), would nod for us to stop playing (a barley wine opportunity) while he started The Thunderstorm Machine.

The designers of The Beachcomber Bar had included a huge papier-mâché volcano in the centre of the bar, complete with a babbling brook, a mountain stream of the South Pacific, Bali Hi type. When Dave flipped the switch, The Thunderstorm would happen. The house lights would go down, and rumblings through the PA system would amplify into thunderous crashes, whilst the lights inside the mountain would flash orange and blue. This would go on for three minutes at least whilst Ron, Pete and I replenished our barley wine supplies and cleared away the empties from The Stage – the Pacific island in the middle of the mountain stream.

We had a laugh, the twelve weeks flew by and it was a successful and quite eventful Butlins summer season.

On August 20th 1968 Warsaw Pact forces, including troops from Bulgaria, the German Democratic Republic (East Germany) Hungary, Poland and the Soviet Union, invaded Czechoslovakia. Approximately 500,000 troops, mostly from the Soviet Union, had poured across the borders in a blitzkrieg-like advance. The Russians claimed that they had been invited into the country in order to preserve socialism, but nobody could say who had invited them. They eventually agreed that they would leave again in October '68, but in fact they were to keep a significant number of troops in the country until 1987.

Hi-de-ho, the big bad Russians had helped to spice up the Butlins summer of 1968 by invading Czechoslovakia in mid-season. That summer Billy Butlin had just happened to employ an enthusiastic team of bouncing Czech chalet maids whose role was to clean and maintain the homely cabins that the happy campers would inhabit for their annual one or two weeks of escape from reality. Funny that World War Two had not long been over and yet the British public was more than happy to be holidaying in a camp not superficially unlike the POW camps we'd seen in those wartime films.

This latest invasion of their homeland obviously threw our Czech chalet maids into some confusion and there was a lot of expensive telephoning home for reassurance. In the event, none of the girls quit their job and went home, they seemed to think things were not so bad for their families – or their country – and they needed the money. Not too many years later, Filey Butlins Holiday Camp and its many restaurants and bars, including The Beachcomber Bar with its wonderful Thunderstorm Machine, were bulldozed to the ground.

As my Filey Butlins 1968 summer season with Ron Snaith's Hawaiian Serenaders approached its end and I was obviously wondering what I should do next, David Bowie left his room at Ken Pitt's Manchester Street flat and moved, together with his new girlfriend Hermione Farthingale, into an attic room at 22 Clareville Grove, South Kensington, London.

Hermione was an excellent dancer, she was a professional dancer after all, and she sang with a soft and harmonious voice. She also played a few chords on the guitar and so she and David decided that they should form a 'multi-media' group. This new group would employ all of their talents, song and dance included, and they could work together.

Tony Visconti provided them with a good guitarist, a friend of his called Tony Hill, and they called the trio Turquoise. The group rehearsed, played one gig at the Roundhouse on 14th September 1968, then Tony Hill left the group. Tony was a heavily mustached rocker, previously with The Misunderstood, perhaps one of Visconti's darker bands, and David and Hermione's acoustic dreamy stuff was probably just not Tony's cup of tea.

Tony Hill was right on the point of leaving when I walked back into David Bowie's life. I had phoned David, told him I'd just finished a Butlins season and asked if there was anything happening, then I'd taken a train to London and watched Turquoise's solitary Roundhouse gig. When asked by David, I decided that I would accept his offer and replace the departing guitarist with immediate effect. Our trio was to be renamed Feathers and it looked as though I was about get into something a little more interesting than just 'Rock and Roll' this time.

Feathers; David, Hermionne & Hutch © Ray Stevenson

Chapter Seven - Feathers: Hermione, Bowie and Hutch

I had handed my Hawaiian shirt back to Ron Snaith and said my goodbyes to Pete Mensel, the bass player who completed the trio line-up of Ron's Hawaiian Serenaders, and to the chambermaids and bar staff, and to the shortly to be bulldozed Butlins Holiday Camp, Filey, forever.

I had decided to retrace my steps and go back to London in search of a good band to play with and I had persuaded my long-suffering wife (now my ex-wife) Denise that we should take our baby son Christian back to the big city. I found an almost affordable furnished flat in East Finchley, and then a draughtsman's job in Hornsey, North London with Smithfield Refrigeration Limited in order to have my independence and guarantee that my family could eat properly. Although I never really considered it at the time, this would take any kind of responsibility for me away from David Bowie in due course, as he didn't have to worry about making sure that I got paid. This detail was to prove a most important feature of our close working friendship during the months ahead, as we were to do more writing and rehearsing than actual gigging, and we consequently made little or no money.

I telephoned David, who invited me over for a chat at his new flat which he was apparently sharing with a new girlfriend, a lady with the wonderful but quite unlikely name of Hermione Farthingale, at an equally posh sounding 22 Clareville Grove, South Kensington.

As I set off to find my way by tube to South Kensington I no longer felt any regrets about leaving Canada. I was happy to be back in London again, and though I still had the sports jacket and a day job, I felt a surge of anticipation at meeting up with David again, knowing how creative he could be and that there might be a role for me to play in his musical career again. Even though I had already visited many socially and economically very different areas of our capital city, I was very impressed with David's new address. South Kensington was quite a social step up for my friend I thought.

David's warm welcome for me at the doorway of 22 Clareville Grove reassured me that he was delighted that I had returned, and his healthy appearance and confident demeanour convinced me that he had got his life together while I had been away on my Canadian wild-goose chase. David to my surprise, and some relief, was dressed very much as I was myself (I had of course left the sports jacket at home) in soft 'flares' and skinny jumper. Also his hair was cut very much like my own, worn quite long but neat and 'feather-cut', and I realised that 'style' in both Canada and the northern provinces of England was not necessarily too far behind London in the autumn of 1968.

As I followed David upstairs, and then up again on a narrow winding staircase to his top floor flat, he told me, "You've come back just in time Hutch, we've got some great things going on." At the top of the stairs there was just the one quite small but stylish room. David and Hermione's flat was a bedsit, a bed-sitting room with a wardrobe, chest of drawers, one cane chair, double bed and bedside table. The room had an unused fireplace, its mantelpiece filled with joss-sticks and glass things, and with a large vase containing tall grasses covering the chimney breast. Pieces of lace adorned the bedhead, and there were hessian cushions on the bed and on the floor. Hermione was not at home, but her personality filled the room.

I still had great faith in David's talent and potential, and I listened with interest over several cups of coffee as he told me of some of the ups and downs in his life, and of his career progress whilst I had been in Canada. He still did not tell however, of the rejections he had endured at the hands of the men in suits at Decca

Records and Apple, to name but two, or of the unexpected return of his half-brother Terry to the family home in Bromley. David didn't say much about Lindsay Kemp either, only that he had been working with Lindsay's mime troupe. This sort of minimal information, on a need-to-know basis, is typical of David, he never wastes words but also he keeps private matters, as they should be, private. The irony, as I relate to you the details of some of David's 'private' moments with me, and with others, is not lost on me.

For my part, I didn't have much to tell David about the past year. I had to admit that my marriage was quite shaky, hardly surprising after many long months of hard winter and night shift in Montreal, followed by a hedonistic summer season at Filey Butlins' Beachcomber Bar playing Bali Hi and drinking gallons of Kings Ale seven nights a week. I had invested my earnings well however in the fares to London, and had come armed with a pretty good finger-style played on a Harmony Sovereign acoustic 6-string that I had traded in return for my electric Fender Telecaster before going to Canada. I also had spent many months listening to Canadian music, mostly of the Gordon Lightfoot and Leonard Cohen variety, and I had somehow become, as David also had, though by a different route, a little less Rock and Roll and more 'Folky'.

We were both now fashionably 'soft', and we were probably both relieved to find that our taste in clothes, as in music, was more or less identical, at that time anyway. David and I never, ever, discussed sexuality as such, but we did talk about 'image' a lot. When I met Hermione a week or so later, I saw right away that we were, in visual terms at least, a matching 'set of three', and I was happy to join him and Hermione in adopting a very natural and androgynous image for our trio.

Having no spare money for the necessary 'stage clothes' to fit in with David and Hermione, I took to improvising by means of buying the likes of 'granddad vests' and kitchen porters jackets from the Army & Navy Stores (the real ones) and cold-water dying them from white to a suitably cool forest green or a pale blue. I would then add an Indian necklace, or beads and leather bought at Kensington or Pimlico Markets, to achieve the intended style. David had always been good at this sort of trick, and I had learned a little about sartorial style on the cheap from him.

We quickly found our musical style too. We were delighted to discover that our three voices blended without effort, and that my new acoustic guitar finger-style fitted well with David's very basic but effective strum on his 11-string Gibson. It had been a 12-string of course, but a machine-head (tuner) had been damaged and was never replaced.

The repertoire for Feathers was developing as we rehearsed. Our starting point was Jacques Brel, whose songs had been translated from French into English by Mort Schuman, the songwriter who together with Doc Pomus had written many of Elvis Presley's hits. Schuman had then recorded an album of his Brel translations, thereby releasing several jewels for consumption by the English speaking world.

David and I worked out the chords for 'The Port of Amsterdam' and 'Next', and I contributed my versions of a couple of Leonard Cohen songs. Hermione joined us for three-part harmonies on David's new song 'The Ching-a-Ling Song' and versions of songs intended for David's next album, namely 'Love You till Tuesday', 'Sell me a coat', and 'When I'm five' – which we segued into from our version of 'Going Back', the Carol King song.

Then there were the mimes. You will appreciate that I knew less than bugger all about dance, but I thought David and Hermione danced, together or separately, wonderfully. I felt that my old pal, the natural frontman, had by no means wasted the past year or so in learning to dance and mime.

Together they danced to a spoken piece called 'The Seagull'. The voice (I've no idea whose voice it was) and some ethereal seaside sounds were on an audio cassette, for which incidentally we carried no back-up. It was my job to operate the cassette player and sit very still whilst David and Hermione danced.

David's solo mime was called 'The Mask', which also had a voice-over on a cassette. No other rock singer, before or since David did it, could have done this stuff, and it knocked me out.

The other element in this new groundbreaking arty-farty multimedia thing was, I was told, to be poetry. Yes, reading poetry out loud. David and Hermione both told me, "You can do it, come on you have to do it!" So I did a poem by Liverpool's Roger McGough called 'Love on a Bus'. It was difficult for me, it was not like singing a song at all, but I did it, very self-consciously, especially in rehearsal with only David and Hermione present. 'I'm a musician, not a bloody actor' I thought, but kept the thought to myself and did my bit so as not to let the side down.

In the middle of our rehearsals, a newspaper interview opportunity had come along, and David and Hermione had gone along and done it without me as I had to be at my job at Smithfield Refrigeration in Hornsey. It was no ordinary newspaper mind you; I was staggered to learn that the article was to appear in 'The Times' and that they wanted a photograph – of all three of us. David could have left me out of the photo shoot of course, but he is a decent chap and he kept Feathers on a democratic basis.

I took the necessary half day off from work and the three of us went into the West End, to the studio of Clive Arrowsmith, the very talented and very famous photographer – who of course I (the lad from The Sticks) had never heard of. Clive was a charming chap indeed, and while he worked he told us funny stories about Eric Clapton buying fast cars in spite of not having a driving licence and other stuff – he was a pal of Eric's apparently.

David had omitted to tell me, as he had been asked to by Clive, to 'come in dark clothing', and I was just dressed as usual in the hippy gear. This did not bother our canny photographer one bit, Clive just set up a small stepladder, set some lights and told me to button my navy blue suede battledress jacket right up to the neck. By these means Clive Arrowsmith produced the most stunning photograph ever taken of Feathers, and there's no doubt that its quality influenced the Times editor's decision to place a large black and white print of it slap bang centre at the top of page 7 on Wednesday December 11th 1968.

The article it supported, written by journalist Sheila More and titled 'The Restless Generation:2', included interviews with (as well as David and Hermione) the likes of Mick Jagger and Mary Hopkin, but there was no room for any photograph of ol' rubber lips or the pretty eighteen-year-old Mary. Just us, Feathers, 'from left to right, Hutch, Hermione Farthingale and David Bowie' it said – and we'd only done three gigs!

David's interview contribution to the Times article was to state that his father's upbringing had been so different that they could not communicate and that: 'discussing religion embarrasses him, and to get emotional about something, well that's only for the servants' quarters, like mental illness'. That must have gone down well in Plaistow Grove, Bromley, but at the time that never occurred to me, I couldn't relate to my parents either could I? The thought never even crossed our minds that possibly it might be the same for every 'Restless Generation' and that the Times could be simply reproducing adolescent bullshit.

Interestingly David also said that, 'We feel our parents' generation has given up, they're scared of the future. I feel it's basically their fault that things are so bad – but we're going to make an even greater mess of it. There can be only disaster ahead'.

101

Hermione had said, 'Now it's more like Shakespeare's time – we question everything in order to discover ourselves'. Her classy comment made it into the article's headline.

The fully grown-up Ken Pitt apparently didn't think Feathers was worth David's time and effort, and regarded the multi-media experiment as 'an innocuous divertissement that nobody wished to pay for', and (as David's manager rightly should) Ken recorded that 'by Christmas (1968), Feathers had done three gigs and earned £56'. Ken's meticulous records show that we had appeared at the Country Club, Haverstock Hill on November 17th for £6, at The Arts Lab, Drury Lane on December 6th for no fee at all, (that can't be right can it?) and at Sussex University on December 7th for £50 (thank God for the education system eh?) I remember the Drury Lane and Sussex University gigs very well, but I have no recollection of that first gig at the Country Club, and I wonder why I don't – was it really awful or did I sleepwalk through it?

Ken Pitt, although he had other clients and young friends like Marty Kristian (soon to become a New Seeker) in his life, continued to work away on David's behalf. I mean of course David Bowie as a solo artist, as Ken had no interest in me (though he appeared to tolerate me) or Hermione (whom he did not). Ken had negotiated that David Platz of Essex Music would finance the independent production of 'Ching-a-Ling Song' for David Bowie's use. Feathers would perform the song and Tony Visconti would be the record's producer.

Hermione and I regarded the session as promotional, and as a potential break for Feathers of course. We never discussed payment or contracts; we just thought we were a team. In a way so did David I'm sure, but Ken Pitt was too slick to even make an appearance when we turned up to record at Trident Studios on October 24th 1968.

Tony Visconti and I just didn't get on. We had met a couple of times at Visconti's flat, and though I couldn't know his reasons he didn't seem to like me very much, right from the start. I certainly had the middle-class young American down as a bit of a clever bugger as he played cello and generally seemed a bit 'highbrow', so maybe it was just as much my fault.

In any case we successfully recorded 'Ching-a-Ling Song' for Essex Music to put away 'in the can', to be sold for large profits in the years to come no doubt. The session produced a good result in spite of Visconti trying to make me sing harmonies well above my admittedly somewhat limited vocal range (a physical impossibility of course) and generally being a prat towards me in the studio. Visconti had apparently told David he didn't want me on the recording, but David stood his ground and kept me in, and seemed to be as annoyed as I was at the rough treatment I was receiving from his producer.

Ken Pitt's managerial efforts had also included talking to Phonogram in Hamburg who had expressed interest in recording David for their Philips label, and also finding his boy a very small part in a film of Leslie Thomas's book 'The Virgin Soldiers'. David cut his hair soldier short for that film; the first time I watched it I blinked and I missed him. It wasn't worth the haircut.

Ken was never Rock and Roll, and never understood what David wanted to do musically, or why, but he diligently kept at the job he did understand, that of artist management.

Ken Pitt very shrewdly took a calculated gamble and booked the Purcell Room, a part of the Royal Festival Hall complex, for David to perform a solo concert almost a year hence, November 20th 1969 in fact. He had also started discussions with a friend from the Manfred Mann days, Malcolm Thomson, now a film producer, about the costs involved in a promotional film of David and his music. This film was to be even more of a financial risk for Ken, for though he apparently had some discussions with a German television producer called Gunther Schnieder, who might have decided to produce the film for German TV, Ken had decided to go it alone, using his own money.

Malcolm Thomson had worked with Ken Pitt during the infamous first 'electric' Bob Dylan tour of the UK, a tour that became known as the 'Don't Look Back' tour, named after D. A. Pennebaker's fly-on-the-wall documentary. He was available, ready and willing to make the Bowie promotional film for Ken as soon as possible. Malcolm Thomson was apparently from a totally respectable background, for when I told him that my home town was Scarborough, Malcolm said his father was a vicar in the town. He told me that yes, he did visit Scarborough now and then to see his father, and he would have to go to the Italian Gardens above the old Spa Ballroom to find the space to smoke a joint in peace. So Malcolm was another sixties rebel. We all liked Malcolm Thomson, and he was good at his business.

Hermione and I were told about 'our' making the film by David, but only once all the financial arrangements were in place and agreed between Ken Pitt, Thomasso Films Ltd and David Bowie. The total cost to Ken was to be, I learned years later, over £8,000, a big layout in those days, but it would prove to be a very profitable long term gamble. As for myself and Hermione, we were once more delighted to be involved in another promotional venture, never for a moment stopping to consider 'contractual matters' or to negotiate payment for our several days work to come in the recording studio, film studio and on location on Hampstead Heath. Perhaps I had become the loyal fool, just like the guys in The Buzz had been.

I arranged the necessary few odd (unpaid) days off from work with Smithfield Refrigeration. The company had originated in Smithfield Market of course, and my boss was a real East Ender called George Impey. I was lucky in that old George was quite used to arranging 'time orf' for another of his employees who was 'sort of involved in show business'. This other chap was in fact a champion ballroom dancer, and he looked the part, very slick indeed.

A few days before filming was due to start, I was given the address of a hairdresser in Sloane Square where, I was informed, 'everything has been paid for'. I found myself in a chair at Leonard's – evidently a 'top people's' salon. Its status was confirmed for me when I recognised the late Maurice Gibb, the rapidly balding Bee Gee (and the talented husband of Lulu) who was sitting a couple of chairs along from me. I tried to be cool, as if I came in places like this all the time, and so I didn't bother Maurice. I came out of Leonard's with a 'bouffant' mod hairdo, and it stayed that way for at least a week.

The next step in my 'makeover' (please note that we didn't actually have that terminology back then) was a fitting session for a pair of tobacco coloured, jersey wool trousers and a flowery shirt, both apparently purchased by Ken Pitt (at no doubt a ridiculous price) from Ossie Clark's shop. In those days I had never heard of Ossie or his shop, but then I'd never read a fashion magazine in my life either. My outfit was completed with the addition of a pair of white loafers by Bally of Switzerland – not my kind of shoes at all, but I was told I could keep them anyway, when filming was finished. That was not to be the case with my 'Ossie Clark Original' shirt however, Ken Pitt took that away from me on the last day of shooting, and then had apparently given it to Marty Kristian, who had by now become a New Seeker and was well on his way to the big time.

I know that Marty probably has the shirt to this day, because he showed me it when I stayed with him and his family in the late 1980s whilst filming for a 'Bowie Documentary' that Marty was co-producing. That proposed production was a television documentary that somehow never saw the light of day, so I will tell you more of that strange story later, dear reader.

Filming for 'Love You till Tuesday' was scheduled to commence on January 26th 1969, and the first day's shooting was to be on location on Hampstead Heath, in order to 'act' some visuals to David's solo recording of 'When I live my dream'. This ballad of David's, the kind of song that Anthony Newley would have been proud of, was taken from his first album 'David Bowie', the album that Dek Fearnley had sweated blood over. The song shows the strength of David Bowie's voice and the breadth of his songwriting, and I think it illustrates my belief that David could have made it as any kind of singer; he is in fact a real singer, not just a pop music singer. Hermione and I were told that we were to accompany David to some sound studios during that week in order to add harmony vocals to some of the tracks, including 'When I live my dream', to be included in the film.

A hired car, with driver, had collected David and Hermione from Clareville Grove at the ungodly hour of 7.30am and then picked me up from my flat at 57 Leicester Road, East Finchley on the way to Hampstead Heath. I had dressed, as instructed, in my Ossie Clarke outfit, but I had wrapped up well in the sheepskin coat that I had bought prior to my trip to Canada. This was just as well as it was a bitterly cold day, although the January light on the Heath was, according to Malcolm Thomson, perfect for his requirements as director.

For David, Hermione and myself the day was less than perfect; it was bloody hard work as Malcolm required the three of us to 'stand next to this tree', 'walk down here', 'look over there', 'look thoughtful' etc. in the freezing temperatures, most of the time dressed only in the flimsy Ossie Clark gear. Hermione's Ossie Clark hippie-style flowing dress was almost see-through, and David wore a sort of schoolboy's jacket over his Ossie shirt, with the same trousers and shoes as me.

I hadn't a clue what exactly we were doing, but the film crew were very professional and they seemed to know what the plan was, so I just did as I was asked, I went 'into make-up' and then 'stood by' quite a lot. I enjoyed my insight into the business of filming though, and whilst David and Hermione would retreat to the back seat of our hire car to escape the cold, I would watch the crew at work when I wasn't required to be on camera.

The next filming was scheduled for six days hence, on Saturday, February 1st 1969, and took place at Clarence Studios, Greenwich. We were in for a long day, as Hermione unusually had some other commitments that week and was only available for the one day. It was my first inkling that all was not well between my Feathers colleagues when David told me curtly that, "She's doing an audition."

The second day of filming started even earlier than the first, the car picked me up in East Finchley at 6am and we collected David and Hermione about forty minutes later in South Kensington en route to Greenwich.

As well as Ken Pitt 'Producer' and Malcolm J. Thomson 'Creative Director', there was a full crew comprising, according to Ken's meticulous records:

David McDonald, director of photography;
Mick Messenger, camera operator;
Robert Carter, film editor;
Des Crowe, production designer;
Jonathon Weston, music supervisor;
Keith Beale, sound recordist;
Paul Owens, hairdresser;
Henrietta Holmes, make-up;
Liz Edmundson, continuity;

and Suzanne Mercer, production assistant (Suzanne was Malcolm's girlfriend).

The performances to be filmed that day were to be of Feathers miming to 'Ching-a-Ling Song', for which of course Ken already had our vocals on tape, and to 'Sell me a coat', another track from the 'David Bowie' album on which Hermione and I had 'overdubbed' our vocal parts earlier that week during our very brief recording session at Morgan Studios in Willesden.

For 'Ching-a-Ling Song', Malcolm had the three on us sit on very large cushions arranged in a semi-circle on a totally white film set. We were dressed, as on Hampstead Heath, in our Ossie outfits, but David had hung up his school blazer for the day. We mimed (strumming acoustic guitars and singing), smiled and acted as instructed on take after take, and 'Ching-a-Ling Song' was soon 'in the can' without a hitch.

'Sell me a coat' required a little more of me in the way of 'acting' I discovered. I was asked to stand nose to nose with the lovely Hermione whilst we mimed our 'back-up' vocal parts. This normally impossible position (she being a good few inches taller that me – she was also taller than David for that matter) was achieved with the aid of a block of wood for me to stand on. This was better than asking Hermione to please bend her knees a little, but it did set us off giggling a bit.

Many years later I was to witness eyeball to eyeball staring between Spiders from Mars drummer Woody Woodmansey and his wife Jean, as part of some Scientology mumbo-jumbo ritual, but for Hermione and me, eye-to-eye with our noses touching, in the middle of the film shoot, it was a slightly disturbing experience. I had to repress the urge to kiss Hermione right there on camera, and Malcolm Thomson (had he really been a soft porn film director? I dunno but have a look at his Space Oddity video…) probably captured that as he had intended.

Hermione made me laugh with a suggestive remark intended for my ears only, and we were like naughty kids. I was always a little careful with Hermione, I always felt that she was out of my league and so I just generally played my 'working class lad' to her upper-middle class and slightly mysterious 'rich man's daughter'. I never knew her real name, though I was curious and so I did once have a look at some mail left on the table in the entrance hall at Clareville Grove. I did see the name 'Miss Evans' on an envelope once and I decided that might be Hermione. When I asked David about it he said he didn't know. I believe it is possible that he really didn't know, certainly when she disappeared he didn't know where to start to look for her. David variously told me that she had 'gone off with a dancer' or 'married a doctor' and on another occasion that she had 'gone to live in Australia'.

Quite recently one of David's biographers (yet another) claimed that David did eventually find Hermione, many years later, possibly some time in the 1970s, and that they had met once more. The story was something along the lines that Hermione is in fact married to an explorer and that they are both working somewhere up the Amazon. Much more recently, I was told that Hermione had turned up at the big 'David Bowie is' exhibition at The Victoria and Albert Museum in London, which ran from 23rd March to 11th August 2013 (the one with all his stage suits and the like on display) so maybe she is back in England now.

Hermione Farthingale, a mysterious lady indeed; she was from another world to mine, and David's for that matter, in 1969. This perceived social gap could have been a part of Hermione's reasons for her leaving David within just days of finishing our film, we will never know. David never discussed it with me, she was here one minute and then she was gone.

The following day, February 2nd 1969, being a Sunday, was a day off for the film crew. It was not a day off for the unpaid 'artists' however, as David informed me that the two of us, without Hermione, were to record a studio version of 'Space Oddity' for inclusion in the film. This was no real surprise to me, as David had shown me the bare bones of the song a week or two earlier, when he had introduced me to his new 'instrument', the Stylophone, and we had worked the new song into the form that everybody now recognises.

It was a song always intended to be sung by a duo – by 'Ground Control' and 'Major Tom'. That was always clear enough, it was two people communicating by radio across open space and in this case it was me playing 'Ground Control' and David playing 'Major Tom'.

We had recorded our first demo of 'Space Oddity', as well as some other originals of David's on his reel-to-reel 'Revox' tape recorder at the Clareville Grove flat. For 'Space Oddity' I had borrowed David's battered Gibson '11-string' guitar and David had played his Stylophone. This was a joke instrument, a battery powered toy which had been advertised extensively by the (at the time) family favourite Rolf Harris, and it made a horrible buzzing noise, the pitch of the buzz being selected by an attached 'stylus'. David, a child at heart, liked stuff like that.

Some of the other songs on the 'Revox' demo had also been the result of our collaboration, and though the song idea, melody, basic chords and the lyrics were always David's, we would work together so that the final shape of the song, and some of its chord inversions and licks were mutually developed. I was the better guitarist and I knew more chords than David, but the songs were his alone.

David told me that our 'Revox' demo-tape was to be sent to 'a guy in the States' who might be interested in us as a duo. I had already realised that Hermione had not necessarily been part of David's longer term musical plan, though she had been his girlfriend. David was however still dependant to an extent on my skills as guitarist and collaborator, and now he seemed to see us as England's answer to Simon & Garfunkel.

For my part I was happy with this, but I also could see the same imbalance of talent in the duo that possibly Art Garfunkel might have seen in his situation, working with Paul Simon. It was to be many years before I was able to fully develop my own performance skills and also to discover that I could write at least a few good songs myself. The title of the new song was a joke of course, a piss-take of Stanley Kubrick's '2001 - A Space Odyssey', but David was I believe saying something valid about the emptiness of infinite space, the loneliness of the long distance spaceman etc. etc., and I liked the idea. The style of the song was pure Bee Gees and we had certainly both been impressed with the Aussies' bleatingly folky harmonies on their early records. The theory that I have read about more than once, that idea that the lyrics were about drugs, or specifically about a heroin trip, is nonsense.

David and I made our way to Morgan Studios, 169 High Road, Willesden on the morning of Sunday, February 2nd 1969, and met up with Jonathon Weston, the music supervisor for the 'Love You till Tuesday' film. Jonathon had been engaged by Ken Pitt to produce what has since become known as 'The Original Version of Space Oddity' by David Bowie. Ken Pitt's published records show that the session musicians that had been hired for the day at Morgan Studios were, Dave Clegg (bass guitar), Tat Meager (drums) and Colin Wood (Hammond organ and Mellotron).

David brought the Stylophone to the session of course, and used it, but he took me aback a bit when he produced what he called an 'Ocarina' on which he intended to play 'a solo'. To me the thing was just another toy, it was a small rounded flute-like vessel filled with water, with an aperture for the player to puff energetically across. In fact the instrument is something like 12,000 years old and variations exist all over the world today. In Japan the traditional ocarina is known as the tsuchibue, the Mayans and the Aztecs played them, and a European example of an ocarina made of an animal horn is the medieval German Gemshorn.

The result of David's efforts can be assessed by anyone who might hear the still available 'Original Version of Space Oddity'. A so-called 'demo version' of this track is today still available – on EMI's 2009 re-release of the 'David Bowie' album number DBSOCD 40 – on Disk Two. I also sing harmony vocals on 'An Occasional Dream' on this album, and prior to its release in 2009 David was good enough to contact me (albeit via a mutual friend) and we agreed a royalty payment for the two tracks. I appreciated the thought, as you can imagine. I have to say that David's Octarina solo on the Space Oddity track from the 'Love You till Tuesday' film was (and still is) just silly, but I've always admired his barefaced cheek.

Once the studio version of 'Space Oddity' – Octarina solo and all – was 'in the can', I was redundant as far as the 'Love You till Tuesday' project was concerned, and I was not needed for anything more on the film. There had been no discussion about performance terms – any payment of fees or royalties – but I felt that I had contributed to a worthwhile artistic endeavour and I thought, well it had only cost me a few days off work.

On Monday 3rd February 1969 I went back to my day job in Hornsey, while David continued with his film making. The visual performances (David miming to tracks from his album) of 'Rubber Band', 'Love You till Tuesday' and 'Let me sleep beside you' were done more or less in one day. Finishing touches to the items that Hermione and I had performed with David on Hampstead Heath ('When I live my dream' and 'Sell me a coat') were made, and David added his Feathers mime piece 'The Mask', dressed like Marcel Marceau in white tights and white face. No surprise to me that 'The Mask' was always Ken Pitt's favourite – there's no music on it and David wears no trousers.

That Thursday, 6th February 1969, David and his film crew worked on the visuals for 'Space Oddity'. I had expected that I might be called in for the day, as the recording, as you already know, is a duet between Ground Control and Major Tom. That is, between Bowie and Hutch. But they didn't call me and in fact I wasn't to hear from David for several weeks. The result of that Thursday's work by David under Malcolm Thomson's direction can be seen by anyone prepared to purchase 'Love You till Tuesday' on DVD (or whatever format might have taken over by the time you read this book!)

My own point of view is that the first few bars where David mimes to the sound of my voice at the very start of the track (I am Ground Control you will remember – I have mentioned it before I think) are really funny. It is a sort of 'before they were famous' teeth joke. The film then develops towards the sort of ending that a porn director (I imagine) might dream up. Major Tom, as the film fades, is shown having his clothes removed by a pair of 'Spacegirls'. I suppose I have to be glad that I wasn't there, but eeh David, you did make us laff.

With 'Love You till Tuesday' in the can, Ken Pitt set about the task of finishing the business end of things, as he had to pay for the printing and publishing of his film. Ken was to find that this part of his project would take more time, effort and finance than he had anticipated. Actually selling the film by turning it into a video, a DVD, an album and a 'Space Oddity' single in all formats was to take him several years.

It was to be those several years later when Ken phoned me at home in Scarborough and asked if I would sign a 'release' for his film. Ken and I agreed a fee for my signature guaranteeing my agreement to the release of 'Love You till Tuesday'. It was after all a promotional film and I wished David the best of luck in his career. I had no idea then that 'Love You till Tuesday' would go on to be sold as a video and later in DVD and CD formats, and that all the soundtracks would appear as an album and various singles. Not an inkling either that the 'Original Version of Space Oddity' by David and myself would be sold to the world as 'by David Bowie' without any performance credit to me.

I will tell you of an interesting phone conversation that I later had with Ken Pitt on this subject, during the year 2000, but that story too must come later in this book.

David phoned me again, towards the end of February '69, to tell me that we had some duo gigs lined up, and that Hermione had left the flat at Clareville Grove. David stayed on at the flat alone, and there we set about rehearsing our act as a duo. We decided that we would call ourselves 'Bowie and Hutch', but in fact the few gigs we played billed us as 'David Bowie and Hutch'. I didn't really mind what they called us.

We didn't need much rehearsal as the material was mostly ex-Feathers stuff, but the evenings of rehearsals round at David's flat provided some light relief from my day job routine as a draughtsman. One evening when I arrived I even found a new girl in David's bed (with David).

Often, before I had to leave in order to catch the tube back to East Finchley, David would nip out to a nearby Indian restaurant and return with a vegetable curry with rice, which we would share. I recall how we ate, on the corner of a bed. In 1969 this was an exotic treat indeed, believe me, and I appreciated David's natural generosity, as well as his friendship, in those days. I had my wife and baby son Christian with me in London of course, but apart from them and David, I knew only the few guys at my day job, and had no friends in the big city. David Bowie, at that time, was my best (and only) mate.

Our first gig as a duo was on 11th February 1969 at Sussex University in Falmer, East Sussex, but the gig I remember best happened a month later on 11th March 1969 at the University of Surrey building in Battersea Park Road, London. The gig was actually scheduled as part of the Guildford Arts Festival; Ken Pitt had booked it, and had arranged a fee of £35 'for David'. I was the hired help again, or maybe just the help, with quite possibly no hire charge involved. Ken sent a minicab to take David and myself to and from the venue, and the driver was a chap called Brian Leeson who had previously worked for Manfred Mann.

David swished into the back of the cab beside me, resplendent in crushed velvet and a very striking curly perm. This kind of hairdo was unusual in those days for anyone who was other than black, and it worked so well for David that evening that people stared into the back of our minicab as we made our way to Battersea Park Road. David responded by waving, in that funny way that the Queen has, at those who stared. This might have prepared me for what was to follow at the gig, but it didn't. David gave me no warning, and from the start of our set he camped it up. Frankie Howerd, Larry Grayson and co. eat your hearts out, David had found himself a character, a gay-comic one that he could hide inside of, and be as outrageous as he wanted to be without embarrassment.

I hid my own only very slight embarrassment behind a Bill Wyman deadpan face. I was totally taken aback, but quickly realised what David was up to, and so played the 'straight man' to David's 'anything but straight man'. "This is Hutch," David told our audience, "I found him in the classified ads in *Time Out* – under macrobiotics!" The gig went very well, and Ken Pitt, who attended the gig, seemed delighted with David's new stage persona.

I was quite used to playing at Folk Clubs. I had done 'floor spots' ever since buying my first acoustic guitar prior to emigrating to Canada, and I would usually play a few Bob Dylan, Leonard Cohen or Joni Mitchell covers as I didn't write songs then. I would sometimes play a couple of 'traditional' songs including a version of

'Scarborough Fair', the traditional song which Paul Simon had not yet borrowed and apparently claimed as his own composition.

David on the other hand had never expressed any interest in Folk Music or Folk Clubs, so I was a little surprised when he suggested that we should both go to one or two 'folk nights' in order to try out and practice our songs to a live audience.

We tried a couple of 'floor spots' to a lukewarm and bemused reception at a couple of forgettable venues before we found that Bounds Green Folk Club would give us a fair hearing, and that we could revisit anytime we wanted to. The resident performer at Bounds Green, who welcomed David and me without any of that teacher/social worker stuff that plagues many folk clubs, was a pleasant and talented chap called Ralph McTell who played excellent ragtime guitar and wrote a few songs himself. I heard him sing one called 'The Streets of London' which was to make him a few quid over the years to come.

David (and I) did cause a few raised eyebrows in the folk clubs; David played stylophone on 'Space Oddity' of course, while I played his 11-stringed, 12-string Gibson acoustic, and our material was anything but 'folk music' to the folkies in those days, but it was our appearance that probably had the most effect on the folky audiences. David persisted with curly perm, crushed velvet flares and tight hippie tops, and I did my best to keep up with him. I probably failed of course, the best I could do was a home tie-dyed granddad vest and a Red Indian necklace or some beads. Very few of the folk music audience in those days ever changed out of the Hush Puppies and sports jackets that teachers and social workers wore as their uniform, and just the odd Aran sweater was proof of their musical preferences.

David's boots were more than a fashion statement; they were possibly the start of a footwear revolution. They were football boots. The fashion world had given us platform soles and kinky boots, but 'trainers' were not available, as they had not been invented yet. Football boots however had evolved from the 'hob-nailed boot' style that David and I had both worn as small boys on the sports field, and had been developed to a high degree of sophistication by manufacturers like Puma and Adidas.

So David wore football boots with his crushed velvet flares. They were black with red stripes and trim and they anticipated exactly the future trainer style. The boots would clatter a bit in the tube stations late at night when there were not many people about, and they can't have been very comfortable, except on grass, until the moulded studs had worn down a bit. They did however make the required fashion statement for David, and the first 'trainers' appeared on the market a year or two later.

Fashion successes aside, the Bowie and Hutch duo were not setting the world alight; we didn't really know how to go about getting more gigs for ourselves. We had no PA equipment, and neither of us had a driving licence never mind a car, and I don't think Ken Pitt was remotely interested in the task of promoting 'Hutch', whether 'Bowie' liked it or not. I believe that Ken was more or less waiting for the duo idea to play itself out so that he might persuade David back to the career path that he saw as the best way forward for his boy, that of an all-rounder, a cabaret singer. David had a great voice for ballads, and in a way Ken was right, David could, if his heart had been in it, have made his mark as a show business 'crooner' in late sixties Britain. This would have been a big mistake; I know he would not have stuck it out for long and the wrong move could possibly have ended David's career prospects for good.

Though David talked to me about the 'show business' idea, and asked if I would act as his musical director in the event that he decided to take the cabaret route, neither of us had much enthusiasm for the plan, and we both regarded a potential move into cabaret as 'selling out'.

Our time together, as Bowie and Hutch anyway, was running out, and though we continued to visit folk clubs in order to try out and practise our material, David also had some solo engagements, and in fact played a short tour with his friend Marc Bolan's group, the emerging Tyrannosaurus Rex. More than one biographer's account of those days has me on that tour, but I was not there, in fact I never met Marc Bolan face to face, though I knew he was around. Some of the tour posters might possibly even have advertised 'Bowie & Hutch', but the guitarist with David on the T-Rex gigs was not me. If I had to make a guess, I would suggest that it might have been Keith Christmas, who later became a Beckenham Arts Lab regular. I never met Keith either, but I believe that David might have been canny enough to line up a potential replacement for me, just in case. David had known that I was reluctantly thinking about leaving London again.

One evening, on our way back from an aborted folk club visit – we found that the 'folk evening' had been cancelled, with no reason given – David took me round to the nearby apartment of a friend of his, having suggested that we might as well make the best of the evening. It seemed that the tube station was very close to this guy's place, and so we could resume our homeward journey later.

David's friend was not expecting our visit, but welcomed us into his apartment. The man was a very striking Chinese-American called Calvin Mark Lee. Calvin's well cut long hair, jewellery and expensive looking hippie-style clothing, together with his very stylish and immaculately furnished apartment marked him out as a man of great taste I thought, but in nothing like the older traditional style favoured by Ken Pitt. Calvin however may have had some things in common with Ken. Calvin was gay, and he made it obvious that he had a thing for David Bowie.

Calvin Mark Lee had been born into a Chinese-American family in San Francisco and had graduated as a pharmaceutical chemist. In 1962 he had come to London on a three year grant, from the US government sponsored 'Office for Scientific and Technical Information', to take a post-doctoral fellowship at Chelsea College, but was quickly drawn towards the more beautiful and creative world of popular music.

Calvin was to be seen around town at all the best music business parties, always beautifully dressed, and wearing a sparkling metallic self-adhesive disc in the middle of his forehead. The disc was made of metallised polyester, which diffracted light into all colours of the spectrum, and it ensured that Calvin would be noticed. The disc idea was to be recycled by David when he invented Ziggy Stardust.

When the US government grant ran out in 1965, Calvin worked for a while in a Kings Road boutique called Dandie Fashions, then was hired by a tall gangling American called Lou Reizner, who Calvin had met and sufficiently impressed at a party. Lou ran the London office of Mercury Records and Calvin, by virtue of his talent for being good at going to parties, was given the overblown title of 'Assistant European Director' together with the job of trying to lure his pop music friends and fellow party animals to sign for Mercury Records.

While Calvin briefly left the room to make us some coffee, David opened up a shallow wall cupboard (which I had thought must be a dartboard cupboard – silly boy) to reveal a bizarre photograph collage of nude or semi-nude young men, most of them posing on Calvin's bed like 'Page 3 girls'. Except these were blokes, and one long-haired nude looked to me very much like the famous lead guitarist in a very famous rock band. I guessed that David was testing for my reaction, so I said nothing, as I did not know whether or not David was telling me that he and this Calvin had some relationship, or was just trying to unsettle his friend from the North, as David liked to do with people, even me.

Calvin brought the coffee and we chatted for an hour or so without any potentially embarrassing gay remarks or innuendo, for which I was grateful. We said goodnight to Calvin and made our way back to the tube station round the corner. It was closed, and had done so well before the usual last train time – according to David's recollection. We were a long way from David's place where I had planned to stay that night as I could not in any event have afforded a taxi to Finchley, so we decided to return to Calvin's and ask if we could sleep on his floor. Calvin, as charming as before, said of course, no problem, and brought me some bedding for his couch. David said goodnight and left me to my couch in the sitting room. Next morning David showed no embarrassment, so I preferred to imagine that David had used a second bedroom (though I didn't think there was another) and we didn't mention the incident or Calvin Mark Lee ever again.

The mysterious Calvin was to reappear (mysteriously) during the 1973 Aladdin Sane USA tour; however he did not even acknowledge me as we passed each other in a hotel swing-door. Maybe he could have said, 'Psst, you ain't seen me, right?' – for that was my impression of his brief 1973 reappearance.

It was during the spring of 1969 that Calvin's boss Lou Reizner met a very bright, high-spirited and vivacious American girl called Mary Angela Barnett. Known as Angie she was then a student of economics and business studies at Kingston Polytechnic in Surrey.

Angie's father, a former colonel in the US army, was a successful mining engineer working in Cyprus, and had sent his daughter to the exclusive St. George's girls boarding school near Montreux, Switzerland. At sixteen, Angie progressed to the Connecticut College for Women in the USA, where she had a very public lesbian affair with a fellow student, resulting in her dismissal from the college. Angie's mother then escorted her to London. Angie, very much like Calvin Mark Lee, once she had been introduced to the glamorous world of 'popular entertainment' that is Rock and Roll, just skipped all her lectures and was consequentially barred from final exams. Lou Reizner naturally introduced Angie to his friend and employee, the dynamic Calvin Mark Lee, and the bisexual pair quickly 'got it on'.

David Bowie's photograph had by this time made it on to Calvin's 'Pin-Ups' gallery on his apartment wall, and Angie, intrigued and attracted, asked Calvin for an introduction. So it was that on April 9th 1969 David met Angie at the Speakeasy Club in London's West End. The headline band that evening was King Crimson, which included the influential guitarist Robert Fripp, who of course was to become a Bowie collaborator himself in due course.

Angie recalls that David appeared to her as 'a lean, blond, enigmatic figure' wearing a pastel striped sweater and mustard coloured sailor's flares. David, Calvin and Angie dined together one evening, then David and Angie became lovers, completing the bisexual ménage. Angie says, 'It seemed predestined,' and 'His character cried out to be explored', while David summarised in a later interview, 'When I met Angie, we were both fucking the same bloke'.

David and Angie were to have a stormy partnership, but at that time I knew nothing of it. As Angie was entering David's world I was leaving again; I told David that my family had to come first, and as neither Feathers nor Bowie and Hutch had showed any signs of making any money, I had to go back to Yorkshire again. David said okay, but would I perhaps come back after I had resettled my family in Scarborough. I told David that I wanted to return and would see what I could do, but my promise lacked conviction, as I knew that I needed a 'proper job' once again, for a while at least.

David lived from day to day, somehow he ate and he kept busy and creative without earning very much money. He was The Jean Genie.

I had to live like a grown-up and so returned to Yorkshire.

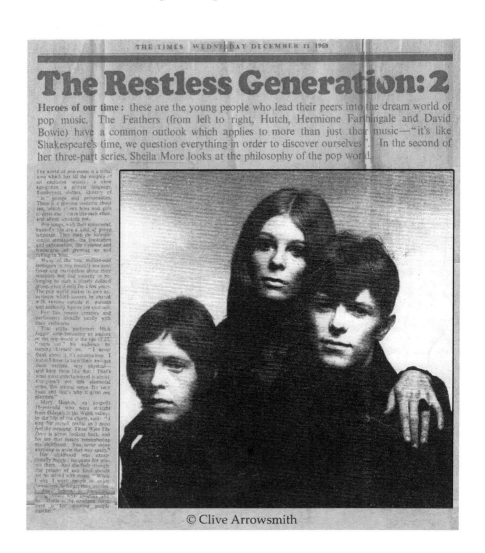

© Clive Arrowsmith

Chapter Eight - The Rise of Ziggy Stardust

My latest retreat to my old home town Scarborough in the summer of 1969 was again difficult. I had to admit to parents and friends that my quest for success in 'music' in London had again failed, for lack of work, and consequently, for lack of money. Of course the 'music' – and by that I mean the creative, roots-inspired kind of rock and roll music that I lived for – was not really regarded as an 'industry' or even a 'business' in those days, it was perceived by both the general public and the music business in the UK as being at the rough end of the entertainment spectrum, and it was certainly not an 'art form'. I told everybody that I knew back in Scarborough that I had great faith in my mate David Bowie however, and that I knew that he would eventually get his big break. People were generally not at all impressed, and the majority said that they had 'never 'eard of 'im'.

Things took a turn for the better for me when to my amazement I managed to get my old job as a draughtsman back, at the company where I had been an apprentice. They even gave me the grand title of 'Chief Draughtsman' as the other lad in the office was a novice. No one at Erskine Laboratories Ltd seemed to remember, or if they did, care less, that I had more or less told them to 'take their job and stuff it' when I'd broken out to freedom and sailed off to become a pop star in Sweden just a few years earlier.

One day, not too long into my rehabilitation, I was at my drawing board (it was of course many years before CAD, that is, a computer aided design system with drawing board graphics) when I sort of half heard the works' handyman in the yard outside, whistling and singing to himself as he cleaned the windows. Next instant I almost fell off my stool. I could not believe my ears, but there it was, drifting into the drawing office, 'Ground Control to Major Tom, Ground Control de-da de-dum'. The handyman was singing our tune. It was out of tune, but unmistakably it was David's and mine, our tune. I walked around the building and questioned the whistling fool who told me that he'd heard 'Major Tom' on the wireless, adding, "Catchy innit?"

I was very soon to hear it myself over the airwaves, again and again that same week and for several weeks to come. My old mate had obviously decided to record a solo version of 'Space Oddity', and he was having some success with it, in fact it was never off the radio. My reaction, after I had recovered from initial disbelief was 'good luck to him, he deserves his success, he's a talented lad and he has worked hard for it'. I was chuffed for my mate, I was back at the drawing board again but our efforts with Feathers and Bowie and Hutch had not been in vain after all.

Even when the record became a Top Twenty 'hit' I harboured no resentment that I had not been asked to do my 'ground control' part on the new recording, I just reflected upon my disappointment that I'd had to leave when I did. It had been bad timing on my part for sure, but isn't that life? I liked what the producer and the session guys had done, especially the lead guitarist, and I could still hear my influence in the finished product. I philosophically concluded that the results of my recent collaboration with David, and my small but significant contribution towards the production of the new 'hit' song would have to pass unrecognised. It didn't matter that much to me, after all the song idea and the lyrics were all David's own. I never really considered the possibility that the song might make a lot of money, and I let it go easily, rather than let any bitterness spoil my recent memories. I had made the decision to leave David to carry on alone in London, and he had tried his best to stop me leaving. Anyway how could I have tried to phone him and ask about some sort of reunion, the song was now published, the record was out and it was too late. I was a grown-up with a family to support, whereas David was very much alone and would live or die by success or failure I was sure, and so he just had to succeed – there was never any chance of turning back for David Bowie. I would not admit to anyone, least of all to myself, that I had missed out badly and that maybe it hurt just a bit to not be singing my part on the new recording of Space Oddity.

On Wednesday April 9th 1969, not long after I had taken off for Yorkshire, and coincidentally the day on which he had first encountered Angie Barnett, David wrote to Ken Pitt about his position. David still believed, as the letter revealed, that I would soon return to London and resume the Bowie and Hutch gigs, having 'dropped the family off' in Scarborough.

David's letter was addressed from his new address at 24 Foxgrove Road, Beckenham, an old house which had been divided into three flats, and in the letter David told Ken that 'Hutch should be back with us during next week so then we can really start the club-zapping month.' David also informed Ken that 'things are a bit grim on the money side. I have just about enough to last me until next Monday'. Ken would usually come up with the cash when things got tight for David, and he would no doubt have recorded the outgoing expenditure accordingly.

Mary Finnegan, a journalist, occupied Flat 1, the ground floor flat at 24 Foxgrove Road. Upon meeting David when he visited an old friend who lived in the top flat at the address, Mary had offered David the use of her spare bedroom. Mary, like David, was more or less 'broke' at the time, but told David to just pay what he could, when he could. Then David had an idea. He told Mary, "I know, let's start our own gig. You can do the organising." Mary did just that, she went to see the landlord at The Three Tuns, a pub in Beckenham High Street, and obtained the use of an otherwise mostly unused lounge bar on a one night per week basis.

It had been a good idea, the opening night of the new 'Folk Club' attracted an audience of fifty people, and they heard David Bowie, as the resident singer, sing for most of the evening. Folk singer Tim Hollier had been engaged as a special guest, and after all expenses had been covered, Mary and David had come away with five pounds each and were well pleased with the success of the evening. The following week the attendance was ninety people, and from then on, no fewer than one hundred and twenty crammed into the gig each week. Barry Mason, the friend of David's from the top flat at Foxgrove Road, had brought a 'liquid whirl light machine' along, and it created a 'super psychedelic atmosphere' according to Mary. It was the dawning of the Age of Aquarius, and Love and Peace were creeping into Beckenham. One evening David told his folk club audience that the gig was now an 'Arts Lab', and it was henceforth to be called 'Growth'. And Beckenham was ready for it.

For as long as I had known David, he had not to my knowledge used drugs, certainly not on any regular basis anyway. It has been said however that around the Arts Lab time David had begun to use 'tincture of cannabis' – a substance that only a capable and unscrupulous chemist (pharmacist) would be able to produce. I have my own suspicions and theories regarding the start of David's use, and misuse, of drugs, but I must keep them to myself. I do know however that Ken Pitt would never have condoned drug use, whereas David's new circle of friends, including Mary Finnegan (journalist), Calvin Mark Lee (graduate pharmacist) and Angie Barnett (free spirit) would have certainly been more 'liberal' and 'progressive' in their attitudes towards drugs during the fast evolving 'psychedelic' era.

Ken Pitt, still assiduously managing David's affairs, had a meeting on April 14th 1969 with Simon Hayes, who although he was an Englishman, was 'Director of Product' in Mercury Record's New York office, and happened to be in London at the time. This important contact with Mercury Records had been made through

Calvin Mark Lee and had been passed on to Ken Pitt by an unusually diplomatic David.

Mercury Records in those days rated low in Ken's estimation. He had heard an untrue and malicious rumour that they were not even a bona fide recording company, and that they were in fact a US Mafia front.

In spite of his misgivings Ken proceeded to act for David in negotiations with Simon Hayes. Having failed to interest Beatles producer George Martin in producing a David Bowie record, and finding that Tony Visconti didn't like the song 'Space Oddity' and wouldn't touch it either, Ken settled for Gus Dudgeon, an associate of Essex Music who were David's publishers, as producer. Ken then, in consultation with his 'love-rival' Calvin Mark Lee, the man who Ken loathed but who was now a Mercury Records employee, proposed and agreed a contract with Mercury Records, the label that Ken mistrusted, to record and release the song 'Space Oddity' by his artist, his boy, David Bowie. The release of the record was to be carefully timed to coincide with mankind's first visit to the moon. We have to assume that Neil Armstrong couldn't sing.

As well as looking after David, Ken was at the same time busy handling the successful career of Nina and Frederik, the Scandinavian folk singers, as well as that of Nana Mouscouri, the Greek 'euro-ballad' singer. Ken's international expertise had also landed him with a job as UK Delegate to the annual 'Malta Song Festival' at the end of July. Although not televised, this event was a forerunner of the ridiculous but extremely profitable Eurovision Song Contest, and Ken made good use of his position by securing a spot for David Bowie as a representative for the United Kingdom. The entire festival was then to go to Italy, where it would no doubt become the 'Somewhere in Italy Song Festival'. David probably went along with the idea of the song festivals to humour Ken Pitt, who certainly still hoped that his boy might yet develop as a mainstream 'all-round entertainer'.

The immediate and quite urgent preparations for recording 'Space Oddity' included hiring an up and coming Paul Buckmaster to collaborate with David in writing the arrangements for the session musicians. Gus Dudgeon made his choice of musicians and submitted a budget to Mercury Records. The cost of recording the solo hit version of 'Space Oddity' was estimated to be (in 'old money', I mean pounds, shillings and pence) a grand total of £493 17s 0d. So it cost less than five hundred pounds for a track that would sell millions of copies and make millions of dollars, pounds, euros, yen and the rest.

The musicians were to be Terry Cox (drums), Herbie Flowers (bass) and Mick Wayne (guitar) each of whom would earn £9 10s 0d from the session. A new lad called Rick Wakeman would play a new-fangled forerunner of the string synthesiser called a 'Mellotron' and would be paid ten shillings less than the others, possibly because the hire of that sophisticated and quite rare keyboard instrument was to cost an exorbitant £35 9s 0d!!

A string orchestra of sixteen musicians were each to be paid the same rate as young Wakeman, and with an estimated six hours of recording time at £25 0s 0d per hour and mixing and overdubbing at £15 0s 0d per hour, plus the hire of a Hammond organ and purchase of the master tape reel, the tight little budget of less than five hundred pounds was accepted by Mercury Records.

The contract, the 'offer they could not refuse' from Mercury Records' office in Chicago reached Ken Pitt's office on June 16th 1969 and the session was booked for June 20th at Trident Studios in Wardour Street. It was a favourite studio of David's and in fact it was the studio where David and I had struggled with Tony Visconti's boorish behaviour on the 'Ching-a-Ling Song' session.

The 'Space Oddity' session was a great success, done in six hours of first takes, but the following day David fell ill with glandular fever and could not sing the 'overdubs' needed to finish the recording until several days later. I wonder if anyone thought of calling me in. Okay it was probably not an option.

The release date for David's 'Space Oddity' single was set for July 11th 1969, craftily timed to coincide within days of the forthcoming and highly publicised first ever real 'moonshot'. Frantic activity at Mercury Records on both sides of the Atlantic ensured that every publicity angle was covered, so much so that Ken Pitt was uncharacteristically persuaded to part with a 'bung' of £140 to a character calling himself Tony Martin. Mr Martin had 'guaranteed' Ken that for one hundred pounds he could buy 'Space Oddity' into the *Record Retailer* chart at number 40 on July 23rd 1969, and up to number 30 the following week. He could also, he convinced Ken, 'rig' the *New Musical Express* chart the same week with an entry at number 30. Thereafter, for every five places he was able to move the record up the charts, he would charge an extra five pounds. For an illegal payment of three hundred pounds, David Bowie's 'Space Oddity' would be guaranteed to make the top ten of both the *New Musical Express* and *Record Retailer* sales charts.

On November 1st 1969 the *Record Retailer* chart placed 'Space Oddity' at number 5, its highest position, the *New Musical Express* had it number 6 – both 'Top Ten' hits, just as Tony Martin had promised Ken Pitt. The *Melody Maker,* which had not been mentioned by Mr Martin during his pitch to Ken, also had the record at number 6 that week.

The British Market Research Bureau who compiled the weekly charts for the music press and the BBC, were said to consult a panel of three hundred record shops in order to assess national sales figures. Tony Martin could not possibly have rigged the reports of three hundred shops, even if he knew which shops were used in the system. Either he had access to the panel, or to the music press, or he was a con man.

Ken Pitt was eventually to admit his error of judgement in falling for Tony Martin's pitch, and concluded that his money had in no way influenced the chart placing. He would though, wouldn't he?

On July 5th 1969, the new recorded version of 'Space Oddity' was played to the 250,000 people who attended the free concert given by The Rolling Stones in Hyde Park. This exposure was worth as much as all the airplay that the single had been receiving, but even better publicity was yet to come. Just as Mercury Records had planned and expected, the BBC's producers for the moon landing took the bait and took the record on board as their moonshot theme song.

On the evening of July 20th 1969 at least a dozen people crammed into Mary Finnegan's flat at Foxgrove Road. As well as Mary, David and Angie, photographer Ray Stevenson, a regular supporter of the Beckenham Arts Lab was part of the crowd. Ray had been close to David throughout the Feathers and Bowie and Hutch periods, and had provided several beautiful photographs of David, Hermione and myself during that time.

At 9.18pm precisely, Neil Armstrong stepped on to the moon. A steady supply of joints had been circulating around Mary's flat, and the little party were as emotional about the amazing happenings as the rest of the planet, if not just a little more so. When the BBC, to accompany their incredible television pictures, played the sound of the opening bars of 'Space Oddity', Angie was said to have become hysterical, laughing, crying and screaming uncontrollably. She knew instinctively that the record would make David Bowie into a star. Not a really big star, not yet, but to Angie he was up there with Neil Armstrong that evening and that was a start.

David Bowie flew with Ken Pitt to Malta on July 25th 1969. The song festival was to require David's attendance in Valetta for one week; thereafter they would go to the mountain resort of

Monsummano Terme for the Italian version of the pre-Eurovision song festival. Ken saw the opportunity for a sunshine break with his boy, and it would get David away from Angie for a few days. The Italians particularly liked David's song 'When I live my dream' (one of the songs Hermione and I had added backing vocals to, and had filmed for on Hampstead Heath) and were proposing to give David an award for it. Ken Pitt's delight was shattered when Angie flew in from London. Angie wept hysterically in the arrivals lounge, then recovered and changed into a see-through dress in which to make her entrance at the song festival awards ceremony. Angie had brought a large white bow with which to transform David's hair for the evening (that bloody Tom Jones-PJ Proby thing again) and the result has been described by Ken Pitt as being 'like a bizzare wedding party'.

When the Italian Job was over, Angie flew to Cyprus to see her parents while David returned to London. On August 3rd 1969 David was to perform at his Beckenham Arts Lab in the back room of The Three Tuns pub to a sell-out crowd, boosted by the success of 'Space Oddity'. Only when the gig was over did Mary Finnegan tell David that she had a message that his father John Jones had been taken to hospital, and that he was seriously ill with pneumonia. Though she had the best of intentions, Mary admits her mistake in not telling David earlier. "It was catastrophically dreadful," she recalls, "He went absolutely ape."

David was appalled to find his father weak and emaciated in the hospital bed. He had taken the Italian award statuette to the hospital in the hope of raising his dad's spirits, and indeed John Jones was genuinely delighted, and proudly told his son, "I knew you'd make it one day." Two days later, as David was starting work on his album for Mercury Records at Trident Studios in Wardour Street, John Jones died, at the age of only fifty-seven.

David attended his father's funeral at Elmers End Cemetery on August 11th 1969 accompanied by several friends including Calvin Mark Lee and Angie, and most of David's family which of course included Terry Jones. David's Auntie Pat and her husband were there with the responsibility of looking after David's half-brother, who had been allowed out of Cane Hill Hospital for his stepfather's funeral. Pat Antoniou recalls that David showed little emotion at the funeral 'he had no tears, no tears at all'. Auntie Pat's published recollection is predictably cruel; I know that David loved his Dad.

Five days later the Beckenham Arts Lab staged a 'free festival' at Beckenham Recreation Ground. The event had taken months to prepare and so David again gave a dynamic performance in the best tradition – that of 'the show must go on'. The festival was a great success, but off-stage David was mourning his father in the only way that he could. Mary Finnegan recalls that, "David was in a completely catatonic state for the whole of the festival – he was vile."

In fact, David was making his journey through what was probably the hardest period of his life. On the one hand he was a successful performer at last, but on the other hand he had lost his much loved father at a far too early age, and in due course was very soon to lose his extremely ill half-brother Terry in equally tragic circumstances.

Predictably, Mary Finnegan had been pulled into (or had pulled herself into) yet another of Angie and David's *ménages a trois*. By the end of 1969 however, in spite of, or maybe because of, the success of 'Space Oddity' the three-way relationship was under some strain, and Mary was beginning to tire of the non-stop party. "I got fed up with people smoking dope and playing music," she said later. "It was like a free festival in my flat."

To Mary Finnegan's relief, in October 1969 Angie found another place in Beckenham for herself and David to live. The new place was a rented house at 42 Southend Road, Beckenham, it was of quite unusual Edwardian architecture and had been grandly named 'Haddon Hall' – possibly after the eccentric who had designed and built it.

David and Angie took the downstairs rooms as their flat, and let one of the spare rooms upstairs to Tony Visconti and his partner. Another room was let to eighteen-year-old Nita Bowles, a student and a dedicated member of the Beckenham Arts Lab. Nita took very little persuasion to join David and Angie in their bed from time to time; it was after all the age of peace and love, and the now freely available cannabis would have loosened any inhibitions.

During that autumn of 1969, David had worked tirelessly with Tony Visconti at Trident Studios on his album for Mercury Records. The album was needed urgently by the record label in order to capitalise on the success of the 'Space Oddity' single. For UK release the album was to be imaginatively titled 'David Bowie', the same title as his previous Deram album. In the USA the album would be called 'Man of words/Man of music'...

One of the bands that had played at the Beckenham Free Festival on August 16th 1969 had been Junior's Eyes, and their drummer was John (Johnny) Cambridge – coincidentally yet another Yorkshireman like myself. Johnny was from Beverley in East Yorkshire and had previously been playing the same coastal gigs from Scarborough down to Hull where I too had learned my trade. Johnny had progressed through The Gonx to Treacle and finally The Rats, based in the nearby city of Hull whilst I had been with The Dave Kirby Five and The Tennesseans in Scarborough. The Rats' lead guitarist was of course a promising young chap called Mick Ronson. So it was that my own connection with both Johnny Cambridge and Mick Ronson dated back to the time before any of us had even heard of David Bowie.

It was some time later, during Johnny's stint with The Mandrakes that I first actually met him face to face – we have been mates ever since and we played together around the north-east of England in my post-Bowie band Hutch & It's Easy. Not a great name. And it wasn't as easy as I'd thought. Soon after Johnny Cambridge's own days with David were over, and while Mick Ronson was still around in Hull, playing with my old chum, the wonderful Michael Chapman as well as with The Rats, Johnny arranged a secret band rehearsal in a Scarborough church hall. It was a try-out with a new line-up and the band that Johnny proposed included singer Robert Palmer together with Mick Ronson on lead guitar. The potential new band didn't really hit it off, and as we know very well, they went no further with the idea.

These band 'try-outs' can be strange affairs, I experienced a strange one myself way back in the mid seventies when Johnny Cambridge again booked a little hall and persuaded Trevor Bolder and myself that we might make a great trio. I turned up with a little acoustic guitar as it was the only guitar I possessed, and Trevor brought a Marshall bass-stack. It was bass and drums rule, my guitar howled and complained with feedback and my original songs made no impact at all on the session. It was a mistake, I had gone all acoustic and Trev and Johnny had no concept of playing quietly, underneath my acoustic. They were still rocking and I wasn't.

It was another of those twists of fate, call it synchronicity or something, but John Cambridge and I, in spite of playing the same gigs and knowing the same bunch of local musicians around East Yorkshire in the mid sixties, had never actually spoken to each other in the old days, and yet we were both playing with this pretty much unknown singer and songwriter called David Bowie within weeks of each other in 1969. John Cambridge came in more or less as I went out of David's life again.

Johnny like me has always had two trades, he is a time-served plasterer as well as a bloody good drummer, and just like me he had decided that playing music was the better option and had headed for the bright lights of London town.

Junior's Eyes went with David on a short tour of Scotland, and when it was over, David asked Johnny Cambridge if he would join him and help to form his next backing band, this one to be known as The Hype. Next day Johnny made the journey back to Hull and went looking for the guitarist who he knew would be perfect for the new band. Of course he had in mind his old mate Mick Ronson, the guitarist from his previous Hull band The Rats. Johnny knew that Mick was still holding down his day job as a council gardener, and quite easily found him, pushing a white-line machine along a football pitch in one of the Hull parks. Johnny made a pitch of his own and it must have been good, for Mick decided on the spot, quite uncharacteristically, to throw all caution to the wind, quit the day job and the horticultural night school studies and join the new band. Both Mick and Johnny also joined the residents at Haddon Hall where The Hype, with Tony Visconti – who was keen to get out of the studio and play some live gigs – completing the line-up on bass guitar, rehearsed what were to be the beginnings of a new era in world pop music. Of course they didn't know it at the time.

At the beginning of 1970, David Bowie and The Hype were a tight unit, ready to rock, and more than ready to go on the road. The band had rehearsed extensively at Haddon Hall, with the two imported Yorkshiremen, Mick Ronson and Johnny Cambridge, sleeping on mattresses on the floor downstairs for the several weeks of rehearsal and planning.

Ken Pitt had surprisingly been the man to give the new band its name, though the overall concept in music and presentation was all David's. The presentation of The Hype was, visually at least, a little unusual and it was certain that before they even played a note the band was to be noticed and not easily forgotten. Johnny Cambridge was nonplussed; he was instructed to dress up in a cowboy outfit, complete with ten-gallon hat, and become 'Cowboyman'. Visconti became 'Hypeman' in a Superman suit, but with an 'H' for Horrible on his chest in place of the 'S' for Super. Mick Ronson wore David's old silver 'Space Oddity' suit and became 'Gangsterman', while David was identified as 'Rainbowman' in lurex tights, cape and pirate boots. This concept of dressing up to play rock and roll was not exactly new, but David's styling of these outfits for his new backing band The Hype was important amid the very beginnings of the soon to be called 'glam-rock' style of presentation that would soon explode upon the world of pop music.

I was to be a little taken aback with the band's appearance myself when I went along to see my old mate David in the spring of 1970, when David Bowie and The Hype played The Penthouse, the only decent live music venue in Scarborough in those days. The town had several dreadful 'discotheques' too of course; they were the inevitable cattle markets where the lads could meet the lasses, and it seemed to me that these were just dark airless rooms with flashing lights and loud recorded rubbish selected by some idiot with a turntable. They had, as they still have to this day, their place in every town. I think they are called 'nightclubs' again at present.

I had eagerly awaited David's visit to my home town ever since Peter Adams the owner of The Penthouse had some months previously told me that he had booked the band. I knew the staff at The Penthouse very well, I was in there a lot, and most importantly I got along fine with Ruby, the lady on the door. So it was that I generally had free admission to the club, and also to 'Ligger's Corner', a preposterous roped-off designated VIP area at the end of the bar. My status as a local celebrity was to be temporarily boosted by David Bowie and The Hype's passing through our small town, and my two previous short tenures as David's guitarist now appeared, to the musicians in the town at least, to have been time well spent after all. They had all 'eard of Bowie by now.

For those of you who have not been in a band, and so will not have had the experience, let me tell you that going to see ex band mates, old friends, at one of their gigs can be a difficult business for all involved. As I climbed the stairs into the darkness of The Penthouse on the evening of Thursday 21st May 1970 I was already prepared to be disappointed with the reunion. I was proven right, for my quite recent and good friend David Bowie – understandably perhaps – was just too preoccupied with preparations for his gig to pay too much attention to my backstage visit, though I was cheered up immensely by Mick Ronson's warm welcome. That was so typical of Mick; we had after all only bumped into each other a few times. By contrast Tony Visconti and I had nothing to say to each other, he had not changed his attitude toward me so I left him alone. There was no sign of John Cambridge, he had been given his marching orders, and for no apparent reason at that, and the new drummer, who was making his live debut with the band that very evening, was a lad from Driffield (the little town just up the road from Scarborough) by the name of Mick 'Woody' Woodmansey

As I watched David and The Hype play their first set, which included of course 'our' song 'Space Oddity', I experienced that complicated emotion, that strange and difficult sensation that can be experienced exclusively by musicians who have no choice but to watch old band mates playing their familiar set, and my memories bubbled up from my subconscious on to the surface. The feeling is best described I think as a mixture of sadness, envy, pride, anger and regret, and probably a couple of other emotions too. In any case that evening it was too much for me and I went home before the band took a break, I just could not say my goodbyes. I did still wish David well, but I couldn't stand and watch the band, and I couldn't take any more of the backstage reunion either.

I suppose I thought that might have been my last meeting with my old friend, and I certainly believed that my musical association with David was over. How wrong I was. There had been lots of changes happening in David Bowie's life at that time, and though I didn't know it that evening as I trudged home from the Penthouse, my own life was soon to be changed too. I would be reconnected with the changes in David's life before too long. David's main life changes were the result of two important decisions.

Firstly, he ruthlessly replaced his old friend and long-suffering manager Ken Pitt with an up and coming, much younger and more aggressively capable character called Tony Defries. David knew that he needed a manager for the times, not one who was plainly living in the past and with consequentially rather low horizons in view for David's future career. In any case David Bowie and Tony Defries were made for each other, the timing was perfect, and they were both ready to conquer the world.

Secondly, on Friday 20th March 1970, David Jones married Angela Barnett. The ceremony took place at Bromley Registry Office, John Cambridge was best man, standing in for Tony Visconti who had a recording session, and David's mum Peggy attended and co-signed as a witness. I don't know that it was really a match made in Hell as some observers have said, as both David and Angie are in my experience essentially very nice people. They both became somewhat eccentric in due course as everyone knows, and maybe they fell out of love as fast as they fell in, but I believe they had hopes and dreams when they married. The fact is that both of them needed to meet US and UK residence and work permit criteria, and their marriage immediately sorted that for them.

Angie got busy and made a home for David, no matter how unusual their three-way sex life might have been, and Tony Defries got busy too; it was to take Tony just two very short years to make

David into a star in both the UK and the USA, and the rest of the world just follows.

Having said that, it is plain that Tony Defries's successful campaign, proactive and determined as he may have been, could not have been possible without David Bowie's timely master stroke, his own unique creation, that of Ziggy Stardust. That Ziggy was a composite fantasy figure who had been made out of influences from several parts of David's rock and roll experience is plain to see, though we all have our different points of view on the subject. For what it's worth here are my own guesses at the component parts of Ziggy. Firstly there were the early sixties rock and roll acts who dressed up in anything that worked for them. The leaders in the presentation stakes were Nero and The Gladiators (yes little skirts and Roman sandals), Johnny Kidd & the Pirates (eyepatch, leather boots up to the thigh) and Screamin' Lord Sutch and the Savages (on-stage coffin, vampire teeth, fake blood and the like).

Secondly there were those leather-clad rockers that David had met and that held a strange fascination for him. They were Gene Vincent (and The Blue Caps – those caps were a band uniform too) who was also a great musical influence, and Vince Taylor, a home-grown Star Club Hamburg rocker who became a big star in Europe, possibly possessing more style than musical substance, but all the same having a remote quality, an intensity that David liked.

The third component was the character that inspired Ziggy's name. A Texan singer-guitarist called Norman Carl Odam had picked as his stage name 'The Legendary Stardust Cowboy' and, probably because Norman was with Mercury Records in the USA (as David was), David had noticed his name among the album releases. Alvin Stardust had nothing to do with it I would say.

The fourth and final component would be Iggy Pop; David was to see Iggy perform in New York and the show would remind David that rock and roll was supposed to shock as well as entertain, and that once in character, on-stage with a great band, for a real performer there are no limits. David's change of stage name had been one thing, but his change of persona was to be something else. Ziggy Stardust was to be the performance.

David's songwriting too had gone through some changes, and the influence of Angie's view of life was coming through. Queen Bitches and Jean Genies were rampant, Ziggy had some killer songs to sing and David was happy to let Ziggy have them all.

Real progress however, as always in the real world, was slow and predictably The Hype were going the way of The Buzz before them. Not enough gigs simply means not enough money to survive on, and Johnny Cambridge, having stayed around long enough to attend David and Angie's wedding, also to witness Terry Jones's rapid deterioration as well as David's real concern for his brother, went back home to Beverley in Yorkshire. Johnny was in fact 'sacked' by David one day at Haddon Hall, but as I have said before, in band business when there are no gigs and no money, there is little or no difference between quit and sacked.

John Cambridge was immediately replaced by the quiet and unassuming Mick 'Woody' Woodmansey, a mate of Mick Ronson's. Woody is a quiet and reliable guy, and though some say he is not the drummer that Johnny Cambridge was (being neither erratically brilliant nor sometimes unpredictably crackers) I would say, having played with both of them, that there's very little in it, they are both very good drummers. It mattered little indeed at the time, as very soon afterwards both Mick and Woody, having helped David complete the second Mercury album 'The Man Who Sold The World', also went penniless back to Yorkshire.

Tony Defries set about revising David's publishing arrangements, thereby laying the foundations for the making of his own fortune in the years to follow. David himself went with Angie to New York, where he made quite an impression on the populace of the city by wearing a dress for press photographs. He and Angie went to lots of parties, and the trip had little to with music, but a lot to do with public image. Upon his return to the UK, David got the music end of things together again. His first step was to recall Mick and Woody to London, and they brought with them from Hull another mate, Trevor Bolder, an ex-hairdresser and very solid bass player, to replace Tony Visconti who had finally tired of the party at Haddon Hall.

The new line-up released the album 'Hunky Dory' to critical acclaim. In some style, resplendent with fur coat and cigar, Tony Defries had secured for David a lucrative contract with RCA Records of New York, and the release of 'Hunky Dory' was to be the start of the real roller-coaster ride to fame. Tony, just like David Bowie, recognised the value of dressing up and becoming somebody else for business purposes.

By the end of September 1971 David had got his ideas together for his next album. He had revisited New York, with both Angie and Mick Ronson along for company, and had with RCA's help and financial support made the rounds again, and he made friends with a lot of influential people in the Big Apple. Significantly these influential people included some members of Andy Warhol's entourage, but also the little known but outrageous singer and frontman of The Stooges, one Iggy Pop, a character in a very similar vein to members of the Warhol group in that his fame was based largely on his ability to offend sensibilities in all directions. David saw something he liked in Iggy, he recognised a kindred spirit, and when he called his new producer Ken Scott to discuss the new album, he told Ken, "You're not going to like it, it's more like Iggy Pop." Ken Scott had never heard of Iggy Pop of course, but when he heard David's proposed material for the album, that detail did not matter.

'What he'd come up with was incredible,' is Ken's recollection of the day he heard the songs that would make up the new album, to be called, said David, 'The Rise and Fall of Ziggy Stardust'.

David Bowie's new band was musically perfect for his new concept, they played the unusual new material with a powerful 'heavy metal' style, and Mick Ronson in particular was to show the strength of his own creativity in producing arrangements and guitar licks to perfectly complement David's musical ideas. David's other ideas for the band, however, were more sartorial and quite understandably were a little more difficult for Mick, Trevor and Woody to embrace with too much initial enthusiasm.

The basement flat at Haddon Hall was occupied at the time by Susie Frost who, as well as being nanny to David and Angie's new baby son 'Zowie' Bowie (real name Duncan Joseph Haywood Jones), was a talented seamstress. Susie was asked to produce a set of band costumes to David's design specifications, and these were based very much on the prototypes that The Hype had worn. David persuaded Mick to grow his hair a bit longer, Trevor to grow and dye his hair black and his sideburns silver, and Woody to turn himself into a startling peroxide blond. These hair transformations would, together with the addition of prototype glam-rock black eyeliner all round and the new stage costumes, achieve for the band the full dramatic effect that David had designed for them. David then told the slightly bewildered working-class lads from Yorkshire that they would from now on be called 'The Spiders from Mars'.

The music was great, and the 'Spiders' very soon took to both their new outfits and their new on-stage alter egos. With the addition of their old pal, ex-Rats roadie Stuey George, a black Yorkshireman from Hull, the band set about setting the world alight.

The first ever 'Ziggy Stardust and the Spiders from Mars' gig was at the Toby Jug pub in Tolworth, Surrey on February 10th 1972, and just seven months later the band were ready for the opening night of their first US tour, at Cleveland on September 22nd 1972. They had come so incredibly far in just those few months; Tony Defries had done the business and had matched David's inventiveness with his own promotional and negotiating skills. The fact that Tony Defries was already making money while David was rapidly getting into debt either escaped David's attention or he just didn't care at that time. Certainly David Bowie's energies were, at the end of 1972, directed towards on-stage performance development as never before.

The first Ziggy Stardust and the Spiders from Mars US tour in 1972 was undertaken by David and the Spiders, at Tony Defries's insistence, in some style and was to cost RCA, who would underwrite the outgoing expenses against David's future earnings, an unprecedented amount of money given that this was a brand new, relatively unproven artist. Tony Defries told the band that if they behaved and spent like stars, then America would believe that they were stars. David, Mick and the others had no argument with that rather attractive theory, and they all took to limos and room service like ducks to water. The entourage was to continue to grow too, as MainMan, the company that Defries had formed to handle David's promotion and tour arrangements, added an extra bodyguard to help Stuey George, a hairdresser/wardrobe mistress, an official photographer and several other administrative staff to the tour overheads.

Whilst his entourage, now swelled to perhaps two dozen people, enjoyed the luxury of living at the Plaza Hotel in New York, David had a real, performance-related problem on his mind. With less than a week to go to Ziggy Stardust and the Spiders from Mars' opening concert in Cleveland, Ohio, David and Mick had decided that they needed to add a pianist to the Spiders' on-stage line-up in order to play live and do full justice to their new album 'The Rise and Fall of Ziggy Stardust'.

They had to move fast and when Ken Glancy, head of RCA in London and an avid Jazz fan, recommended an experienced and talented New Yorker called Mike Garson, David and Mick asked Defries to call him in for an audition at RCA studios that very same day. Mike Garson recalls that, 'I must have played for about eight seconds when Mick said, "You've got the gig." ' When Tony Defries asked him how much he wanted to be paid, Mike, an experienced studio and jazz-group player, had guessed that the Spiders, being rock stars, must be earning at least $2,000 a week, and so asked for a comparative $800 per week. Defries' deadpan expression, then his immediate agreement to the generous weekly wage, plus on-the-road expenses, made Mike instantly wish he had asked for more. In fact, at that time, though the Spiders had all their high-living expenses paid for them, Woody and Trevor at least were still being paid only a £30 per week retainer. Mick Ronson, always important to David, might possibly have earned a few quid or so more than the rhythm section, but he would have had to keep it quiet.

Tony Defries had instructed the Spiders, "You've all got to learn how to look and act like a million dollars," but in reality there was no money coming in to pay his phoney millionaires even a fair living wage at that time. David Bowie's accounts, if anyone had bothered to look at them, would have shown that David himself was deep in debt. David's previous manager, the capable and careful Ken Pitt, would never have contemplated such a risky promotional strategy, but the confident Tony Defries's style was of course destined to pay off big-time for all concerned. In retrospect, I suspect that there was probably no other way to achieve that perception of glossy 'international stardom' for David in such a short period of time, and anyway it wasn't Tony Defries's own money that he was gambling with was it?

The tour was as a whole a great success, though there was the odd *non* sell-out, as in St. Louis where only 250 people turned up to experience the beginnings of a world phenomenon. The new 'auxilliary Spider' Mike Garson was giving the band his extraordinary musicianship to great effect. David and Mick's overtly sexual on-stage antics might be wowing the already screaming audiences, but Garson's rippling piano style was inspiring David musically. David had already begun to assimilate the influences that he saw and felt around him in the USA. Particularly so the more 'seedy' aspects of life at street level in the cities of America, and the lyrics to the songs that were to make up his next album 'Aladdin Sane' were taking shape and were benefiting immensely from Mike Garson's imaginative piano stylings.

Work on the tracks for 'Aladdin Sane' was started in the RCA studios in New York, and when the tour party eventually returned to London, while Tony Defries remained in New York to arrange David's next, bigger and longer tour for 1973, the band went into David's favourite Trident Studios in Wardour Street to finish off the album.

For some time, David Bowie and Mick Ronson had been discussing the idea of augmenting the Spiders' on-stage line-up even further. The addition of Mike Garson had been so successful that the prospect of having a horn section and backing singers on-stage to exactly replicate several of the new album tracks in live performance was just too tempting for David and Mick. So it was that when David was interviewed by the UK weekly music paper, the *Melody Maker*, he talked about 'enlarging his band' with sax players and backing singers, and David added that he would 'probably get a guy to play 12-string guitar with us – so I can move around more freely'.

The *Melody Maker* was in those days very much a musicians' paper; it even included intelligent 'jazz' and 'folk music' sections and its journalists were both talented and genuinely interested in music. The paper was to eventually lose its direction and it became an awful teeny-music magazine in the nineties before closing down completely, but in 1973 any provincial semi-pro guitarist like me could be guaranteed to buy it every week.

So I bought it that particular week, and I read the front page 'Bowie' article, including the bit about 'we'll need a guy to play 12-string guitar'. Okay, I thought, I can do that, but he surely must have somebody lined up by now? My next thought was 'now where did I put Johnny Cambridge's phone number?'

Chapter Nine - Hutch Becomes a Spider

David Bowie had successfully spent the last couple of years, 1971 and 1972, working hard at making Ziggy Stardust and the Spiders from Mars famous. He had also, for convenience sake, married Angie Barnett. I had been working hard at being a draughtsman again in Scarborough, whilst watching my own marriage disintegrate.

By the autumn of 1972 I was to find that I had little or no choice but to move out of my comfortable but sadly no longer happy family home, and into a cold basement flat beneath a 'trendy boutique', a clothes shop called 'Surf-in Scene' in the South Cliff area of Scarborough. Although I knew that my marriage was finished and irreparable, I also knew that I would miss my two young sons a lot. Christian now had a baby brother, Jesse, to keep him company, and on the day I left I thought that my heart was broken.

My new abode smelled badly of the old portable paraffin heater that was my only source of heat in the seaside holiday flat. When the heater was off, the place just smelled of damp. I had never learned to cook properly, my first wife had simply replaced my mother in that department, and so I was eating badly. I did have a girlfriend or two, and I did appreciate some of the immediate benefits of life as a single person again, but in general terms I knew that my life was going nowhere. I did have some sort of consolation in that I played with a dinner dance band three or more nights a week, even six nights in the summer season, and that was in addition to my day job in the drawing office at Erskine Systems, so fortunately I didn't have too much spare time to sit around and feel sorry for myself.

The Roger Dean Five were very good at the dinner dance job, and we earned good money from entertaining the better off amongst the hotel owners, shopkeepers and amusement arcade owners in Scarborough every Saturday evening at The Royal Hotel, which in those days was the top hotel in town, and much grander than The Grand Hotel just over the road. It wasn't a bad gig, the head chef was one of the good guys and during our breaks, taken in the hotel kitchens, he would secretly supply us with chips – I mean French Fries, not gambling chips – there were not yet any casinos in little seaside towns like Scarborough. We would also play engagements around the area for the small town Round Tables and Rotary Clubs, to the business types, young and old (Round and Rotary Clubmen respectively), who had 'made a few bob' – and the women who had married them – with the occasional birthday celebration, society wedding or hunt ball thrown in. Roger Dean knew how to run that kind of gig, he was a decent piano player but more importantly he was a good bandleader. Roger would tirelessly talk to the people who had booked us, and to the punters who came to patronise us, and all musical 'requests' for silly pop covers or favourite dances, foxtrots, waltzes and the like, would be diplomatically handled by him. If I didn't already appreciate the 'us and them' state of English 'county' society, then I certainly learned all about it during my time with The Roger Dean Five. All musical experience is useful though; you have no idea how many rock and roll guitarists have played the 'Gay Gordons' in their time. And neither have I.

It wasn't so bad, both my old mate from the Tennesseans, Roy Piper, a panel beater who was our bass player, and Dennis Hitch, who was an architect and our drummer, would always have us laughing, and their humour and friendship was good enough to keep me going during the early days of my new-found freedom, or loneliness, depending on what day it was. These guys knew what I was going through, Roy had already divorced, and every one of the other band members, Dennis and both the Rogers, Dean and Maughan (trumpet and vocals) were all later to follow suit, thereby completing a full set of divorced band mates. Not that unusual for working musicians perhaps, but we were a hard-working, family-type outfit, we weren't doing drugs and shagging groupies (well, rarely anyway – in both cases) so how come? At least ten different answers would be given by the five musicians and their long-suffering ex-wives no doubt.

My first Christmas on my own without the family, that of 1972, was a tough one and I was ready to take the first opportunity, no matter what it might be, to take a new job, leave town, whatever. The New Year's Eve celebrations were as they always have been and always will be at The Royal Hotel, and the big hit at the time was 'Jump up and down and wave your knickers in the air'. 1973 was going to be different I thought, something would turn up, I was certain of it.

It was during the first or second week in January 1973 when I read the *Melody Maker*'s front page article about David Bowie's (apparently quite late in the day) requirement for a 12-string player and backing vocalist, and I was more than ready to have a go at getting the gig. I realised that I probably was too late, that I'd most likely missed the boat and that they must surely have somebody lined up by now. Still I had to try to get hold of David's phone number, or Mick Ronson's number, as quickly as possible – just in case.

My first instinct was to call David's ex-drummer John Cambridge. I knew Johnny was back at his job as a plasterer in the little market town of Beverley, and though I knew that he would be perfectly happy being at home with his wife Angie again, Johnny would almost certainly have contact numbers for David and Mick. He did have the numbers, and Johnny said no problem he would get back to me. I had no doubt that he had been asked not to give the rising stars' phone numbers away – even to old friends – without checking first, and I left the matter in his capable hands.

Two days later, it was not long after my twenty-ninth birthday in January 1973, I picked up the phone next to my drawing board and our receptionist said, "There's a call from a Mr Ronson." It was my birthday present. Mick's cheerful voice came on the line, "Alright Hutch? You still got that Telecaster? Okay, you're coming with us then? That's great mate, here…David wants a word."

David sounded chirpy too, they had obviously decided between them that I would join them; there was no time for auditions and they both knew that I could do the job. David said, "Give 'em a week's notice Hutch, we're in the studio, can you come down?" I said I would, and so I went to see the works manager, Howard Hunter. Howard was a decent sort and a good boss, and actually offered to see if he could get me a wage rise if I would stay, then asked me if I was sure that I should be doing this sort of thing at my age. I told Howard that I didn't think an opportunity to visit the USA and Japan would come around again and that I was giving just a week's notice and that I needed tomorrow off to go to London to see David Bowie.

Next morning, instead of getting into my draughtsman's outfit (you know, the old sports jacket and Hush Puppies uniform) I put on jeans and T-shirt and caught the early train to Kings Cross. When I got to Wardour Street and walked down past the Marquee Club towards Trident Studios, it was like coming home again, though I still didn't allow myself to believe that I was definitely going to re-join David, to actually join his Spiders from Mars band. 'Not till you're on the plane' I told myself 'you know that things can always go wrong in this business'.

I waited in the reception area at Trident Studios, a place of course that I knew very well, for a break in the recording session so that the receptionist could tell David of my arrival. After fifteen minutes or so David came through to reception and welcomed me warmly enough. He had his mind very much on the recording session, the job in hand, and so did not waste much time with me apart from telling me that he was pleased to see me again and would see me in

New York in a couple of weeks time. I happened to be wearing a 'Surf-in Scene' (the shop upstairs from my little flat in Scarborough) T-shirt with an appliquéd radio set on the front, and David paused to compliment me on it as he went back into the control room. He was inclined to do that, I mean notice my clothes, from time to time over the next few months. We could go for days on tour without even exchanging greetings at a sound check, then he would comment on something I was wearing as he passed me. On the road I did tend to buy leather jeans and the like in order to look a bit less like a draughtsman. I think David had long since given up on my poor dress sense, but perhaps he noticed that I was still trying.

Before I left Trident I managed to have a few words with Mick Ronson in the studio. Mick told me I could have played some rhythm guitar on the album in progress, which was apparently to be called 'Aladdin Sane', if I hadn't had to go back to Yorkshire that same day. 'Oh well, can't have everything' I thought, and caught the train back to Scarborough in order to work my notice at the day job.

Mick had told me that when I came back down to London the following week I could, for the few days until we left for the USA, stay with him and the other Spiders at the house they shared in Beckenham. Mick Ronson's naturally friendly nature reassured me that I would be okay in my new band, in spite of the slightly offhand reception that Trevor and Woody (and to an extent, David himself) had given me at Trident. It was to be several years later before I learned that Trevor had wanted to bring his own younger brother into the Spiders to play 12-string, and presumably Woody would have supported him in that. Fortunately for me, David and Mick had the last word and preferred to take me with them, but somehow I think neither Trevor nor Woody ever forgave me, being an 'old pal' of David's after all, for getting the gig.

Back in Scarborough I had to tell Roger Dean that I wouldn't be able to play the dinner dance at the Royal Hotel in Scarborough the following Saturday as I had to go to New York with David Bowie and the Spiders from Mars. Roger took it quite badly; he obviously wanted more notice than I could give him. I enjoyed telling Roger I was leaving though, because although I liked him and got on with him well enough, he was a typical band leader of the old school, not one of the lads, and I felt he perhaps underrated me as a guitarist because I am not a proper reader, and not a natural dance band player. I can follow a written arrangement, play all the fancy chords and fake a melody solo but Roger made it no secret that he had preferred his previous guitarist, an old-school player, a good reader who played it straight.

I was the small town star again in Scarborough that week. The Scarborough Evening News had always kept the local population informed of my comings and goings, to Sweden and the like, and my old mate Barry Hampshire, himself an excellent saxophone player, had generally written good reviews of my local gigs. 'Scarborough musician to join David Bowie in New York' was a story too good to miss and the paper was to keep track of my movements for the next year or so. I could have sent them a weekly diary for them to run as a column, but then isn't hindsight a wonderful thing?

I said goodbye again to my parents, who seemed a little bemused by my latest stroke of good fortune, and I guessed they had been phoning round family and friends to let them know that I was on my way back on track to find fame and fortune after all. Just a bit of a shame that it had to be with the notorious bisexual pop vocalist David Bowie I guess.

It was harder saying goodbye to Christian and Jesse, my two lovely boys, but I promised to send them lots of postcards. Of course kids adjust quickly to new circumstances, and I thought at the time that my leaving would not hurt them as much as it was hurting me.

These days I'm not so sure about that, and guilt is a permanent thing.

I packed just one suitcase, as instructed by MainMan Management. I didn't own much more than one small case would hold anyway, and with just that and my Telecaster I caught the train to Kings Cross, then made my way south to Beckenham.

Mick, Trevor and Woody, the three East Yorkshire lads known to the world as the Spiders from Mars, were sharing a large semi-detached house in Beckenham, not too far from David's house, Haddon Hall, together with their roadie Pete Hunsley who was another old mate of theirs from Hull, and they very generously made room for me for a few days. Both Trevor and Woody's wives were visiting when I arrived, though mostly they were back at home in Hull and not generally around the house, so I didn't feel that I was intruding too much. The 'band wives', and also Mick's girlfriend Denise from Hull to a lesser extent, were a little stand-offish towards me, but I had expected it and I wasn't complaining. Mick Ronson on the other hand made me feel very welcome, as he had done before, and Mick kindly took me to the MainMan offices at 2 Gunter Hall Studios, Gunter Grove in leafy SW10 where I was required to sign a contract of employment – it was just a typewritten agreement on a MainMan letterhead – with no witness and no copy for myself. In those days I couldn't have cared less what I signed.

The offices were located in part of an old former church with stained-glass windows and ivy around the door, very stylish though very tiny. The office manager introduced himself as 'Hugh' and said that Tony (Defries) had asked him to 'sort my wages out'. Knowing that there was no way that I would be afforded any 'star' status in my new job I asked Hugh what the other 'extra' musicians, the sax players, were to be paid. He told me, "Eighty pounds per week into a UK account, plus generous on the road expenses paid cash-in-hand, and all transport and hotels paid for." This was pretty good when compared to a 'day job' in those days, so I said that would be fine for me, and I signed the sheet of MainMan letterhead. A day or two later Hugh was to call me to say that I should have been offered sixty pounds, not eighty pounds, per week, and could he change it? I said no, he couldn't, and that I wanted the same as the sax players or I wasn't joining. Hugh called back and said okay, eighty it was. Looking back, I think I might have worked for next to nothing, but I hate for people to get one over on me, and I thought at the time that it was a strange bit of penny-pinching by the MainMan office. When, years later, I learned of the precarious state of MainMan's finances at that time, I could see why Hugh might have been trying to save money.

Mick Ronson told me that David and Angie's house was just walking distance away in Beckenham and suggested that I should pop round and introduce myself to David's new wife. David was not at home as he was preparing to set sail for New York on the QE2 on 25th January 1973 (having vowed never to fly ever again following a panic attack on a flight the previous year) but Mick told me that perhaps I could be fitted for my stage outfit while I was round there. I had phoned first, then walked the few hundred yards to David's house, the impressively named Haddon Hall. It was not really a large house, but it did have a lot of style, vine-covered walls, stained-glass windows, wrought iron gates and the like, in fact it had pretty much the same features as the MainMan office in Knightsbridge. Except that Haddon Hall had never been a church.

Angie Bowie answered the door and welcomed me warmly into the quite grand 'main hall' of the house. It was the stately-home style of the ornate central staircase and the surrounding minstrel gallery that would impress any visitor, and my first impression was further confirmation of David's new star status. Big staircase = big star. Angie was very New York, very American, lively and blonde, bright and friendly, and she told me that she had heard so much about me from David, and that he was so pleased to see me back. We had coffee in David and Angie's living room and chatted about the exciting times that were taking over all of our lives. I liked Angie from the start, and throughout the next few months of touring, although we never really 'socialised' together (I preferred the quiet life) we would remain on friendly terms. Although Angie could be quite outrageous and would show off for the benefit of the press, the public or anyone else who might take notice, I never saw any bad side. I never got close enough.

Angie told me that arrangements urgently had to be made to have me fitted for my stage outfit, as there was very little time left before I had to leave for New York with the other Spiders. I was informed that the stage clothes were being made by a chap called Freddi Burretti, a friend of David's and apparently a sometime 'vocalist' himself. Freddi was occupying one of the rooms at Haddon Hall whilst he did the job, so when we found that he was in the house at the time, Freddi agreed to do the measuring-up business right there and then.

Freddi Burretti was a very young man, a small person with highlights in his hair and he was wearing the bits of spangly jewellery that I was beginning to recognise as being an important part of my new band's, and for that matter their entire entourage's, 'Image' – this being so essential to their presentation to the drab world on the streets outside. Freddi, a little to my surprise, kind of gave me the cold shoulder – pretty much as Trevor and Woody had done – and it turned out that it could have been for a similar reason. It appeared that Freddi had been hoping to be included in a proposed 'backing vocals' unit, to have been called 'The Astronettes', for the upcoming tours. The vocal group's name was to be borrowed from Lindsay Kemp's 1972 dance group of that name, and David would later use it yet again for his filmed and televised 'Midnight Special' shows at the Marquee Club in 1973. The

Astronettes would have featured a couple of black girls as well as Freddi and another of David's friends, an old school chum from Bromley, Geoff MacCormack. The backing vocals group idea was ultimately rejected for the upcoming tours, but Geoff did actually come with us, to play congas and share backing vocals duty with me (our black-chick replacement falsetto harmonies were to be hilarious rather than authentic sounding, but more of that later).

I knew nothing of all that upon my first visit to Haddon Hall, and I don't think that Freddi said anything about it as he measured me up. He huffed and puffed about my 'shape' though, which I thought was a little unfair as I was still getting into 28-inch waist jeans in those days. The 'saxophone section' had already been in for their measure-up and Freddi told me that they were not of 'male-model' proportions either. David himself would in the old Feathers days ask me why I didn't 'greyhound down a bit' (his phrase) – usually when I was wearing my elephant cords and a chunky jumper. Hell I was skinny enough, I hardly ate anything, I was just not pop star shaped.

Next, my unruly hairstyle was to be attended to by an unfashionably voluptuous and strikingly beautiful dark-haired girl called Suzi Fussey. Suzi occupied yet another of the rooms at Haddon Hall, and was to come on tour as the band's wardrobe mistress, as well as being David's hairdresser and make-up person. Suzi took pity on me and at my request just cut my hair a little bit, rather than follow whatever her instructions might have been (I shudder to think). I was happy to take on the trappings of being an auxiliary Spider, off-stage and on, but I didn't fancy one little bit a silly space-haircut of the kind that Trevor and Woody had agreed to.

I was acutely aware that in my street clothes I didn't look anything like a Spider from Mars. I looked like a Draughtsman from Scarborough. I asked Mick Ronson what he thought I could do about my off-stage clothes as a temporary measure, as none of us had any money and I was not due any wages for another couple of weeks. Mick went upstairs to his wardrobe and returned with a pair of UK size 9 green patent-leather boots and a fitted kid-leather jacket with a snakeskin collar. Despite my protestations, Mick insisted that he no longer wore the boots or the jacket and that I must wear them. The boots fit like a glove; they were the ones Mick had worn in The Hype and also on the Spiders' first US tour during the previous year. They had plenty of life left in them and would go perfectly well with the green satin and lurex stage outfit that Freddi Burretti was grudgingly making for me in his room at Haddon Hall. The jacket on the other hand was a very close fit, but it was such a beautiful handmade designer garment, and it did make me appear more pop star shaped, as well as more pop star looking generally, so I gratefully accepted Mick's generosity. It was very typical of the man, and I have never known anyone else quite like him.

With the addition of a few wrist-bangles borrowed from Suzi Fussey, I was now one of the team. At least, I was beginning to look like one of the team. Apart from showing me some chord sheets that he was writing, and giving me some David Bowie albums to listen to, Mick had no time to rehearse me. My homework, listening to the classic albums that had somehow evaded me was to be 'The Man Who Sold The World', 'Hunky Dory', 'Changes' and 'The Rise and Fall of Ziggy Stardust and the Spiders from Mars'. Rehearsals would have to wait until we got to New York, and even then we were to have very little time. I was going to have to read the chord sheet arrangements on-stage. I had not, ever, bought any of David's albums, my musical tastes have rarely followed popular opinion, and though I had heard some of the songs on the radio, they were by no means familiar to me. Mick assured me that this would not be a problem, as the two sax players who would be joining had told him that they hadn't heard any of David's songs, so they would be sight-reading their parts as well. In fact specially designed 'Aladdin

Sane' music stands were to be a part of the tour stage set. Even richer was Mick's confidence to me that David had selected the sax players because, in addition to being good players and sight-readers, they both wore square glasses and looked nothing at all like pop stars. They looked like sax players.

Though I had intended to return to Sweden in the probably unlikely event that a proper musician's work permit had come through for me, I had foolishly not noticed that my passport would quite soon need renewal; certainly it would expire before the tours had finished. I needed a new passport fast, and as there were no photo booths in those days I went to see Brian and Mal Cooke, old friends from Scarborough who were now living in London and doing very well in the business of taking photographs of pop stars and designing record sleeves. Before leaving Scarborough behind, Brian had taken over from Ron Gillette as manager of The Mandrakes, and so had to cope with the departure of their star-bound singer Robert (Alan) Palmer. I still have the old 1973 passport, and Brian's photo shows a wasted and dissolute person that I no longer recognise as me.

A lady at the Passport Office in Liverpool had told me that they could turn my application around within the week given the 'special circumstances' of my pending tour with the famous David Bowie. The same special treatment was obviously given to MainMan's requirement for my US visa and work permit too, and all the papers were delivered to the US Embassy for me to collect with just a couple of days to spare. These seemingly last minute arrangements would have normally driven me up the wall with worry, but with MainMan running the show, I found it easy to leave the responsibility to Hugh and his staff at the office. In addition to that, I still wouldn't let myself believe that I was definitely going to the USA, not until I found myself on the plane with the rest of the band.

That day did arrive. It was the morning of 11th February 1973 when the UK based members of the enlarged band, the four new 'auxiliary Spiders' and the three full-time pop star Spiders, met up together for the first time at Heathrow Airport and boarded a New York-bound plane. Also on board was an entourage that included ex-roadie and newly designated 'stage manager' Pete Hunsley, David's bodyguard Stuey George, who had famously been the only black roadie in Hull, two wardrobe girls, Suzi Fussey and 'blonde Susie' Susie Frost, and half a dozen or so road crew who I was informed, by one of the more personable of them, a young chap called Will Palin, were being 'loaned' to David by the new up and coming band Queen who were not touring at the time.

Mike Garson, our American piano player, was at home in New York, and David Bowie, who had disembarked from his QE2 transatlantic crossing, was waiting for us in The Big Apple. On the plane I took the opportunity to chat to the other members of my new band. The saxophone players, apart from the previously mentioned facts that they both wore glasses and played saxophones, were two very different characters.

Brian Wilshaw, the younger of the two preferred, so I had been told, the nickname 'Bux', though I never heard anybody ever call him anything but Brian and I suspected that David had been at his nicknaming games again. Brian, in appearance at least, could have been the prototype for Nigel Planer's long-haired hippy character in 'The Young Ones', or maybe Cheech or Chong. The lank shoulder-length hair and slouching stance draped in flares and washed-out T-shirt marked Brian out as a likely member of the Woodstock generation. He said very little to anyone except his room-mate and fellow saxophonist Ken Fordham, and from the day I met Brian on the plane to our last gig together at Hammersmith Odeon, we never exchanged more than a few syllables in spite of standing shoulder to shoulder on the auxiliaries' rostrum behind Mick Ronson every night for several months. I gathered that Brian was not at all impressed with superstardom and its attendant fuss, and that the 'Aladdin Sane' world tour that we were embarking upon was 'just another gig'. He did have a point.

Ken Fordham I would say had a similar point of view, but was a more affable and rounded character altogether, in fact he was more like my old band mates in the Roger Dean Five in Scarborough. Ken was a fine musician with a powerful tone and a confident and flexible solo style. David Bowie, as a sometime sax player himself, obviously admired Ken Fordham's musicianship a lot, and he would talk to Ken from time to time on the tours, about whatever sax players talk about.

Both our sax players wore heavy rectangular glasses and, when standing together behind a pair of our 'big-band style' music stands complete with 'Aladdin Sane' flash artwork on the front, dressed in big-shouldered stage suits, they achieved the effect that David had intended. We were an eight-piece Space Orchestra, a nine-piece if you included our vocalist Ziggy Stardust.

On-stage, viewed from the audience, we were always positioned stage right on a rostrum beside and slightly behind Mick Ronson, and we were rooted to the floor behind our Ziggy flash music stands. Brian Wilshaw would stand furthest right, then Ken Fordham, then there were the congas played by Geoff MacCormack and then me with two guitars (my Telecaster and David's Harptone acoustic 12-string) on stands, with a classic Sound City amp-head together with an Orange 4x12 speaker cabinet just behind me.

David and Mick had asked me if I wanted to bring my own guitar amplifier on tour, but I had told them that my little dinner dance amp, an old Vox AC30, was a little past its best, not really up to much, and so I would be happy with whatever they had. I didn't know it at the time, but in fact they didn't have very much stage equipment at all, and no money to buy more, and so I was just to use Mick's spare amp and speakers, hoping that neither his amp nor mine blew up in mid-performance. I had suggested that we get hold of a twin-neck Gibson of the type made famous by Jimmy Page, so that I would not need to keep changing instruments, but the idea fell to earth like a lead Zeppelin, both David and Mick insisting that the sound of David's Harptone 12-string was a well established part of their on-stage sound. I think they might have been intent upon saving money there too.

I met Geoff MacCormack for the first time upon my arrival in New York, he came over and introduced himself and told me that if it was okay with me, we would be room-mates on the tours. It was to be tour policy that most of the band members and the roadies were to share, two to every hotel room. This policy would prove to have some disadvantages, but it saved a lot of money and was probably intended to at least reduce the frequency of the inevitable on-the-road shenanigans. Geoff had been at school with the young David Jones, and as a life-long friend he was bound to know all about my own friendship and previous musical involvement with David. Geoff and I got along fine right from the start, we were as different as chalk and cheese but we gave each other enough space to be ourselves, and Geoff possessed the essential for any band mate, he had a good sense of humour. Fashion-obsessed as Geoff was in those days, his sense of humour was the saving grace. To his credit Geoff never once told me what my own faults were, and God knows I have plenty of them.

Pete Hunsley, the ex-Rats roadie from Hull, was an easy man to get along with too, and it was Pete, now working as our stage manager, who described the planned stage set-up to me during our flight from London to New York. The four additional musicians would, as I have already described above, occupy the right-hand side of the stage (viewed from the audience's perspective), all standing on a 2ft high rostrum, stage space permitting, with

Woody's drum kit centre stage upon a drum riser – as a drummer's rostrum is known in the trade.

Mick Ronson's guitar amplifier, another Sound City amp-head and a pair of 4x12 speaker cabinets would stand between my amp and Woody's drum set-up, and so Mick would have the whole space, stage right, in front of the auxilliary Spiders' rostrum, to pace around in. Mick always played his favourite guitar on-stage, an old Gibson Les Paul with a sanded-down front and its scratch-plate removed. Between Mick's guitar and his amplifier, a wah-wah pedal was used as a sort of pre-amp, achieving a precise tone quality by means of careful positioning by Mick at every sound check. He rarely if ever used the pedal as its designer had intended – that is, as a wah-wah device.

Mick Ronson never stood still on stage, he would grimace and contort his body and thoroughly enjoyed showing off. Mick, with a lot of encouragement from David, had adopted a stage persona very different from his own character, very much as David himself had already done. Mick's stage outfit generally comprised a frilly, ruffled white shirt open to the waist, baring his hairless and fake-tanned chest, and a pair of sequinned knee-length britches worn with white stockings and black patent, high-heeled and buckled shoes. It was a costume straight out of Pantomime really, but the effect was dramatic and it perfectly complemented David's own dressing-up adventures.

The pair of them would prowl and spar around the stage, making whatever exaggeratedly comic homoerotic moves and poses that might occur to them as the band pounded on. David was to make at least two costume changes per concert on the Aladdin Sane tours of 1973, and although one change was ingeniously done without leaving the stage, other changes had to be made backstage. The five minutes or so whilst David was off-stage would be covered by a quite fiercely improvised 'jousting dance' or 'guitar-fight' by Mick and Trevor in centre stage, made all the more dramatic (and even more dangerous for the participants) by the use of a flickering white strobe light. A little error of timing could result in a bang on the head from a heavy guitar machine-head for Mick or Trevor, and very occasionally there would be a minor wound to the forehead. It was all great fun of course, and Mick would regularly turn to me (I was always just behind him to the left) with a huge grin on his face and with a wink he would exhort Woody, the 'horn section', Geoff MacCormack and myself to greater effort. Certainly, though the sax players were happy to be rooted to the rostrum and believed that they were getting paid to just be there and play their stuff, both Geoff and I, being more inclined to be show-offs, would have needed very little encouragement to join in with the on-stage looning about. David and Mick however, quite rightly would never have tolerated any running around the stage by the auxiliary Spiders; it was a very professional show after all.

At the other side of Woody's drums, stage left, was Trevor Bolder's bass-rig, it was very much the same as Mick's set-up, a Marshall or Sound City valve-amplifier with two 4x12 speaker cabinets. Trevor, who played a Gibson SG-type bass, was generally much less mobile around the stage than Mick, and would stand quite close to his speakers, leaning slightly forward, nodding in time with the beats he and Woody were laying down.

Woody remained impassive, he even looked somewhat disinterested as he drummed. He looked good though, under the lights, up there alone on his drum riser, with bleached blond hair and glittery outfit. As indeed did Trevor, who sported huge silver-dyed sideburns and a spiked-up jet black mullet, and he balanced precariously on the highest pair of platform boots I had ever seen. Trevor never came down from those boots. He may have been, to put it in the language of his beloved home town, 'a short-arsed 'airdresser', but he was a powerful bass player and he had made himself look like the pop star that he had become. David Bowie had created and designed the Spiders from Mars. They had been The Rats, the nobodies from Hull really, but the three Yorkshire lads had responded magnificently to David Bowie's science-fiction imaginings, and had grown into their characters very quickly. Their musical contribution to David's development had been invaluable, beyond estimation, as David could not have made it happen without Mick, Trevor and Woody. The three Spiders from Hull were perfect for the characters that David had created for them, and those characters were perfect for the musical times we were living in.

The two full-time star members of the Spiders' rhythm section, namely Woody and Trevor, were friendly enough towards me and the sax players but they obviously regarded us as additional tour musicians, just auxiliaries not full band members, and so they were not inclined to socialise or talk to me very much, neither on that first plane journey to the USA, nor throughout our world travels. This was possibly as much my fault as theirs, for I carried my own arrogance around with me in order to help me deal with my situation, and I wasn't prepared to waste time trying to persuade them as to what a great bloke I am, or for that matter try to show how good a guitar player I am. Whether or not this was a mistake on my part I don't know, but the result has been that neither Woody nor Trevor really had any knowledge of my musicianship or ability (or otherwise) as a guitarist. We just never jammed together and they almost certainly never heard my guitar on-stage, they would not have needed to hear much of my 12-string or rhythm guitar in their stage-monitor mix. Woody and Trevor must have thought that I was just along for the ride, as Geoff MacCormack was, and to an extent, though I did my best to do a professional job for the band, they were right.

I was just a few years older than the three Spiders from Hull, I was from Scarborough, a softer kind of home town than theirs and my musical tastes and influences were not the same as theirs. Nor was my general perspective on life in general, or on rock and roll in particular, the same as theirs. Despite this, I resolved that none of the perceived differences between me and my new band mates were going to get in the way of my having a bloody good time, for as long as it lasted. I was getting along just fine with my new friend Mick Ronson, and well enough for the time being with my reunited old friend David Bowie, and in my own mind at least – never mind the reality that I was in fact just a hired-hand auxiliary – I was now a Spider from Mars.

Chapter Ten - With Ziggy in the USA

What a buzz! We landed in New York and were met by a small army of very loud and very excited MainMan Management people who whisked us as VIPs through Customs and into waiting limousines. I had never been in a limo before, never mind been whisked into one like a pop star, and I felt as though I had landed in the middle of a movie. Yes, I had been to North America, to Montreal in Canada a few years earlier in 1967, but that had been a quite different experience. I had arrived last time as an immigrant, a would-be new citizen of the new world, the new frontier, and it had been a difficult year and a tough learning curve, living in the real world. This time it was not reality, this time it was a kind of dream sequence, on a set in an American movie. Mick Ronson had done his best to prepare me before we left Beckenham. "You won't believe it over there Hutch, the chicks and the dope and that." He warned me, "You 'ave to watch out."

The two limousines for the musicians, and the station wagon for the road crew, took us to the Gramercy Park Hotel which was located on the edge of Greenwich Village in New York City. It was a smallish hotel by American standards and quite classy, sort of old-fashioned colonial in style, and given that it was my first sight of an American hotel, I was impressed. We were told that the hotel staff had been sworn to secrecy about our stay, and we in the band and crew were all asked to 'keep a low profile' so that the city of New York would not get to know where our famous little group was staying – just in case the entire city came round at the same time.

It immediately became obvious that the secret had not been that well kept as within minutes of our arrival there were incoming phone calls, and 'parties' were being discussed even as we checked in. Geoff MacCormack and I unpacked in what was to be the first of our many shared twin-bedded rooms. Geoff was to use his designated bed quite rarely on the tours (no, I don't know where he got to) and I was quite often to enjoy the luxury of a room to myself. We were to get along fine though, as fortunately Geoff never took anything too seriously.

We shaved, showered and changed quickly, keen to get downstairs as soon as possible to see what our first evening in the Big Apple had to offer. Geoff's wardrobe put mine to shame of course; he wore designer label clothes and shoes, and had been shopping at Yves St Laurent in anticipation of his new life attending celebrity parties. Geoff was a natural show-off with very good taste; he put a lot of thought into his clothes, and so reminded me that I was not too clever when it came to the fashion requirements of my new job. As my costume for my latest role in the rock business I had only the green boots and the kid-leather jacket that Mick Ronson had given me, an old sheepskin coat, a blue-dyed cotton kitchen porter's jacket from the Army & Navy store and some T-shirts. These few items, plus a few borrowed bangles around my wrists, would just have to do until I had been paid my first week's wages.

We had all been given a tour hotel 'contacts' sheet for everyone on the tour with all the phone numbers plus extension and room numbers, so the first thing Geoff did was to call David Bowie in his room. David asked if we both fancied going with him to see the early variety show at Radio City Music Hall. It was to be the first venue on our tour itinerary, with our opening concert due in just two days time, and David wanted to see the layout of the place for himself. I felt flattered to be asked by my old friend on my first night in New York, and said I would love to tag along. When I called round to his room I found David to be in fine form, he was bright and apparently healthy and he warmly welcomed me along on his latest adventure, adding, "Who'd have thought we'd end up here together Hutch?"

David asked me to listen to a new album that he had just acquired. "Listen to this guy, Hutch, he's from the North East of England, he was just an art student, but he has some great ideas." The band was apparently called Roxy Music, and Brian Ferry had made a big impression on David. "Yeah, it's great," I lied, although in Roxy's music, in the core of their songs, I thought I could hear a kindred spirit to David himself. Show me another art student, and I'll show you another potential groundbreaking conceptualist.

David made me feel welcome in my new job and promised me that I would enjoy it. "The only problem with touring, Hutch," David told me, "is that you never want it to stop. You'll find that you want to go on forever, I do anyway."

David, Geoff and myself, along with Stuey 'the bodyguard' George, took a taxi to Radio City, where Stuey then went to the box office and collected four tickets for seats in the top balcony (seats in the topmost gallery, known where I come from as 'the gods'). Nobody took any notice of David Bowie as we made our way to the cheap seats, and we were all enjoying the anonymity of our night at the show, away from the rest of the entourage. The rest of the band and crew must have wondered where we had got to so early on that first evening in New York.

The main feature of the Music Hall was reputed to be the appearance of the resident dancing-girl troupe, the famous 'Rockettes'. The girls, there must have been two dozen of them, were pretty spectacular alright, dressed in sequinned and feathered outfits that would have shamed Mick Ronson, and they high-kicked higher than any BBC Television Toppers (a fifties thing dear reader, ask your granddad), however the venue itself was by far the star of the show.

It was a grand auditorium, as ornate as any theatre in the world, but there was more to it than that. The stage was not just a stage, there were several sections of stage, all movable by means of hydraulics, old technology certainly but faultless. Some sections of the stage would rise up from basement level and could become rostrums at the rear, while some moved front to back, or sideways on the stage space. Apart from the full range of lighting effects, the stage also had a selection of spectacular 'steam curtains'. These were literally vertical blasts of hot steam, vented through grids in the stage floor itself. They erupted high into the air behind the Rockettes with a whoosh of old-fashioned exuberance and David immediately turned to me and Geoff and said, "We'll use that." What seemed like only moments later the show's finale featured a kind of rotating gyroscope device, which descended slowly, glittering with light, from the centre of the roof of the stage. "And that," said David, in a whisper, "we *have* to use that."

I had enjoyed the show, it had been a good old-fashioned variety show of the kind that I had presumed to have died out altogether, but I thought no more of steam curtains, gyroscopes and the like as we went to dinner at the hotel later that evening. David however, ever the true professional, had already discussed with his manager Tony Defries the possibilities that the spectacular Radio City stage effects had to offer, and arrangements were being made to use all the magic that we had seen that evening. If David wanted something, Tony made it happen, right there, right then.

After a few drinks in the bar at the Gramercy Park Hotel with most of the tour party in attendance, and just a few very well-connected New York groupies, we were all ready for an early night. In the morning we were due to rehearse for the first time as a full nine-piece band, and jet-lag was already kicking in.

The rehearsal, which was to be the band's only pre-tour get-together and was scheduled to last all day, took place at the RCA studios in downtown New York in a huge, high-ceilinged room which had been purpose-built for large symphony orchestras to record in, primarily for film scores. Fortunately the band sounded basically fine, right from the first count-in, which must have been a great relief to all, and to David Bowie and Mick Ronson in particular. The three-piece Spiders knew their stuff of course, and Mike Garson, a brilliant and adaptable piano player in any case, had already done the short tour with David and the Spiders not many months back.

My own role was simple enough, I would play 12-string on most songs, reading from the chord and arrangement sheets that Mick had written out. On a few of the more rocky songs, I was required to imitate, as closely as possible, Mick's rhythm style on the Fender Telecaster that I had last played at the dinner dance at the Royal Hotel Scarborough a couple of weeks previously. My Telecaster was not the same one that I had used with The Buzz, although I had customised it in exactly the same way – I had stripped off the Fender paint job and applied a clear protective grain sealer, giving the guitar a 'natural wood' appearance. That just gave the instrument a more personal touch really, and in fact Mick Ronson had done the same with his own Les Paul, but then I had also replaced the standard Fender neck pick-up with a Gibson Humbucker pick-up. I have seen that Keith Richards, along with many other players, does the same thing with his Telecasters. I didn't copy Keith in any way, it's just that we are from the same era musically and the idea was circulating around the UK in the sixties. Some old American blues guitarist would have started the fad no doubt, but the idea worked well for me on the Spiders gig, as the rhythm/backup guitar sound I got from the Gibson pickup was pretty much the same as Mick had achieved with his Gibson Les Paul on his recording sessions.

Upon our arrival at the RCA studios, Mick Ronson had handed me a jumbo-sized acoustic 12-string guitar with a fitted De-Armond sound-hole pickup. It was a nice-looking, blonde-finished instrument with an unusual harp-like headstock shape, and was in fact a 'Harptone' guitar. This was a new name to me, but Mick said the manufacturer was in New Jersey, and if I wanted to I might negotiate a sponsorship deal with them for some more of their guitars. I said I would certainly do that, 'I'll give Harptone a call before the next US trip' I thought. The Harptone 12-string was fine, it was the one David had been playing on-stage himself, and would therefore produce the sound that the band was used to, and that had been heard on all the albums they had made. I told Mick that I fancied a double-neck, one with both 6-string and 12-string necks on a solid body, so that I didn't have to change guitars, but he wouldn't hear of it. Mick was our musical director, our camp boss, he was good at it and he would have things his way. He had a little trouble getting me to hit the exact rhythmic nuances that were a feature of his style, as I naturally tried to play the feel of the rhythms in my own style. Mick was always good-humoured though, and we invariably sorted things out to our mutual satisfaction.

Less satisfactory however were the black-chick falsetto harmonies that Geoff MacCormack and myself, assisted by Mick Ronson where possible, were supposed to produce. It was immediately obvious that Geoff and I would have to work on our backing vocals outside of the rehearsal on that day, or we would have stopped all progress with the full repertoire. Work on it we did, right through the tour, but our falsetto ooh-ooohs were always hilarious when heard in isolation, and became only passable when the entire band was playing, and playing very loud indeed. Very loud was the only way the Spiders ever played anyway, which was fortunate indeed for the backing vocals department. Geoff and I were not really ever found out until somebody started recording from the mixing desk, live at gigs, in England later in the year. 'Like cats on heat' was the verdict of Robin Mayhew, the Sound Control chief sound engineer, and I had to agree with him, even though I knew that Geoff was probably a little more at fault than myself – his ooohs were generally a little sharp. After all nobody had ever paid good money to hear old Geoff sing, and I reckoned he was just a talented bathroom singer with no real sense of pitch and lacking the advantage of live gigging experience that guitarist/singers like Mick Ronson or myself had. I heard on the grapevine that Geoff had somehow convinced Mick and David that I was the one with the off-pitch vibrato, and in fact a few years later David attempted to launch Geoff on to the world stage – as 'Warren Peace'. A great name I thought, recalling the days of Larry Parnes' stable of adolescent Furys, Wildes and Gentles – and David of course, like myself, has always enjoyed a good pun.

We had been thrashing guitars, hammering drums, blowing saxophones and ooh-ooohing in the RCA studios for more than three hours when the studio-live red light went out, someone called 'break', and in walked Harry Belafonte. Harry Belafonte! I felt I had always known him and was somehow hardly surprised to see him, and yet I was dumbstruck. I would eventually get used to the occurrence of this phenomenon, as we were to meet stars with famous faces on an almost daily basis on the USA tour, but Harry was the first. He had come to ask David, very nicely, if he could ask his band to turn the volume down a little, as the sound of Ziggy Stardust and the Spiders from Mars could be plainly heard in the studio upstairs where Harry was recording for an album. We took a break and David apologised to Harry. It was bizarre, it was great, we were in New York, ready to rock and roll, and all was well.

At dinner that evening, David again suggested to Geoff and me that we might like to go out on the town with him. This time it was to be a visit to the Village Gate, the world famous old jazz venue where composer and legendary jazz bassist Charlie Mingus would be playing that evening. I was again surprised by the friendly invitation, and happy to be included in David's small party. My old friend was indeed making me very welcome, and the bleakness of my lonely life in Scarborough just a couple of weeks before was already barely a memory. I was in another world, this really was another planet.

The Charlie Mingus group was brilliant of course, and the man himself surprised us by playing a solo on a large, flexible steel saw. This is an old music hall trick; the saw is bent over and played with a bow, thereby producing an unearthly whining sound. As Charlie Mingus was never famous for his high spirits, we had witnessed a rare joke – he must have been having a good night. Or maybe it was something else after all – "You people want entertainment, get this then." Mingus was said to be a difficult and sometimes arrogant man, but I believed that the musical saw was just a joke, the guy obviously had a sense of humour in any case, and later I was to feel that I had been privileged to hear the great man play (play bass I mean, not really the saw so much) and we had all been lucky to catch him, as Charlie died three years later.

After the Village Gate gig, David, Geoff, Stuey and myself went on to a Greenwich Village nightclub called Max's Kansas City where David had arranged to meet 'a few friends', including the now notorious New York Dolls. I had been leading a quiet life in the provinces for a few years remember, playing dinner dances and hunt balls, and had never heard of the 'Dolls' – or for that matter any other of the freaky musical celebrities in the city of New York. I was not concerned though, I was beginning to enjoy my own 'instant celebrity' as a friend of David Bowie. Or should that have been 'a hanger-on' with David Bowie?

As the four of us walked into Max's, incidentally creating quite a stir amongst the locals, I saw an interesting gig poster and was disappointed to learn that I had just missed, earlier that week, a solo gig by an up-and-coming singer/songwriter called Bruce Springsteen. I had heard of him, he sounded interesting and I thought that perhaps he might do well. David Bowie had caught Bruce's gig though, and thought that 'he was marvellous' –

particularly in his second set, playing electric with his band. David had apparently hated Bruce's first set, which he had played solo with an acoustic guitar.

A pretty waitress approached and asked me what I would like to drink. I ordered some drinks and she said with a smile, "That'll be twelve dollars," or something like that. I gave her twenty dollars, and I never saw the drinks, my change, or her again. I was going to have to wise up fast in this city.

Max's Kansas City was in fact quite a dangerous place and you had to be with people who knew the ropes. I saw a guy open a briefcase and sell hard drugs openly in one of the bars, and most people there seemed to be smashed. I felt uneasy, and without the reassuring (even though often somewhat comical) presence of David's bodyguard Stuey George I would probably have decided to return to the comparative sanity of the Gramercy Park Hotel right away. David Bowie on the other hand was now in his element. He had set up court at a group of tables and had a new kind of entourage around him. These people were serious posers; they made Freddi Burretti look straight. The guy with his shirt undone and his arm around David's neck turned out to be David Johansen, the singer with the New York Dolls, and Geoff MacCormack told me that Wayne County, as she was known before he became Jayne County, was there too. We were freakin' at the freakers' ball, and though the proceedings were entertaining enough, I was happy when it was time to leave.

Later, I lay awake in the Gramercy Park Hotel listening to the night sounds of the city four floors below me. I heard a succession of police and ambulance sirens, and the sound of junkies screaming, like cats in a backyard, came from the leafy park nearby. I wasn't sure, in the wee small hours of that morning, that I liked New York that much after all. Maybe the junkies and the transvestites really did own the city; maybe David Bowie really preferred the seamy side of life, and it began to occur to me that maybe David and I no longer had that much in common anymore.

Things became a lot brighter again next day, the morning of 14th February 1973. Mick Ronson had asked me if I had considered that I might need another guitar as a back-up. Mick always had another Les Paul on-stage in case he broke a string, or a pick-up failed, or a switch broke in mid-performance. Mick told me, "Just go downtown and get whatever you need 'utch, Tony Defries says we buy what we need." I needed no further encouragement, wow, a new guitar on the company! 'I'll have some of that!' I thought, so I got a lift downtown with Pete Hunsley and I walked into Manny's Guitar Shop like a kid looking for sweeties.

From the Aladdin's Cave of fabulous guitars at Manny's I selected a Gibson 'black beauty', a two pick-up Les Paul guitar. I had started out on Gibson guitars, first a Les Paul Junior then an SG followed by an ES175, and then I changed to Fender Telecasters, so I thought it would be amazing to have one of each – a Gibson and a Fender at the same time! You see in those days, every guitarist I knew just 'traded-in' their old guitar for whatever new one that they coveted. We could not afford to do otherwise, only the stars owned lots of guitars. If I'd kept all the guitars I'd owned in those days I'd have maybe thirty genuine vintage guitars with a total value today of who knows what, tens of thousands anyway.

Manny's put the Gibson Les Paul in a Gibson case, Pete Hunsley signed for it and I walked out with it, feeling on top of the world again. I enjoyed the illusion at the time, then some many months later Hugh at the office would start deducting the cost of the instrument – in instalments – from my wages. Fair enough really, there was still a real world, operating normally somewhere after all.

The road crew had gone into Radio City Music Hall at 9am that morning to set up the sound equipment and rig the lighting. The sound crew were under the control of Englishman Robin Mayhew, who had been working for the up and coming band Queen, and had now set up his own company called Sound Control. Yes, Robin was Sound Control to Major Tom. I was to meet Robin Mayhew again many years later in 2011 at a charity gig in Hull, and Robin told me that he had packed in the sound business and now did portable toilets as his retirement job. "More money in umm...that," he said.

The lighting crew for the 1973 tours on the other hand were working for a very large Hells Angel sort of character, an American by the name of Bob See. Bob suffered no fools, and his crew to a man were Vietnam veterans, good reliable guys but all equally as hardbitten as their boss.

During the day the theatre was prepared, our stage set was put together by the Radio City staff, and the wardrobe girls Suzi and Susie took in the costumes and arranged them in the dressing rooms. An outside caterer delivered the contract 'rider' of crates of wine and beer bottles, and chicken-wings, ribs and rolls to the dressing rooms in readiness for the evening.

After lunch, at 2.30pm precisely, all musicians, Spiders and auxiliary Spiders alike, were rounded up and corralled in the lobby of the Gramercy Park Hotel in preparation for transportation by limousine to Radio City Music Hall. The musicians, for the record, were listed on the official tour literature as follows:

David Bowie – 'The Artist', vocals, guitar, mini-moog, percussion

Band:
Mick Ronson – Musical Director, lead guitar, vocals
Trevor Bolder – bass guitar and vocals
Woody Woodmansey – drums
Mike Garson – piano, mellotron
Brian 'Bux' Wilshaw – tenor saxophone, flute
Ken Fordham – tenor, baritone, alto saxophone

John 'Hutch' Hutchinson – rhythm guitar and vocals
Geoffrey Alexander MacCormack – percussion and vocals

The round-up of rock musicians on any tour, just finding them and getting them all together and ready to get aboard a bus or into a limousine or a Transit van, is no mean feat, and is probably by far the most difficult and most important task of all on a tour. This thankless task would be achieved on the Aladdin Sane tours by means of tireless badgering and hectoring of eight – or nine, if we include the main man David Bowie – sleepy and argumentative musicians by the tour management duo of Tony Zanetta and Jamie Andrews.

Both Tony (known to the other Americans in the tour party as 'Zee') and Jamie had been part of Andy Warhol's troupe of actors for his controversial play 'Pork', a production that had made a great impression upon David Bowie in London. Both Zee and Jamie were still part of Warhol's little circle at that time – as was a very bubbly lady called Cherry Vanilla.

Cherry Vanilla (originally Kathleen Anne Dorritie) had worked with iconic superstar personalities before. Both the very famous photographer Bruce Weber and the very infamous jazz trumpet star Chet Baker had kept her busy before she tied up with Andy Warhol and then David Bowie. Cherry sure knew how to pick 'em.

Cherry appeared to have some sort of management role with David Bowie though nobody could tell me what exactly her job was. It transpired that she was David's 'publicist' and that made sense because she mostly hung out with Leee Black Childers who took all the photographs. They all did a great job, their style was a little unusual perhaps but they were real pros.

Tony Zanetta had played, to some critical acclaim, the part of Andy Warhol in 'Pork' and had appeared in some of Warhol's movies. Zee was a natural actor I thought, and it seemed to me that all he did, and very successfully too, was to play the part of a management executive, and he played as our 'Tour Manager' to perfection. I found Tony Zanetta to be a helpful and positive character though, and in fact he went on to become a Vice President (whatever that means) of MainMan Incorporated, Tony Defries's artist management company. Zee also was to write his own Bowie book, years ahead of this one of course – though I have not yet found and read a copy. Tony Zanetta could maybe have become a film star, he had the qualifications in his dark and slightly sinister looks, and he was of course gay. That was a given, anywhere near Andy Warhol, apparently.

Jamie Andrews was more the New York stereotype gay, and somehow he reminded me of Peter Pitts, the Tennesseans' old manager in Scarborough. Jamie highlighted his hair and wore the bright clothes, but his main talent, and his main job on our tour, was to make people take notice. Jamie would sweep into a hotel or concert venue lobby and make everybody 'listen-up!' I guessed that both David Bowie and Tony Defries had realised that an entourage which included a tour management group comprising Zee, Jamie and Cherry was bound to get people talking about the tour, all over the USA – all over the world in fact – and they were right, it worked a treat. Zee and Jamie could play up and be outrageous at the drop of a hat. Any encounter with a pompous hotel manager, or some jobsworth at a concert hall, would spark off a fabulous display of gay-powered outrage, a torrent of New York streetwise abuse, backed up with threats to cancel the gig, pull the entire tour group out of the hotel, and inform the world's press and so on. They would stand no nonsense; they had enough of their own nonsense to look after.

We didn't generally see Cherry Vanilla around as much, but she would appear occasionally after dark, and could be as conspicuously outrageous as the other Warhol gays when necessary.

The lady had style, she had a pair of cherries tattooed on one of her breasts (it was to be many more years before many other women found the bottle to do that sort of thing) and would show her cherries on demand. I liked Cherry Vanilla and her more or less constant companion Leee Black Childers too. Leee was, and continued to be until his passing, at the age of 68 in April 2014, a photographer of some reputation and talent. He was also an ex-Warhol man, though I was never sure of his role – Andy's staff photographer I would guess. As I've said before I don't need to know who does what, with what, etc. and that goes double for Warhol's crowd.

Leee took my photograph whilst I was sitting in the auditorium lacing up my boots prior to our sound check at Radio City, and he and Cherry Vanilla signed the back of the picture with 'Happy Valentine and welcome to America' and 'Would you please be my Valentine' (and a pair of cherries). It was Valentine's Day, 14th February 1973, and I had forgotten. Leee must have gone out and had the photo developed within the hour so that they could give it to me on the day. I kept the photograph; Leee and Cherry may have been notorious Warhol people but they were also really nice people.

The gig at Radio City, our first concert, was sensational for audience, band and tour party alike. Over the coming months we would all become a little blasé perhaps, but on that first night, the realisation that we were a part of a groundbreaking display of rock and roll showmanship by David Bowie, a tremendous piece of rock and roll theatre, was an unforgettable experience.

Our support band for most, though not all, of our dates on both the US and UK tours was Fumble, a four-man guitars, bass and drums band from Weston-Super-Mare in the west country of England. Their talented young keyboard player Sean Mayes would eventually join David Bowie's band later on in the seventies. Fumble had successfully supported David and the Spiders on some of their tour dates during the previous year and they were a decent bunch of west country lads who probably reminded David Bowie of his own happy and more carefree days back in the sixties. Fumble would work their way through a short opening set of straightforward rock and roll kind of pop songs, they were always cheerful in their work, and good to get along with on the road. The support band was under no illusion however; they knew that every crowd, on every night of all the tours, was impatient to see David Bowie arrive on-stage.

On that first night, our first gig on the 1973 Aladdin Sane tour of the USA, we were called from our dressing rooms in the bowels of Radio City Music Hall by Zee and Jamie, and then handed over to Pete Hunsley who took us into a darkened area and showed us, the auxiliaries, me and Geoff MacCormack, Brian Wilshaw and Ken Fordham, where to stand. We were positioned behind the 'tabs' (the stage curtain) down in the stage basement upon a rostrum, which we were told would begin to be lifted to two feet above stage level when we began to play the intro to David's opening song. The theatre was in darkness when the overture music was started up. The music that had been chosen by David was the dramatic Walter Carlos version of Beethoven's 'Ode to Joy' – previously used for Stanley Kubrick's notorious film 'A Clockwork Orange' – and the bass sounds, played through our Sound Control PA system, thundered through the floor and walls of the Radio City Music Hall. The revered old venue had never heard the like before, and the sheer volume must have been just a little alarming for the theatre management, though they would almost certainly have already had the Zee and Jamie treatment. To their credit as professionals, when MainMan hired a concert venue, the place effectively belonged to MainMan for the entire term of the engagement, and all theatre employees were made aware of that when we arrived. Stuey George would not stand for any interference backstage either, and he generally barred all theatre staff from entry to our dressing room area.

Sound, lighting and stage management were co-ordinated by walkie-talkie radio headsets, that for me at least was a first and I realised that now I really must be in the big time.

When the Spiders and auxiliary Spiders were all in place below the Radio City stage, Mick Ronson gave the 'ready' thumbs up signal to Pete Hunsley, Pete relayed the instruction, the overture tape faded and Mick counted the band in. As the opening bars of 'Hang on to yourself' pounded through our PA system, the lighting crew went into business, and we heard the gasp from the audience as the band came up through the floor of the stage. It's a good bet that the majority of the audience on that evening had never been to a Radio City gig of any kind before, there had never been a rock concert in the place before, and the old theatre was already playing its intended part in the success of our 1973 USA tour's opening concert.

Nobody had seen David for a good half hour before the start of the gig. We thought nothing of it really, after all he had his own dressing room, and maybe he was preparing in his own way, and maybe that included a bit of peace and quiet.

When we heard the next sound from the audience, it was more than a gasp, it was a graduated rumble which grew to a roar of amazed excitement. David had not been preparing quietly in his dressing room after all, in fact for more than half an hour he had been balancing in the roof of the Radio City stage on the gyroscope device that David, Stuey, Geoff and I had seen on our visit two nights previously.

The band repeated the opening riff over and over whilst the gyroscope, glittering and turning, descended slowly to the stage with David Bowie on board, resplendent in the first of several spectacular stage costumes and nonchalantly holding on to the

181

contraption with one hand. In fact David suffers, as I do myself, from vertigo, a fear of heights, and was repressing his terror for the sake of his performance. It was the most sensational rock and roll stage entrance that anyone had ever seen, and one that probably has never been bettered – not using standard stage props anyway – and at no extra cost.

The first half of the concert was over in a flash. We had worked our way, to a barrage of enthusiasm from the New York audience, through just nine songs; in fact the set was a selection from all five of David's albums. The first half set list read:

Hang on to yourself
Ziggy Stardust
Changes
Soul Love
John I'm only dancing
Drive in Saturday
Five years
Space Oddity
My Death

The first half, probably thirty-five or forty-five minutes long, seemed to have flown by in ten minutes at the most. I had hardly heard most of these songs before, let alone played them at a gig, and I enjoyed the music immensely, though I couldn't hear anything much of what I was playing or singing. Mick's lead guitar was everywhere, and our monitors – the wedge-shaped speaker cabinets providing the balanced and individually adjusted on-stage sound – or perhaps the soundmen responsible for them, were almost useless. The monitors were never to improve much throughout our world tours, and there is no doubt that this would have contributed to the 'cats-on-heat' quality of our backing harmonies. Trevor Bolder simply couldn't sing – although he always had a microphone – Mick Ronson didn't sing backing vocals very much, and Geoff MacCormack and I just struggled to stay on pitch. After initially trying to persuade the sound men to get the monitors' fold-back sound right, in the long run Geoff and I decided, as did the other experienced auxiliaries, saxophonists Ken and Brian, to just make the best of it and not let the problem spoil our enjoyment of the tour – especially on that opening gig. The fact is that both Mick Ronson's lead guitar amps, and Trevor's bass rig, were way too loud to allow any real control of monitor speakers for backing vocals or saxophones.

During the intermission the whole band was jubilant backstage in the dressing rooms, and we opened a few more bottles as we exchanged our observations on minor performance problems – for example the on-stage monitors problem. Jamie Andrews called us back for the second set and I, together with the other auxiliary Spiders, took up my position on the rostrum. The second set was, as it should always be, even more powerful than the first. The eleven strong second set list (which I still have) scrawled by Mick Ronson on the back of a MainMan memo, was:

The Supermen
Moonage Daydream
Aladdin Sane
Panic in Detroit
Width of a Circle
Time
Let's spend the night together
Jean Genie
Watch that man
Suffragette City
Rock 'n' Roll Suicide

For me, the second set was memorable mainly for three things, and two of them were concerned with David's costume changes. The first change was achieved when David stood motionless in centre stage, with arms and legs outstretched. The two Susies, Suzi Fussey and Blonde Susie, both dressed entirely in black, ran on-stage from the wings at opposite sides and with a loud shriek (to aid timing possibly and for dramatic effect certainly) they ripped off David's costume, which had been held in place by velcro fasteners. This trick had been cannily copied from the Japanese traditional Kabuki theatre that David had been studying.

All of David's new costumes for the Aladdin Sane tours had been designed and made to measure by the famous Japanese designer Kansai. I saw the designer briefly at the start of our tour, he was just leaving our hotel as I came in, and I was surprised at how tall he was (not your stereotypical Japanese!) Kansai's costumes, no doubt very expensive ones, were invaluable to David Bowie at this stage of his career. The outfits were an integral part of David's concept for Ziggy Stardust's Aladdin Sane tours and they were a sensation in their own right. A roar of approval from the audience would greet the skimpy bits of costume that David was obliged to wear underneath the ripped-off ones.

The second costume change required David to leave the stage altogether, and Mick and Trevor's stroboscopic guitar duel, in the middle of 'Jean Genie', was incorporated to cover David's three or four minutes absence. The auxilliary Spiders were not required for 'Jean Genie', and so in the darkness we were all able to slip off our rear-stage rostrum and into the wings where we had a few minutes to have a drink, go for a pee, whatever. The little break was great from my point of view, it enabled me to see the show from the wings, and I took in more detail than I could see from my position on-stage. It also gave me an opportunity to have a look at some of the excited young ladies at the front of the audience, the ones who would kill to meet someone who played guitar with David Bowie.

The audience by this time would be extremely hot and crushed up against the edge of the stage, and Stuey George would from time to time run on-stage to grab a stage invader and return them to their place in the crowd. Stuey and others of the on-stage crew would also try to pull out anybody who showed any distress in the hysterical crush.

The third memorable piece of excitement we experienced at Radio City Music Hall, our very first USA gig, came when David, at the end of the 'last' song 'Suffragette City' (false tabs you know) just before we played the intended encore of 'Rock 'n' Roll Suicide', appeared to have a repeat of the 'fainting' attack that I had seen him suffer (or perform) with David Bowie and The Buzz, light years earlier. It wasn't exactly James Brown, but it was very theatrical and, real or not, it went down a storm, then we played the encore and the concert was a resounding success – it was to be the talk of New York for days to come. The press called it 'a triumph'. The second concert, at Radio City on the following evening, 15th February 1973, was an even more successful gig, in terms of David's performance, the band's performance, and the audience response.

We were a happy little band, and when the second gig in New York was over, we all, with the notable exception of Mike Garson, got ready to party. Mike would always have his own agenda, as I will explain later in this chapter. The road crew meanwhile, though happy too no doubt, had to set about the next phase of their soon-to-become exhausting tour schedule. They now faced the task of taking everything apart again that they had brought into the theatre and put together, then packing it all into flight-cases and loading up the transport before commencing their journey south to Philadelphia in the early hours of the following day. This operation by our sound and lighting crews, at every gig on all the tours, would take all night, and then they would have to sleep as best they could on the road, taking turns to stay awake and drive. The road crew was listed in the tour programmes too, written exactly as shown below:

Crew:
Robin Mayhew – sound engineer
Peter Hunsley – stage manager
Mick Hince – equipment manager
Willie Palin – equipment manager
Stuart George – personal security to Mr Bowie
Sue Fussey – wardrobe mistress, hairstylist
Bob See – lighting director
Ron Meadows – lighting operator
Stephen Hurston – lighting operator
Jamie Andrews – Road Manager
Tony Zanetta – Tour Co-ordinator (MainMan)

The foregoing lists of musicians and crew were the on-the-road members of the organisation, and were just the tip of the Aladdin Sane Tour iceberg. Quite apart from Tony Defries's staff at MainMan in both the New York and London offices, the tour was also very much an RCA Records responsibility. At least another twenty-five people also had an immediate interest in our progress, as the following heading to an RCA memo (I still have the copy given to me in lieu of a USA tour itinerary) clearly shows:

Memo
February 9, 1973

To: R. ANDERSON   *N. LAPATIN*
    R. BATTOCCHIO   *T. POTTER*
    G. BREUER   *P. RUSH*

W. COCHRAN	*B. STEBBINS*
N. CHACKER	*B. SPENDLOVE*
T. DEFRIES	*P. SKLAR*
E. KAHANEK	*K. VENTOUR*
S. KAHN	*D. WHITTEMORE*
R. KRUEGER	*D. WHEELER*
G. LANDON	*F. O'DONNELL*

From: PAT KELLEHER

Cc: H.Helman, M. Hoffman, M. Ilberman, B. Keane, F. Mancini

Subject: DAVID BOWIE U.S.A. TOUR II – TRANSPORTATION AND HOTEL INFORMATION

SHOW GROUP:
The show group will be travelling by air. Listed below is the schedule, city by city.

New York – Philadelphia
Transportation Info: The entire group including David Bowie will leave by Greyhound Bus Friday, February 16 at 11:00 PM in front of the Gramercy Park Hotel. Estimated time New York to the Bellevue Stratford in Philadelphia is two hours.

(A note from Hutch: this '11:00 PM' was just an office typing error, this memo reads as though it was dictated by Mr Kelleher, and in fact we had to leave New York at 11am in order to play Philadelphia that same evening.)

Hotel Info: Hotel reservations at the Bellevue Stratford, Broad and Walnut Streets. Contact Mr. Wilson – 215-PE5-0700.

Comments: (Note Chacker: as we discussed I need one station wagon plus one Hertz car upon arrival. Also will need a contact for limo service for David for concert times only. Please advise. Exact times for use of limo to be discussed.

(Another note from Hutch: The Bellevue Stratford Hotel was in 1976 to become almost as famous, or as notorious, as David Bowie – that is within just three years of our stay there. Read on!)

Philadelphia – Nashville
Transportation Info: (Show group) – Leave Philadelphia February 20, Allegany 997, leaving Philadelphia 9:15 PM – arriving Nashville 10:04 PM.
Hotel Info: Hotel reservations at the Ramada Inn, James Robertson Parkway. Contact Mrs. Patsy Nevels – 615-224-6130.
Comments: (Note: Wally, Elroy and Bob Spendlove – we will need two wagons plus a Hertz car at the airport upon arrival. Wally, per our conversation please have a big Cadillac plus a chauffeur available for David for the afternoon of February 21. The car will be used for the Nashville concerts on the 22nd and 23rd. On the 24th we will use the car to drive David to Memphis and keep the car for the concerts on the 25th and 26th. The car can then be released on the 27th with the chauffeur going back to Nashville. I would appreciate estimated cost on both the car and chauffeur for the five days.

Nashville – Memphis
Transportation Info: (Show group) – Leave Nashville February 24, Allegany 871 at 4:25 PM – arrive Memphis 5:20 PM.
Hotel Info: Hotel reservations at the Holiday Inn Rivermont, 200 West Georgia Street – Contact Mr. Ryan – 901-525-0121.
Comments: (Note: Bob Spendlove – per our conversation please have two station wagons plus a Hertz car at the airport upon arrival. As you can see

David will be arriving by limo from Nashville and will have the limo during his stay in Memphis so that's taken care of.

(Yet another note from Hutch: This Memphis gig was in fact to be cancelled at the last minute, due, we were told, to very strong protests by the 'Daughters of the American Revolution' – the protectors of America's morals. I suspected at the time that there was another explanation for the very late cancellation, maybe it was something to do with money or bookings – a 'protest' would surely not have stopped us.)

Memphis – Detroit
Transportation Info: *(Show group) – Leave Memphis February 27, Delta 360 at 12:25 PM – arrive Detroit 2:51 PM.*
Hotel Info: *Hotel reservations at the Detroit Hilton, Bagley Avenue at Grand Circus Park. Contact: Mr Sarno – 313-965-7800*
Comments: *(Note: Dave Wheeler & Kelvyn Ventour – we will need two station wagons and a Hertz car at the airport upon arrival. Will also need a limo for the concert time only. Please advise of limo service.*

Detroit – Chicago
Transportation Info: *(Show group) – Leave Detroit March 3, United 603 at 2:55 PM – arrive Chicago 2:55 PM.*
Hotel Info: *Hotel reservations at the Hampshire House, 201 E. Delaware – contact: Norma Deary – 312-943-5000*
Comments: *Note: Bud Stebbins and Tom Potter – please arrange to have two station wagons and a Hertz car at the airport upon arrival. I will also need limo service for David for the concert. Please advise as to limo service.*

(Note from Hutch: The Chicago gig was also cancelled, much to my own disappointment. This time we were given no explanation.)

Chicago – Los Angeles
Transportation Info: *(Show group) – Leave Chicago on March 5,
American 197. Leave at 1:00 PM arrive in Los Angeles at 3:05 PM*
Hotel Info: *Hotel at this time not decided. You will be advised.*
Comments: *(Note: Ray and Don – please arrange to have two station
wagons and a Hertz car at the airport. Also we will need limo service for
the show for David. Please give the limo contact and you will be advised as
to when the limo will be needed.*

(Just one more note from Hutch: There were to be some other
changes to the intended tour itinerary. The enforced changes to Pat
Kelleher's plan will be revealed in due course, as my story makes its
way westward across the USA. Using a sensibly cautious opening
sentence, Mr Kelleher signs off his memo with this note to all
recipients.)

*That's where we stand as of now. If you have any questions please get back
to me or Gustl. All the hotels have been sent the manifest. Attached you
will find one for your use. I am asking the hotels to pre-register the group
before arrival. I would appreciate your checking on that to see that it is
done. David Bowie train schedule will be on a separate sheet.*

End of memo

As one would expect, both RCA Records and Tony Defries's
MainMan organisation ran their operations very efficiently, and
from David Bowie and his tour party's point of view, the travel and
accommodation arrangements generally went quite smoothly. Tony
Defries himself was a pretty smooth character I thought. Tony had
modified himself, in a very short space of time, from a humble
solicitor's litigation clerk into a sort of Colonel Tom Parker kind of
star manager figure (younger readers, the Colonel was Elvis

Presley's manager). Tony wore fur-collared coats, a white-boy's afro haircut and fair-isle patterned tank tops. He smoked huge Cuban cigars and ran a tight ship. Tony had instructed his Warhol extras, Leee, Cherry, Zee and Jamie, to behave as outrageously and as extravagantly as possible, and he played a similar part himself.

Tony would fly in and out of the cities we played, accompanied by his very young and very boyish looking girlfriend Melanie. Melanie wore her hair like David's, carrot-coloured and spiky, she wore tomboy clothing, and she added very well to the general impression of sexual ambiguity that surrounded the operation of our tour. She was actually very nice I thought, and as was so often the case with people around David Bowie, not what she appeared to be.

Tony Defries called a meeting and instructed all of the tour party, with the notable exception of David Bowie himself, to attend. The meeting had been called, said Tony, in order to give everybody, musicians and road crew alike, details of when we would be required to make ourselves available for work during the remainder of the current year 1973.

We learned that we would be working for a total of approximately twenty-five weeks of the coming year. We would, as we already knew, be touring Japan when we had finished the present US tour, preceded by a short break in England while David sailed across the Pacific from California to Japan. Then, immediately before we started our tour of the UK, it was possible that we might be required to make a short trip to Australia. In any event, David Bowie would be travelling only by land or sea. David would never fly again, said Tony. The tour of the UK would be followed by a European tour in June and July, then following a month off, we would be beginning our next tour of the USA in September. The next trip to the USA would be a very long one, warned Tony, but we were assured that we would return to the UK occasionally for a couple of weeks off.

There was a very brief mention of a possible salary increase, probably in response to an enquiry by a member of the saxophone section, but Tony said that he 'did not want to talk money right there and then'. Personally I didn't care about money too much, but I did scrawl a note, again on the back of my 'itinerary' sheet, and although nowadays I don't remember exactly what it meant, the note says 'Salary £50 increase frozen? thru Mick Ronson'. I suppose I'd meant to ask Mick to be shop steward on our behalf – he was after all our bandleader.

Mick had in fact already had his own discussions with Tony Defries about money. The original Spiders, Mick, Trevor and Woody, had complained to Defries after Woody had discovered how much the tour was paying Mike Garson. They also must have asked how much the other auxiliary musicians were being paid. Trevor and Woody particularly didn't like the way that the Americans now regarded The Spiders as an eight-piece backing band, with no distinction between themselves (the stars) and the hired help (me and Geoff, Brian and Ken, the auxiliaries) who were, it turned out, earning more money on the road than they were.

Predictably, Tony Defries was too sharp for Trev and Woody. He had already taken Mick Ronson to one side and told him that MainMan would make Mick himself into a solo star, as they had done with David Bowie, when the current workload had been completed. Trevor and Woody were given a small raise in salary, and some story which kept them on-board for the time being. They were though beginning to understand that they too were now becoming regarded as David's backing musicians, and not as part of the act, as they had been until now. It was becoming plain that David Bowie was now a star, and that there would be only room for one up there.

A 'New York reception' had been arranged to follow the highly publicised Radio City Music Hall concert as a high profile celebration of our tour. As this appeared to us in the band to make a change from the already boring old Gramercy Park Hotel bar, we all, having been transported back from Radio City by limo, showered, changed and prepared to attend the reception as requested by Management.

Unfortunately, as was to be the case with a few officially pre-arranged 'tour parties', this party was to turn out to be a bit of a damp squib, and it was not to be long before we all headed back to the good old Gramercy Park Hotel to see what was happening in the bar. Something almost always was.

Before we abandoned the official reception however, I was lucky enough to find myself talking to Annette Peacock. Annette was a famous artist and musician in New York and she was very interesting, an inspirational kind of person I thought. Annette was a good friend of Mike Garson's, so maybe New York was a small world after all. Another interesting attendee was Allen Ginsberg the finger-cymbalist, poet and Woodstock-generation guru, though I didn't get to speak to him as Allen had quickly already gathered a small and admiring crowd around him.

I spotted two young guys sitting together at a table, they looked like musicians alright and they looked vaguely familiar, so I went over and said hello. The famous faces turned out to be Rick Springfield, formerly a guitarist in Johnny Winter's band and himself a big star in the USA, and Todd Rundgren, pop-star guitarist and record producer. Our conversation did not amount to much, as they were plainly not particularly interested in the Spiders' auxiliary backing vocalist, 12-string and rhythm guitarist, and were both understandably a bit miffed that David Bowie had not turned up. Someone told me much later on that while Todd, with Rick and me, had been attending this damp squib of a reception, David had been shagging Todd's girlfriend, Bebe Buell (who incidentally is lovely actress Liv Tyler's mum). Bebe was said to be a serial shagger in her day, she collected pop stars and would eventually in the year 2000 publish her own book on her lifetime's work.

We returned, early by all-night rock and roll standards, to the Gramercy Hotel, and so I dropped into the bar for a couple of Irish coffees, a whiskey nightcap that Mick Ronson had recently introduced me to. I found myself for the first time, along with several of the tour party including Mick and Geoff but not David, in the lively company of some attractive New York party people, both girls and boys, and all up for it.

Most rock and roll tour musicians (well almost) just went along with the groupie phenomenon which surrounded every famous band, particularly in the USA – and although to different extents, it was the same the world over. It seemed to me that all these great looking and intelligent ladies must have led a comparatively boring existence for most of the year, so that when a 'famous band' came to town it became top priority for the girls to meet and greet the lucky visitors.

There was always a pecking order for the girls to target mind you: first choice of course the famous singer, second the famous lead guitarist, then the drummer and so on down the list to the likes of me, an auxiliary guitarist. I wasn't complaining. The list went on down by the way, descending through the sound, lighting and road crews. The roadies were generally accommodated too, in spite of their heavy workload. They had a saying, even had T-shirts with the slogan, 'no head no backstage pass' – hey don't ask me what it's about.

Sure enough, as promised in the RCA memo, there, outside the front of the Gramercy Park Hotel the following morning, Friday 16th February 1973, was our very own Greyhound Bus. It was ours for the day anyway, a private-hire. The journey down to Philadelphia gave me my first real sight of America outside of the city, and all of us enjoyed the bus ride, even David, who was 'slumming it' on the bus with the lads on that particular day.

The journey gave some of the band members the opportunity to get to know each other a little better. In my case, I got to know our pianist Mike Garson. I had heard that Mike was some sort of 'priest' in the cult, or 'church' as they liked to call it, of Scientology. I liked Mike and respected him immensely as a musician, especially following his performances on our opening gigs in New York, his home town. Mike was easy to talk to, so it was easy for me to ask what this 'church' was all about. The thing was evidently a sort of self-help or self-improvement system that an American science fiction writer called L. Ron Hubbard had dreamed up in his spare time. I had some difficulty in believing that tens or even hundreds of thousands of 'converts' to Scientology had been persuaded into accepting Ron's home-grown brand of mumbo jumbo on a grand scale, in order that they achieve the advertised personal improvement. Mike gave me a little starter book written by good ol' Ron – it was titled 'Dianetics'. With just a small temporary suspension of disbelief I was able to read the book and get the gist of what Ron was selling. As Mike knew that I did not subscribe to any of the well-established churches or their sub-divisions, he probably also knew that I wasn't about to consider joining the Church of Scientology. We got on fine though, and Mike would regularly throughout our tours come over and talk to me, sometimes about music, and sometimes about self-improvement or whatever. He did not talk about sex or drugs, except to say that I should not do either of them.

Mike had more success with both Trevor and Woody. Our rhythm section seemed to naturally perform as a pair, so it should have been no surprise to me that Mike Garson, as Scientology's fisherman, should catch both Spiders from Hull in the same net. I think that Woody swallowed L. Ron's hook, line and sinker a little more than Trevor did, but they both took the bait and spent much of their time on our various journeys around the world reading their new testaments and practising the 'exercises' that ol' Ron had invented for them. One of the exercises involved long silent periods of expressionless staring at each other on the tour bus. Woody and Trevor appeared to be made for it.

Philadelphia
The band settled into the Bellevue Stratford Hotel in the centre of Philadelphia for what was effectively a week's residency at the famous Tower Theatre in the city. The Bellevue Stratford was an old place and it reminded me of at least one of the old Victorian hotels I had known in Scarborough – dodgy plumbing, faded carpets, faded glory.

As long as the beds were clean and comfy and the water was hot, real hotel standards did not matter too much to the Aladdin Sane tour party, our main requirement was that the management left us alone to get on with our own business. Jamie and Zee would see to it that the hotels understood and accepted this requirement. We were not a room-trashing band, no TV sets were ever thrown from bedroom windows, but we followed our tour management's initiative and would not tolerate any restrictions concerning our comings and goings, or who we came and went with.

Hotel restaurants too were of little importance to the band as we were hardly ever able to eat during normal restaurant hours. We played and stayed up late, and we slept late into the mornings if we could. We would though regularly call room service for food and drink at ungodly hours of the night, and we could otherwise more or less survive on the food provided in the dressing rooms at the gigs. The 'rider' was often a very good buffet and was a part of the contract with the individual venues – something that is common in the music business by the way.

Jamie and Zee were supposed to ensure that we paid our own room service bills before we checked out of our hotels. When this proved to be unenforceable in the general confusion of the morning round-up they mostly gave up trying to catch us, paid the bills for us and attempted to clear it up later. And they generally failed.

The auxiliaries, Ken Fordham, Brian Wilshaw and I (Geoff MacCormack was a different case as he hung out with David almost all of the time) had already worked out that, even when a hotel's restaurant facilities were open and available to us, the prices were too high for our liking. Remember, this was 'just another gig' for the saxophone section, and for me to an extent, and though we were being paid a reasonable allowance for on the road expenses, there was little point in wasting it all on expensive food. We soon came up with a system that would avoid unnecessary expense.

When we arrived at our latest hotel, having been transported by limo direct from the airport, Ken, Brian and I would check in at reception, take our bags upstairs, then walk straight out of the hotel and into the first suitable eatery down the main street.

This miserly behaviour was after all entirely in keeping with a Yorkshireman's natural frugality – we are tighter than the Scots. I do regard food as one of life's greatest pleasures however, and I was happily to experience a handful of top restaurant meals on the tour. These culinary adventures would occur on the odd occasion that I happened to be in David Bowie's company and at his table. Spiders, musicians and liggers alike were well aware that all of David's expenses were naturally added to the hotel bill. The guarantor for all tour expenses was not MainMan of course, but RCA, a blue-chip company with limitless funds. RCA was paying through its corporate nose.

Our own noses, and even more crucially our lungs, were lucky in that we enjoyed the comforts of the Bellevue Stratford Hotel in Philadelphia in the year of 1973, and not just three years later. In July 1976 the American Legion, the association for old soldiers, held a convention at the hotel to celebrate America's bicentennial year, the 200th year since the birth of the United States of America. Within two days of checking in to the Bellevue Stratford Hotel, one veteran after another became ill with acute pneumonia-like symptoms. 221 of the Legionnaires were stricken with the mysterious disease, and of those 54 of the veterans tragically died.

It was suspected that the illness had been caused by a previously unknown bacterium which thrived in cool damp places; traces were discovered inside the hotel's abandoned nuclear bomb shelter (they were a sixties thing, to protect the rich and famous in the event of Armageddon) and it was found that the hotel's air-conditioning system had spread the disease throughout the hotel.

It was to take a congressional committee and their team of experts, led by a Doctor Joseph McDade, six months to trace and isolate the bacterium that had caused the disease. The bacterium was named Legionella and the disease, which is still around today lurking in very old pipes and water systems in very old places, was named as 'Legionellosis' or Legionnaires Disease – after the first victims, the American Legionnaires.

What would they have called it if the outbreak had occurred three years earlier when we stayed at that hotel? Spiders from Mars Disease? – Ziggy Stardust Disease? – Bowie's…? Okay it isn't funny, we were all very lucky, and all respects are due to The American Legionnaires who tragically died in the incident in 1976.

I should say here that the Bellevue Stratford Hotel subsequently totally refurbished and replaced all their old plumbing arrangements, and it has been rightfully returned to its former glory as one of Philadelphia's best hotels.

The Tower Theatre Philadelphia was a nice, cosy old venue, well used to the behaviour of travelling rock musicians, and we settled in there for a straight run of five concerts on five consecutive nights. A residency! It was like being back at The Royal Hotel in Scarborough. The Tower Theatre had a seating capacity of 2,500 and all five concerts had apparently sold out within hours of going on sale. Many children of the well-heeled residents of Philadelphia had bought seats for all five gigs perhaps, but in any case 12,500 tickets went like hot cakes, or like cream cheese on crackers perhaps (sorry).

I met a cracker of my own in 'Philly'. The after-gig parties in Philadelphia were entirely different affairs to those we had experienced in New York. Things in Philadelphia were provincially reserved, and the population seemed to be much more relaxed about life in general. The red-haired lady that I met at a light and airy after-gig soirée in the city, turned out to be living alone, and was apparently a self-supporting, successful business type. The Philly lady was not too provincially reserved, in her apartment she had a water bed, a widely hyped and expensive thing in the seventies, and actually an overrated idea I thought. It was not made for sleeping much on anyway. The red-haired lady was intelligent and pretty, and again was a disturbing contradiction, not what I had expected – not what I would have said to be a 'groupie' at all. Still, although the lovely lady was not a man-eating Bebe Buell type, I did feel later that I had perhaps been collected. At the time though, I didn't mind at all.

As I had been paid at last by MainMan, and had some time to walk the streets of Philadelphia, I was able to look around the shops. I bought a pair of black leather trousers, which went well with my new Spider from Mars image I thought, and in a sailing equipment shop I found a zipped and hooded waterproof blue jacket with a bright yellow towelling-type lining. The jacket pre-dated the sports gear fad in much the same way as David's football boots had done some years before. I hate the whole sports-label-in-the-pub thing nowadays, but in 1973 the jacket was the dog's bollocks and, along with the creaky leather trousers, the new (slightly bizarre?) ensemble was to receive my style-inspector's (Mr Bowie's) nod of approval, in passing, at the sound check later that evening.

David Bowie and I though were already losing touch with each other. The tour was rolling, David was busy, and consequently it appeared to me that our renewed friendship was sort of on hold. Geoff MacCormack saw David every day however, and partied with him every night too. That suited me; it meant that Geoff rarely used our shared hotel room at that time. Also I had discovered that I was just not cut out for a role as hanger-on with my old chum. I still valued David's friendship but I was never sure whether to tag along with him or not. If I wasn't asked I didn't go, and so I accepted that I had to become, for the time being at least, just another musician, an employee on the tour.

Nashville

I have always seen the good side of country music. When I was growing up I listened to the Everly Brothers' harmonies, and to the style of brilliant country-influenced guitarists like Jimmy Bryant, James Burton and Cliff Gallup, among many others. Most of the guys in the tour group however, and particularly the Spiders from Hull, thought 'country' was just Jim Reeves and Slim Whitman, and that music from Nashville, the home of the Grand old 'Opry after all, was to be avoided.

Nobody on the tour was interested in coming with me to visit the famous recording studios in the city. I had spoken on the phone to somebody at one of the studios who said that they would be happy to show one of Mr Bowie's Spiders from Mars around their studio, and they could perhaps introduce me to some of the resident session musicians. I couldn't go downtown to the studio in the end however as I was told by management, Zee or Jamie, that I couldn't just borrow one of the station wagons and take off just like that on my own. My consolation was that I got to tag along with some of the road crew and we all went riding in the hills outside Nashville. These guys, mostly Bob See's guys, the Americans in our crew, were experienced riders and it was to be a wild-west ride alright. I just hung on to that big saddle for dear life as we charged around the hills like the James Gang. It was nothing like 'riding' in England, but it was great fun. I had of course been very disappointed not to get to meet the legendary session guys and maybe even see them at work, but I resolved to pre-arrange these kinds of things much better when we returned to the USA for the next tour, later in the year.

I was to regularly make the mistake of postponing things during our tour in 1973. I had no reason to not believe what we had been told by Tony Defries – that we were already engaged for another US tour later that same year, following an extensive tour in Europe, not to mention the possibility of a brief visit to Australia.

Behind the scenes the reality of our situation was quite different, and in fact our prospects were not so rosy. Ticket sales had not been going at all well in Chicago, nor in Memphis which was to be our next port of call.

There had been, quite apart from a certain amount of disinterest in the Ziggy Stardust phenomenon on the part of the citizens of Memphis, a campaign by a group known as 'The Daughters of the American Revolution' to have our concert cancelled. The Daughters sought a ban on the grounds that David Bowie's performances were lewd and obscene, and for fear of corrupting the youth of Memphis. In the southern states we were finding that public opinion, as displayed in the local press and on television was divided between the excitement of the younger generation for the new phenomenon from England, and the disgust of the older generation. I wasn't sure that I agreed with either polarised position, but as the older generation were classifying me, along with the other members of the tour party, as a 'cock-sucking English faggot', I tended to side with the younger generation.

Our concert in Nashville, at the War Memorial Theatre, was equally as successful as all the previous shows had been. We could have been anywhere in the USA, there was not a cowboy hat to be seen, and David achieved a resounding acknowledgement of his 'triumph over bigotry' in the Nashville press next morning.

Our stay at the Nashville Ramada Inn was during midweek and it was February so we pretty much had the place to ourselves. There were no groupies to be seen, or to be had either, and very few other guests in the place.

My first visit to a tour hotel bar, in fact any hotel bar, generally held few surprises. They were always very plush, and always dimly lit. They had evolved to an identical formula, all over the USA. Quite a surprise then to discover that a guy with an acoustic guitar had been engaged to play in the rose-tinted and leather-seated bar of the Nashville Ramada Inn. It should not have been such a shock of course, Nashville is a town full of guitar pickers isn't it? (I think John Sebastian counted sixteen hundred and eighty-five of them, and that was back in the sixties.) I talked with the guitarist when he took a break, and he explained to me how he was getting his guitar to sound a little 'doubled' – a bit like a 12-string. As every guitarist in Nashville would have known, he was using a Nashville 'high strung' stringing, which simply involves exchanging the third string for a first string, then tuning it right up to G, an octave higher than the normal string. The guy was a brilliant player, it was just another bar gig for him, and pop stardom was probably not on his agenda.

When our Memphis gig was cancelled we found that we had a night off and so would spend it in Nashville. David, Mick, Trevor and Woody had stayed at the Ramada Inn during their tour the previous year and they had discovered a previously unknown Black Nashville. David had befriended one of the hotel bellhops (always a good strategy), a tall and handsome black guy, and so on our unexpected night off we were all invited to a night club where a live band would be playing some soul music.

Mick Ronson had decided to stay in and wash his hair, but a small group of us, comprised of David, Geoff MacCormack, Stuey George, Trevor, Woody, our drivers and myself, piled into our two station wagons, the one in front carrying David, Stuey George and our navigator, the bellhop. We left the bright and glitzy Country and Western main streets behind, and soon we entered an obviously black neighbourhood on the outskirts of town, an area that reminded me of any poorly lit industrial estate, anywhere in the world. Our station wagons pulled into a dark and muddy car park outside a single storey unit, and the building turned out to be the nightclub. Faces in the gloomy car park glowered with surprise and anger at the intrusion by this bizarre little group of white boys dressed in faggot gear, and unfriendly warnings were to be heard from somewhere in the shadows. Fortunately our bellhop was obviously well known and very well respected at the club, for he quietened all the protesters, and explained who David Bowie was, and told them that the five white boys and the one black one from England were his personal special guests for the evening.

Our five white faces were quite possibly the only white faces that had ever seen the inside of that club. I had thought that Max's Kansas City in New York had felt dangerous, but Max's at least had been racially integrated. In this nightclub in Black Nashville, or more precisely in its car park, I had feared for my life when we had been approached. People in this neck of the woods were known to be armed, and this included the 'security staff' at the door of the club. In those days there were no black policemen in Nashville, and no policemen at all in Black Nashville after dark.

Things lightened up inside the club after a few drinks, and most of the customers accepted us or forgot that we were there. They remembered that we were in the place however when the house band proudly announced that the famous David Bowie and his Spiders from Mars were in the club, and that their famous drummer, Mr Woody Woodmansey, would now join them on-stage for a few numbers. I was gobsmacked, and very impressed with our Woody's courage. He climbed behind the drum kit, expressionless as ever, and went about his business for two or three numbers in his own powerful, capable and reliable style. The entire black population of the club gave Woody a generous and appreciative ovation as he climbed down from the stage, just as much for his nerve as for his performance I thought. Woody had done his bit for race relations in Nashville and he had done The Spiders from Mars proud.

My own attempt at a contribution to race relations in Nashville was certainly less commendable. When I found myself talking to a pretty girl in that nightclub, she inevitably happened to be a pretty black girl. We sat together and chatted for a while and we danced to the soul band (I have always hated dancing, but I will do it in a good cause). Suddenly I was pulled roughly to one side by a friend of our bellhop. The guy asked me what the fuck did I think I was doing, did I want to get myself killed? His strong advice to me was to leave the pretty black girl alone, and return to my place with the other white boys. My drink-induced courage enabled me to protest about it being 'a free country blah blah blah', and so the guy whispered to me, "Listen, make arrangements with this chick for later if you like man, meet her back at the hotel, but do it quietly, and don't be seen leaving the club together."

We broke the unwritten rules in Nashville, though we broke no laws of the land. Black Nashville opened my eyes to the state of America at that time, and it was some experience, believe me.

Memphis

We did not go to Memphis. MainMan management blamed the obscenity ban and played that for all it was worth to the music press.

I was very disappointed, this was the great music city, the place where Elvis had started out, and I'd missed it. Never mind, I thought, I'd see it next time round.

Detroit

David had written 'Panic in Detroit' on the occasion of his previous visit, and both the young and the gay residents of the city were thrilled to find that the track appeared on the new 'Aladdin Sane' album. This had established forever a kind of personal link with their new hero David Bowie. Everyone was saying that Detroit was going to be a blast, and as the tour party checked into the Detroit Hilton, we could feel the vibes. This was David Bowie's kind of city, we could feel the anticipation of a wild evening all around us, and the raw excitement seemed to be circulating around our hotel through the air-conditioning system.

Jamie Andrews was a good barometer in this respect, if Jamie was excited and louder than usual, it meant that wild things were likely to turn up; something for everybody and somebody for everybody that needed somebody. I don't criticise Jamie, he may have preferred boys, but I was no better, I was myself becoming a one night stand, totally selfish and necessarily without any conscience. I wasn't going to worry about groupies; they knew what they were doing. And casual sex on tap is addictive, as both David Bowie and Mick Ronson had already discovered on their previous USA tour. Mick had warned me, and now I was finding out for myself.

I was in the 'tour bubble'. I had regularly sent postcards to my young sons Christian and Jesse in Scarborough from each hotel lobby that we had passed through, but generally I did not think about life in the real world much, even though I knew I would return to it when all this Ziggy nonsense was finished.

The Detroit gig, at the Masonic Auditorium, was a near riot, almost 'Panic in Detroit' indeed. It was a hot one and it was over in the blink of a bleary eye. We all, including David, had some difficulty in getting away from the theatre, we were surrounded by fans and in the confusion, for some reason (I can't remember what), I had some kind of a falling out with big Bob See, the lighting boss. It was probably nothing to do with his lighting, and I think he was taking his frustration out on me. Maybe he wanted to be a guitarist, maybe he was even a guitarist himself and hated working on lights, or maybe he just didn't like me. It was probably a misunderstanding, but he seemed to be angry, very close to the point of getting physical, and so I did my best to give Bob a wide berth for the rest of the tour.

When we eventually got back to the Detroit Hilton, the place was almost as busy as the gig had been. The hotel had obviously decided, in interpreting Jamie and Zee's stated requirements, to have open house for the one night only. We were knee deep in groupies, all on offer, for one night only. David Bowie had arranged a small party 'for friends', and although Geoff had been invited I had not, so I made for the hotel bar as usual. I was not really in the mood for the bar, groupies included, so before too long I was off to my bed. I discovered however that several of the Detroit groupies had positioned themselves in the hotel corridors, and were lying in wait for any band member, sound engineer, or lighting man, or anybody else who might take them closer to the buzz surrounding David Bowie. I would not have believed that girls (and boys) could stoop this low, although I never did understand the mentality of the groupies, and I just hoped that they would eventually grow out of it. I climbed over and around the kids in the corridor, passing by my old chum Cherry Vanilla, who was just coming out of her room and was obviously in full party mood.

I watched television for a while; in the States they had twenty-four hour television, unlike at home where we had just three channels and they all shut down at midnight. As I was getting ready for bed, my phone rang. It was Cherry Vanilla, who asked did I 'wanna come and party'? I said no, I was ready for bed, but thanks for asking. Cherry asked was I going to bed alone, and I said yes, and goodnight. Fifteen minutes later there was a knock on my door. Sleepy-eyed I answered the knock, and a girl who I recognised as a friend of Cherry's walked straight into my room and closed the door behind her. Cherry had sent her. I managed to get the young lady out in less than half an hour. That's just the way it was on tour with Ziggy in 1973.

Chicago

We didn't go to Chicago, the gig was cancelled, to my own extreme disappointment, and with no explanation given this time. In fact, I was really gutted as I had been looking forward to Chicago ever since a conversation I had with Mike Garson some days earlier. Mike had told me that a friend of his was playing in the windy city with Stan Getz's jazz group, and did I fancy coming along to hear some amazing music. Mike told me that his friend was a string-bass player from England by the name of Dave Holland, and had I heard of him? Heard of him? He was my old mate! I had lost touch with Dave, since the summer in the sixties when he would come to the Cricketers pub on his night off to listen to my band The Tennesseans. We had almost formed a band together, but instead of going with Dave to The Midlands, I had gone to Sweden.

Dave Holland had gone to London; he had attended Music College and played a residency in a Chinese restaurant in order to pay his way through college. He had progressed quickly and gone

207

on to play with the likes of pianist Roy Budd and singer Elaine Delmar at Ronnie Scott's in the West End of London. There he bumped into Miles Davis, who had watched Dave play a couple of sets, then called him over and told him that if he came to the USA he would give him a job with The Miles Davis Group. Dave had gone for it, he had bought the plane ticket and he never looked back. The prospect of walking, along with Mike Garson, into Dave's gig with Stan Getz in Chicago was mouth-watering, and I had been looking forward to seeing the surprise on Dave Holland's face.

Dave would probably never have known of our near miss, our almost reunion, to this day, but in January 1999 I saw a poster for an upcoming Kenny Wheeler jazz gig at The Leeds Irish Centre. The gig was promoting an album called 'Angel Song' and the band line-up was to be Kenny Wheeler (trumpet, flugelhorn) Lee Konitz (alto sax) John Abercrombie (guitar) and Dave Holland (bass). I had heard that the album was making a big impression, so when I saw that Dave Holland would be playing bass I bought tickets and sent an email to Dave via his website. His reply was a bit vague, and I realised that Dave had not immediately remembered who I was. My message referring to Stan Getz, Mike Garson and David Bowie in 1973 most likely would not have helped Dave remember his first summer season on double bass at Scarborough back in the early sixties!

Susie (my wife by the way, since 1980) and I took my bass player John Precious and his wife Wendy along to the Irish Centre in Leeds on the evening of 28th January 1999 to have a look at Dave Holland and the band, and in spite of the venue (the Irish Centre is a cavernous old hall, a bit like an old working men's club or a factory cafeteria) we were knocked out by the freestyle jazz the guys were playing. It seemed that 'Angel Song' was a loose sequence of themes, to be improvised on freely – without any rigid chord structure or arrangement – and the time to move on to the next part, the next theme, was decided when all the band had played all they wanted to play on that section. I decided that the changeover into the next theme must be somehow signalled by the bandleader when he was ready, a nod or a wink probably. In any case I really wanted to ask Dave Holland that basic question – and some other questions about 'free jazz' and I knew that he would not mind me asking.

When the intermission came around, in spite of my curiosity I decided that I could not go backstage as Dave had instructed me to. I knew he would remember me when he saw me, but backstage after gigs, or even after any old pub gig, there are people who just have to get to talk to the performers, while all any performer wants to do is sit down quietly and chill out. Or in the case of a pub gig, pack up the instruments, microphones, amplifiers and leads then sit down and chill before packing the van then driving home for an hour or two. And so, at the end of the 'Angel Song' gig when fans were gathering around the backstage entrances, I really didn't fancy trying to talk my way in to see Dave, and we just drove home to York. Next day I emailed Dave again, to say how much we had enjoyed the music and to say sorry I didn't get backstage. Dave replied, 'Now I remember you Hutch of course, and the days at the Cricketers in Scarborough – you should have tried harder to get backstage. You just have to come and see me next time I'm in England'. Well of course I intended to, but you know how it is, I don't see any gig posters or get hold of any jazz magazines out in the sticks where I live nowadays so I have no idea who is playing anywhere. I do though tell every arrogant bloody jazz expert anorak that I meet that many years ago I played with the greatest jazz bass player on the planet – my old mate Dave Holland.

Los Angeles

L.A. the city of angels was next up, and the flight from Detroit would be a long one. The tour party, with the exception of David

Bowie who travelled by train or by limousine, flew everywhere in the US. It was the quickest way of course, but I actually envied our support band Fumble, who were travelling by station wagon (the cheapest travel option) and who on the trip from Detroit to L.A. would get to see the desert, Las Vegas and the Grand Canyon. And they had a lot more laughs. Their bass player, Mario, was a character to keep the spirits up, he would keep the band laughing like Roy Piper or Dennis Hitch did back in my days with the Roger Dean Five. Or like my old mate Ron Snaith did with the Hawaiian Serenaders in the Beachcomber Bar at Butlins, Filey. I could have been happy playing guitar for Fumble probably, but had I been given the choice, my vanity in those days would have had me pick the Spiders every time. It's just human nature.

I had for most of the tour, since Philadelphia in fact, been carrying a small acoustic guitar around as my personal hand luggage rather than sending it with the rest of the band's equipment. I was never sure whether it actually belonged to Mick Ronson or to David Bowie, but Mick had told me that it was okay for me to use it, to keep it with me to write songs with on the road. The airlines generally allowed me to take the guitar on board as cabin luggage, and the American Airlines staff found no problem with me carrying the instrument aboard for the long flight from Detroit to Los Angeles.

In spite of my short career at Montreal's Dorval Airport in 1967 I have never been very well up on aircraft types and numbers, but the plane which took the Spiders from Chicago to L.A. in 1973 was a bloody big one. We were delighted to find that the plane had a fully stocked lounge bar upstairs above the flight deck, and that the bar amazingly had an electric piano in the middle of it. This was not an American Airlines special arrangement for the benefit of the famous Spiders from Mars, it was apparently by pure chance that our plane had the piano in its bar. My guess was that they may have had some sort of cheesy corporate entertainment on a previous flight.

Brian Wilshaw, or Ken Fordham, I'm not sure which of them, had bought himself a shiny new soprano saxophone in New York, having possibly been under the same misapprehension as myself regarding the purchase of instruments, and Brian (or Ken) would carry the small instrument around with them everywhere. The soprano sax therefore was also on the flight, and in the cabin, in the lounge bar, with us.

We were flying at who knows what speed, at who knows how many thousands of feet, and we were playing a jam session in the clouds. The pilot and Mike Garson were not drinking, but Mike was playing a mean electric piano whilst Brian and Ken took turns with the little soprano sax and Mick Ronson and I both tried, more or less in vain, to make the little acoustic guitar audible. Mick and I, as it was daytime, drank a lot of Bloody Marys during the three or four hour (or maybe it was more, I don't remember) flight. We reasoned that these drinks were mostly tomato juice after all and were obviously a healthier alternative to proper alcoholic drinks during daylight hours. Woody and Trevor read their Scientology books and did their staring exercises.

"Ladies and Gentlemen, welcome to Los Angeles," came over the plane PA system and in a flash we were whisked through Customs into Los Angeles. It was just like landing in the middle of so many movies, and strangely L.A. was an even more familiar movie set than New York had been. We had left the real world behind some time ago.

The usual pair of station wagons took the band to L.A.'s infamous rock and roll hotel, the Hyatt House on the famous Sunset Boulevard. As I climbed out of my station wagon in the Hyatt House forecourt, I saw an instantly recognisable Jimmy Page climbing into a limousine. Okay fine, we had arrived in tinsel town, and I was up for it.

We were, as was the routine, all counted up and checked in at the Hyatt House hotel reception, all that is except for David Bowie who was already settled in his hotel suite somewhere up in Beverley Hills. There was no sign of Geoff MacCormack, so I guessed that I would probably have the hotel room to myself again. I took my key and got into the lift, together with a man in a suit and a smartly dressed foxy sort of lady who was possibly in her late twenties or early thirties. No sooner had the lift door closed when the lady said, "Hi, I'm Dee Luxe, welcome to California." She then handed me a joint and said to me, "Don't worry, this guy is the house detective and he is a friend of mine." Dee came to my room a little later with a big bag of grass, and we became friends. I was to see Dee going about her business around the place for the week or so that we spent in Los Angeles, and we remained friends. We were particularly friendly the day she called round and asked if I had ever 'done cocaine'. I had not, and so we did cocaine, and although it was a great buzz funnily enough I have never done it again since. Dee was well known in L.A. rock music circles, and it turned out that Dee had also been an in-house friend of Jimmy Page's during the previous week. Jimmy had left as I had arrived, and no doubt the procession of rock and roll friends and lovers would have continued for Dee Luxe at the Hyatt House hotel long after the Spiders too had left town. It all worked a bit like Butlins really.

We had been delighted to discover that we were to have several days off in Los Angeles before we actually had to do a gig, a very big one, at Long Beach Arena. I had some time off for a change and so I called the two old friends from England that I knew to be living in the Los Angeles area.

The first old friend was Rod (The Sod) Pearson, a sound technician from Filey, a small seaside town just up the road from

Scarborough, who now worked for all kinds of big stars in the USA. Rod was unfortunately out of town, on tour with somebody like Frank Sinatra. It was a shame, I had last seen Rod in the Beachcomber Bar at Butlins a few years earlier, and it would have been good to see how he was living the good life in sunny California.

Next I called Paul Downing, my old pal who had taken my place in The Tennesseans when I had gone off to live in Sweden in 1965. Paul was originally from Hull of course, and although Mick, Trevor and Woody knew of him, and certainly would have watched him play in Hull in the old days, Paul was just a little older than the Spiders (as I was myself) and he was not really a contemporary of theirs – anyway Paul did not seem too bothered that my band mates, the three Spiders from Hull, were not that interested in meeting up with an old Hull guitarist from the past. Paul had been a Tycoon, I had been a Tennessean and Mick had been a Rat before becoming a Spider. It's a funny thing about band names, I wonder if they always have a deeper meaning.

Paul, who lived in one of the canyons at that time, drove over to the Hyatt House and picked me up in one of his classic cars (he is a collector). It was a great feeling; I was off the roller-coaster ride, if only for a few hours. Paul told me he was still playing regularly and he took me to his house in a lovely wooded canyon, not too far out of town, to show me all kinds of vintage Fender guitars and amplifiers that he had collected over the years in the USA. Together with a local pal of Paul's, a guitar player in his current band, we had a bit of a jam, and then we went out for an excellent Chinese meal – one of the best I have ever tasted – in downtown Los Angeles. Paul and I decided that we should really have been in the same band together, not been in the same band but at different times, and that we might re-form the Tennesseans as a four-piece, or that I might move over to California for a while. I would wait and see what happened when our next US tour was over – maybe I would come out to California then.

I had met yet another intelligent groupie, who I will disguise as Jeanette, at the Hyatt House hotel. She was not really a groupie at all actually, she was just a fan and I had misjudged her – maybe I had met too many groupies recently. Jeanette lived in the San Fernando Valley and she had a proper job, nice parents and all the good things that California can bring. The sun was, as always, shining in Los Angeles and we were on holiday. One day I went horse riding again, this time in the Hollywood Hills, and this time with Jeanette, not with the James Gang. On yet another sunny day Jeanette suggested that I might enjoy a visit to Disneyland. Most tourists did that, and we, the band, were no different, we were touring. The rest of the band, together with some of the road crew (we all got along quite well as a 'team') were planning to use the day off to make a visit to the local cinema to see the much talked about porn movie 'Deep Throat'. I declined and instead decided that I would go with Jeanette to Disneyland for the day. Ken Fordham asked if he could come along too, so off the three of us went in Jeanette's little 'compact' ladies car. It was a fantastic day out at Disneyland; we had rides in a submarine, a white-water raft ride, visited a haunted house, and all kinds of kids stuff. Ken, Jeanette and I had a really good time, and being outdoors in the California sunshine made a welcome change from sex, drugs and rock and roll.

Sex and drugs were not to be avoided in Los Angeles. We never saw David Bowie for a few days, but I was reliably informed that he was keeping his end up out in Beverley Hills, and he would have been well supplied with all essential commodities. The provision of essentials would have been a job for bodyguard Stuey George. I knew that Stuey would often carry David's recreational grass, because Stuey was regularly billeted in the hotel room next to Geoff and I, and Stuey told me that he had it. And I probably smoked it too. Stuey George was an ideal gofer for David Bowie, he had lifelong insomnia and he figured that he might as well be out and about keeping busy as sitting in his hotel room with the TV set switched on all night. Both Geoff and Stuey were often out and about, Geoff just being the good mate to David that he was (and still is I believe) and Stuey taking care of David's requirements. Stuey always admitted to 'getting chicks' for his master, 'five at a time if necessary' so he said. I was never sure of Stuey's own sexual orientation, he was apparently not gay, but he was a mystery all the same. One morning he walked into our room, through an adjoining door, and said to Geoff and me 'what time is it guys?' I looked up to see that Stuey had wrapped his oversized willy around his wrist, like a wristwatch. That was his kind of joke, and Ol' Stuey did like a good laugh.

I went to David's hotel in Beverley Hills only once, and I didn't even get out of the car, but on that occasion I saw two very young looking 'chicks' being escorted out through the foyer by Stuey. I was to see the same double-girl act more than once in L.A., and later I discovered that they had been two of California's most famous groupies, one young Lori Mattix, who was later to live-in with Jimmy Page for a couple of years, and her friend Sable. Some others of the more high profile scores for David Bowie while we were in California were said to have included model Cyrinda Foxe, the critic Lillian Roxon and Ava Cherry, a black girl with peroxide-white hair. Ava was to sing backing vocals on David's 'Young Americans' album in 1975, and both she and Cyrinda, at different times of course, were engaged with David and Angie's favourite line-up, the *ménage a trois*. Stuey George also provided David with an inexhaustible supply of pretty suckers. Mick Ronson reckoned that David 'craved chicks' to bolster a chronic lack of self-confidence at that time.

One day I bumped into, or rather almost fell over, another very good friend of David's at the Hyatt House. Somebody had said to me 'Iggy's up on the roof', and I was intrigued, so I took the lift to the top floor of the hotel. I found the opened fire escape door leading to the flat roof of the building and I climbed the stairs. I found a sleeping, or possibly unconscious, Iggy Pop sprawled across the top step of the stairway. Iggy had his shirt undone and his bleached hair was wet through, as though someone might have tried to revive him. I had never met Iggy, I hadn't seen him around the hotel, but this guy looked a bit like an older, totally wrecked version of Mick Ronson, and I knew that it was Iggy. I went downstairs and had a quiet word with one of the hotel staff, who told me not to worry, they knew that Mr Pop was on the roof, and they had the matter in hand. What he meant was that they were letting Iggy sleep it off in the sunshine.

When I didn't see Jeanette, I had a couple of other friends apart from Dee Luxe to keep me company at the Hyatt House Hotel. Whilst not exactly 'craving chicks' as David Bowie was said to, I was by now quite used to 'chicks on tap' – I had decided within hours of arriving in the USA that I would enjoy the fringe benefits of life on the road for as long as they were on offer. One afternoon, a little friend decided that she wanted a joint and left me in bed while she went away to get some grass. I found out later that she had gone to see none other than Bob See, my old ex-mate, the lighting boss, who had demanded and received payment in kind for his dope whilst I dozed in my room down the corridor. I was to pay double for Bob's generosity; this free love business was bound to have a downside, and eventually I was to require the services of a doctor. The ever patient and understanding Tony Zanetta, our tour manager, arranged this service for me, and the good doctor subsequently gave me enough penicillin 'to kill anything on the planet'. As I had arrived at the doctor's surgery, I had passed a man on his way out, and the face was vaguely familiar. The receptionist had told me, quite unethically I suppose, that another English guitarist by the name of Big Jim Sullivan had just been in the surgery, did I not know him? Of course I did, it's a small world this rock and roll touring business.

I spoke only briefly to David Bowie the whole time that we were in California, but I did ask him in passing (as I had decided that he could be a man of some experience of the subject) about his view of the inherent perils of casual sex on the road. I told David that I had to wear this really smelly ointment that had been prescribed by a local doctor to clear up a mild social complaint, and I was concerned that everyone would smell it when I was out socialising. David roared with laughter and told me that he just wore his ointment throughout the daytime, but showered it off every evening before going out.

Our Los Angeles gig, on Saturday 10th March 1973, eventually came around, it felt as though we had been on holiday for too long and we were glad to be playing again. The gig was huge, the Long Beach Auditorium was an 18,000 capacity stadium and we were all set to enjoy the special occasion immensely. The venue was of course located on the seafront at Long Beach, a few miles out of Los Angeles. Our management had decided that we would use a hotel not too far along the beach from the venue as a nearby base of operations, mostly for the benefit of the road crew I believe. We used the hotel during the break between the sound check and concert time, so we didn't have to hang around the remote venue, or drive all the way back into L.A. and back out again.

David as usual was on top form, we had heard that Mick Jagger was in the audience, and the Long Beach gig was another storming success; it was great fun and as always it was over in no time at all. As the applause and the cheers and calls for 'more' following our encore 'Rock 'n' Roll Suicide' were dying away, I wondered why everybody, strangely including the sax players (who usually would fiddle around on-stage collecting mouthpieces or whatever), seemed to have left the stage before I had even unplugged my guitar. Just a little puzzled I went backstage with my new Les Paul Black Beauty, the 'spare' guitar that I only occasionally used, still around my neck. I was amazed to find our dressing room completely empty. My clothes had all gone, there was no one there – the place was deserted. I walked around backstage and eventually found one of our English roadies, the young Mick Hince. Mick stared at me, looked as surprised as I already was and said to me, "Hutch. What the fuck you doin' here?" At that point a slightly flustered Tony Zanetta showed up and asked me exactly the same question.

There had been a plan, but for some reason I had not been present when it had been unveiled to the band. Incredibly everybody on the tour, except for me, knew that three limousines, complete with a Los Angeles Police Department motorcycle escort, were to be waiting backstage and would depart the gig through the big backstage double doors at high speed and with sirens blaring, just a matter of seconds after the last chord of 'Rock 'n' Roll Suicide' had rung out.

The spectacular Beatles-style escape convoy might have impressed the crowds waiting outside the stage doors, but it was in fact only going as far as the temporary base, the hotel down along the beach. Tony and I had to catch up with the rest, but we had no transport and no taxis were available, as thousands of fans were milling around the venue, slowly making their way back to their cars which were strung out all the way along a very long car park on the beachfront. Tony Zannetta made a tour-management decision. "Follow me," he said, and he led me out through the stage doors, still wearing my green satin and lurex outfit and carrying my un-cased Gibson guitar. Tony had decided that we would walk the mile or so to the temporary hotel, where my clothes and a guitar case, would be waiting for us. This was fine by me, I felt reasonably safe in Long Beach, after all we were not in Nashville on the wrong side of the tracks, but it was a bizarre experience all the same. As Tony and I walked along the car park, we passed hundreds of fans, just a handful of the 18,000 who had just watched our gig. Several of them spotted me as they got into their cars, and they all did a double take. Americans generally, as we all know, are a gregarious people, and the ones in the car park fortunately saw the funny side of the situation. Many of them said something along the lines of, 'Err, goodnight, thanks for the gig man'. They were cool. I was eventually also cool about the whole experience, but not until I had been reunited with my clothes, my guitar case and my wallet at the beachfront hotel. Mind you, as everyone had already left for Los Angeles I had to wait in the hotel room for an hour or more (with no clothes at all as somebody had to take my stage outfit away) for my street clothes to be driven back to me from the Hyatt House Hotel.

Next morning, the band was surprised to learn that we were to do one more gig, an extra gig arranged at very short notice, before leaving Los Angeles for London. It was to take place next day, Monday 12th March 1973 at a very small venue, the Hollywood Palladium on Sunset Boulevard. It was just a small ballroom and somehow it felt like coming home to a reality-sized place. We were told that it was to be a special gig for just a small audience of close fans, as a thank you for their support in California. They all paid good money just the same though and it was in fact a profit-making venture.

All good things do come to an end, and the tour of America had been a good thing. If I had been at all interested and paying proper attention to my future prospects in the rock and roll business, I might just have figured out that although the tour had been a tremendous artistic success for David Bowie, and a terrific promotional success for MainMan Management, it had most likely been a financial failure or even a small disaster for RCA Records who were picking up all the bills.

Nobody in the tour group talked about money however, we were on a roll and next up was Japan. David Bowie was to board the *SS Oronsay* which would take him, with Geoff MacCormack along for company, across the Pacific to the port of Yokohama in Japan while the rest of us caught a plane home to London's Heathrow Airport. As David Bowie sailed across the Pacific Ocean (we would not see David again for almost two weeks) the band would have a few days off before we too had to leave for Japan. Meantime I was going home to Scarborough to see Christian and Jesse Hutchinson, my two lovely boys.

I had been keeping my new guitar, the black Les Paul that I had bought at Manny's in New York, close by me ever since the Long Beach car park incident, and had decided to carry it back to England myself rather than leave it with the road crew for shipping to Japan. I had been given, by various well-meaning individuals, a choice of stories to tell the UK Customs upon arrival at Heathrow Airport which would, I was assured, avoid having to pay customs duty on the brand new instrument. As the sax players had also bought new instruments in the USA and were carrying them aboard our flight, I was not too concerned over which particular customs deception device I would finally choose, and I forgot about it until we touched down. Unfortunately, by that point I had been drinking steadily, had fallen asleep, and was jet-lagged, barely properly awake when I was stopped by a customs man as I was walking through the green 'nothing-to-declare' channel. In my half-asleep state I had followed the rest of the band, including the sax players who had not been stopped, through the wrong channel and I was in trouble. As I tried to put forward my on-the-spot choice of story, I knew that the official was not buying it. The officer asked me if I would 'please step this way sir' and the rest of the band watched me disappear into the custody of Her Majesty's Inland Revenue, Department of Customs and Excise.

The customs officer took me into a secure interview room and read me the official caution. I was under arrest, and I was amazed; I was very naïve and had absolutely no idea that these customs guys had the power of arrest! Silly really, of course they do. I did my best not to crack, not to admit my guilt, rather I tried to modify my cover story a bit to suggest that I had realised, before being arrested, that I had made a mistake in my jet-lagged confusion. The reasonable though firm customs man left the room, to be replaced by a less reasonable character, who told me that they were going to keep me overnight in the cells, before my appearance in court the next morning. They were doing nice-cop, nasty-cop, and I couldn't believe it. My situation might otherwise have seemed just a little funny, but nasty customs man told me that I should expect a heavy fine and the confiscation of my beloved new Gibson guitar. I did not need to try and act anymore, I was now really worried. I would find myself with a criminal record, and they would take my guitar from me. Hell, I had thought that conning the customs was a national sport, with some lightweight punishment, even just a ticking off as punishment if I was caught. I thought it would be like school, and I had been wrong. They left me to sweat for some considerable time; the Spiders from Mars would be home by now I thought. Nice customs man came back and he told me that this time I was to be very lucky, and would not be prosecuted after all, though I would have to pay the duty on my instrument before I could be released. He warned me to be very careful in future, and they let me go.

Some homecoming I thought dejectedly, and made my own way to Kings Cross railway station, the gateway to the North. By the time I got to Scarborough however I had more or less recovered from the experience, and I thought little of it for the rest of the world tour.

The experience must have stayed with me though, for I never tried to 'con' the customs ever again, not even with a few bottles of wine over the allowance when returning from holidays in France! The customs men at Heathrow Airport had sorted me out for life – in respect of smuggling I mean. To sort me out in most other respects would take years yet.

My Funny Valentine © Leee Black Childers

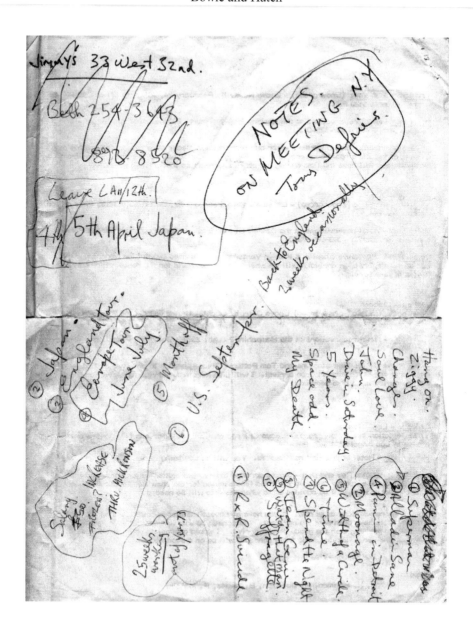

2 Gunter Hall Studios
Gunter Grove
London SW10
01·352·7629

240 East 58 street
New York· New York
10022
212·371·0531

March 12, 1973.

MEMO TO ALL STAFF (U.K.)

Please note that from now on all Mainman U.K. Staff are to make their own way to and from gigs (unless otherwise instructed from either Hugh in London, Zee in New York or Lee in L.A., and of course Tony), that also includes getting to any of the offices or anything.....unless otherwise told. Any taxi costs incurred will be taken off wages.

Clockhouse and Mercedes Hire have been notified and only David has the authority to sign for a taxi (including Tony and other heads of our various offices).

Long Distant phone calls, collect or transfer ones, will no longer be accepted. If an emergency should occur, send a telegram.

Therefore anyone sending a telegram collect, or phoning collect or taking a taxi should be aware of the fact that it will be deducted from their wages.

Also, individual members of staff have NO authority to make any arrangements for money of purchase of ANY goods. Any arrangements made for hire or puchase or labour must be made by Hugh in England, Zee in the U.S. and of course, Tony.

MainMan Ltd.
London Office

/mg

Registered in London No. 1013819.

Chapter Eleven - With Ziggy in Japan

It was towards the end of March 1973 and, along with the other Spiders from Mars, stars and auxiliaries and road crew, I now had almost two weeks off in the UK as David Bowie, refusing to fly anywhere, would spend the time travelling by sea to Japan. My time was to be spent in my home town of Scarborough, well away from the confines of the world tour party, before we were all required to fly to Japan to meet up with David again.

It was a paid holiday too. It seemed that MainMan was being careful to keep the team together, for we had a whole year's work ahead of us didn't we? The truth however was that the financial excesses of the whole David Bowie operation in the United States were beginning to take their toll on the accountants, who are always the real decision makers in the end – in every business. Somehow RCA had been persuaded to carry the losses incurred on both of David's tours in the USA, but the relationship between Tony Defries and the money men at RCA was now beginning to deteriorate. Most of the tour party had taken after the example set by Tony Defries and David Bowie, and whilst not necessarily ordering champagne and caviar every night, they had charged everything that they could get away with to the MainMan/RCA account. I had dodged a few room service bills myself; everyone else pulled the same trick, and a few other tricks to boot.

Another staff memo, given to all of the tour party as well as management staff, was sent out by MainMan's office in Gunter Grove during our holiday break and – with hindsight – it was very revealing:

March 12, 1973

Please note that from now on all MainMan UK Staff are to make their own way to and from gigs (unless otherwise instructed from either Hugh in London, Zee in New York or Lee in L.A., and of course Tony), that also includes getting to any of the offices or anything...unless otherwise told. Any taxi costs incurred will be taken off wages.

(Note from Hutch: So that's why Zee made me walk a mile back to the hotel at Long Beach instead of calling a cab.)

Clockhouse and Mercedes hire have been notified and only David has the authority to sign for a taxi (including Tony and the other heads of our various offices).

Long Distant (sic) phone calls, collect or transfer ones, will no longer be accepted. If an emergency should occur, send a telegram.

Therefore anyone sending a telegram collect, or phoning collect or taking a taxi should be aware of the fact that it will be deducted from their wages.

Also, individual members of staff have NO authority to make arrangements for money or purchase of ANY goods. Any arrangements made for hire or purchase or labour must be made by Hugh in England, Zee in the US and of course, Tony.

Who knows perhaps that memo was written the week that MainMan received Manny's bill for my new Les Paul guitar, although presumably that would have been just one more small straw, and not the one that broke the camel's back.

Back in my old home town of Scarborough it was fantastic to see my two sons again, and they were happy to see me too, though the reunion hurt quite a lot, and that was not something I had anticipated. I had landed back in the real world again and I found that I quickly had to make a few adjustments to my expectations and to my behaviour. I had to find my own way around again, and make my own day to day decisions. It was a little strange, after only a few weeks on the road in the USA as a member of Ziggy's band I had become kind of institutionalised.

Never one to waste money myself, I stayed with my parents in Scarborough for a few days. They expected me to stay with them of course, but I was in culture shock, back in my old bedroom and all that. I was the star at my old gig the Penthouse again though, and both Peter Adams the owner and Cedric the manager made me 'right welcome' in Liggers Corner. I went on the pull as usual, but very quickly I was made to remember that the Scarborough girls were not like the California girls. In Yorkshire a man has to pay for his pleasures in one way or another and he is generally expected to earn a lady's affection in time-honoured fashion – with 'nice girls' anyway. So I did my best to avoid nice girls – of course that wasn't always a great idea.

The short break in England flew by. I watched my eldest son Christian play football and I took my youngest, Jesse, to feed the ducks, and then suddenly, whilst I was still 'readjusting' to the real world, it was time to rejoin my teammates the Spiders from Mars again.

The tour party reconvened at Heathrow Airport check-in desk and so began our long journey to Japan. The first leg of our journey was to Paris, and from there we took an Air France flight to Japan, via Moscow, where we were asked to disembark whilst the plane was refuelled. Although we were not allowed out of the confines of the International Departures area, and were technically not in the country, we certainly knew that we were in very grey communist Russia. Armed guards were everywhere, and they watched our glittery little group like hawks. The dour-faced Russians just stared at us in amazement.

The journey was indeed a long one, it really did feel like a trip to the other side of the planet, and when we landed in Tokyo it was not at all like arriving on a movie set, as had been our experience in the USA. Jet-lag apart, entering Japan was a real culture shock – and we realised that we had come to another world altogether.

TOA Attractions Incorporated, the tour promoters in Japan, were as we might have expected, determined to run an extremely efficient operation. Their organisation was not going to be outfaced by MainMan, and they had obviously decided that they were not going to be messed around by a bunch of western rock and roll degenerates.

The following memo, specifying precise timings and instructions and including the tour itinerary, was duly issued upon landing to everybody involved:

TOA ATTRACTIONS INCORPORATED
2-A UEMURA CO-OP
13-2 SAKURAGAOKA, SHIBUYA-KU
TOKYO, JAPAN

TELEPHONE 463-4261, 463-4262
CABLES: "OHNOASIASHOW"

DAVID BOWIE JAPAN TOUR NUMBER ONE
for spring 1973, April

Welcome to Japan! We sincerely hope that this visit to Japan will be an enjoyable one and especially a successful one. Please be advised that this itinerary has been planned for with extreme care and in detail, and we would sincerely appreciate your kind attention on the times mentioned in this itinerary especially when travelling to other areas in Japan as trains run on time here, and each and every individual seat has been reserved. We thank you very much for your close and kind co-operation and understanding. Please be advised also that space has been provided after each date on the itinerary to make personal notes etc.

....

April 5th
Thursday

David Bowie arrival in Yokohama 'Oronsay'.....................4:00PM

Arrive Yokahama pier C
Meet the fans, press pictures for news prior to boarding car.
Proceed to Imperial Hotel in Tokyo by cars.
Check-in Imperial Hotel (tel. 504-1111)

....

April 6th
Friday

Mrs. Bowie and son arriving with other members 10:35AM

Mrs. Bowie and son/other members arriving AF Flt. 270.
Proceed to Imperial Hotel by bus and car.
Check-in Imperial Hotel (tel. 504-1111)

PRESS CONFERENCE: to be scheduled at 2:00PM – 3:30PM
Conference to take place at FUKUNO-MA on the 3rd floor of Imperial Hotel.

Other members to arrive on NorthWest Airlines from Los Angeles and New York.

....

April 7th
Saturday

OFF

....

April 8th
Sunday

<u>Shinjuku Koseinenkin Hall</u> .... <u>Show time: 6:30PM</u>
<u>Rehearsal</u>......................................

Will advise rehearsal time after conference with management.

For concert: Pick up hotel lobby.................
Will advise after concert pending rehearsal.

Proceed to concert hall by car and bus.
After concert, return to hotel by car and bus.

NOTICE: IF REHEARSALS ARE TO BE HELD PRIOR TO THE CONCERT, IT IS EXTREMELY ADVISABLE TO STAY AT THE CONCERT HALL TILL PERFORMANCE TIME.

....

April 9th
Monday

OFF

....

April 10th
Tuesday

Shinjuku Koseinenkin Hall .... *Show time: 6:30PM*

Pick up hotel lobby..*4:45PM*
Proceed to and return to hotel by car and bus.
....
April 11th
Wednesday

Shinjuku Koseinenkin Hall .... *Show time: 6:30PM*

Pick up hotel lobby..*4:45PM*
Proceed to and return to hotel by car and bus.
....
April 12th
Thursday

Nagoya City Kokaido .... *Show time: 6:30PM*

Pick up hotel lobby..*9:50AM*
Proceed to Tokyo Yaesu Station by cars.
Board Bullet Train "Hikari No.67" departing......10.30AM
Arrive Nagoya...*12:31PM*
(THE ABOVE RESERVATIONS HAVE BEEN MADE FOR THE
LIGHT AND SOUND CREW)

(THE BELOW RESERVATIONS HAVE BEEN MADE FOR DAVID
BOWIE ENTOURAGE)

Pick up hotel lobby..*10:50AM*

Proceed to Tokyo Yaesu Station by cars.
Board Bullet Train "Hikari No.71" departing......11.30AM
Arrive Nagoya..13:31AM
Check in Nagoya Miyako Hotel.........(tel. 052-571-3211)
Pick up hotel lobby.....................................4:45PM
Proceed to concert hall and return to hotel by cars.

....

April 13ᵗʰ
Friday

Travel day to Hiroshima

Pick up hotel lobby.....................................12:15PM
Proceed to Nagoya Station by cars.
Board Bullet Train "Hikari No.33" departing......13.03PM
Arrive Okayama Station.................................3.20PM

Depart Okayama "Ltd. Exp. Tsubame 7"............3.35PM
Arrive Hiroshima..5:40PM
Proceed to Shin Hiroshima Hotel by cars.
Check in to Shin Hiroshima Hotel (tel. 0822-41-5181)

....

April 14ᵗʰ
Saturday

Hiroshima Yubin Chokin Hall .... Show time: 6:30PM

Pick up hotel lobby.....................................4:45PM
Proceed to and return to hall and hotel by cars.

....

April 15ᵗʰ
Sunday

<u>*Travel date to Kobe City*</u>

Pick up hotel lobby..*12:00 Noon*
Proceed to Hiroshima Station by cars.
Board "Ltd. Exp. Shiojo 52"..............................*12:40PM*
Arrive Sannomiya Station................................*4:42PM*
Proceed to hotel by cars.
Check-in Kobe Oriental Hotel (tel.078-331-8111)
....

April 16ᵗʰ
Monday

<u>*Kobe Kokusai Kaikan*</u>..........................*Show time: 6:30PM*

Pick up hotel lobby...*4:45PM*
Proceed to and return to hall and hotel by cars.

....
April 17ᵗʰ
Tuesday

<u>*Osaka Koseinenkin Kaikan*</u> ....*Show time: 6:30PM*

Pick up hotel lobby...*12:00 Noon*
Proceed to Osaka by cars.
Check-in Osaka Grand Hotel (tel.06-202-1212)

Pick up hotel lobby...*4:45PM*
Proceed to and return to hall and hotel by cars.
....

April 18th
Wednesday

Shibuya Kokiado .... *Show time: 6:30PM*

Pick up hotel lobby..9:30AM
Proceed to Shin-Osaka Station by cars.
Board Bullet Train "Hikari No.60" depart............10:25AM
Arrive Tokyo...1:35PM
Proceed to and check in Imperial Hotel (tel. 504-1111)

Pick up hotel lobby..4:45PM
Proceed to and return to hall and hotel by car and bus.
....
April 19th
Thursday

OFF
....
April 20th
Friday

Shibuya Kokaido .... *Show time: 6:30PM*

Pick up hotel lobby..4:45PM
Proceed to and return to hall and hotel by cars and bus.
....
April 21st
Saturday

David Bowie departure for London

Pick up hotel lobby..9:00AM

The contents of this letter do not constitute a contract.

And that was to be exactly the way of it. The memo may not have actually constituted a contract, but it certainly informed us all as to who was going to be the boss on this trip.

There was a lot of smiling and bowing at the airport. This was obviously the custom in Japan, and we were just going to have to get used to it. The same gentlemen from TOA Attractions Inc. who had issued the pompous introductory memo were now giving us the traditional courtesies of welcome.

Our honourable tour promoters had also booked us into a quite prestigious hotel in Tokyo. The Imperial Hotel is sited across the road from a large and leafy public park in the centre of the city, which in turn has at its centre the private grounds and buildings of the Imperial Palace, Tokyo's own Buckingham Palace no less.

The lobby of the Imperial Hotel was filled with people, and while the three star Spiders were permitted to talk to members of the press, I found myself cornered by two young Japanese girls. They both were wearing what I took to be a traditional costume, including Geisha-like Kimonos and a traditional sort of hairstyle. The girls' smiling and bowing routine was accompanied by 'Welcome to Japan' spoken in very soft voices, then they completely took me by surprise when they presented me with a small collection of apparently very ancient Japanese coins. I took this to be a tradition, but felt both humbled and embarrassed by the girls' generosity. I still have the coins somewhere, and I still have no idea of their value as antiques or whatever. They are though, of great value to me – as no doubt was intended.

The formal and possibly traditional nature of their welcome gave no opportunity for talking to or getting to know better the doll-like girls who had come to welcome us. What I really mean is that there was no chance of pulling – absolutely no chance.

The members of our tour party who were interested in, not to say addicted to, casual sex on tour were to soon discover that Japan was, in 1973 anyway, not an easy hunting ground. The Americans amongst our road crew, those guys that had been in Vietnam, had already sown seeds of doubt amongst us by questioning the wisdom of one night stands on the Japanese tour. They had given us graphic information about a virulent form of clap that was said to be circulating in these parts, and that was known to the Yanks as 'Tokyo Rose'. This was, we were told, a venereal disease that would not surrender easily to a single blast of penicillin, California-style.

The result was that later that evening when Mick Ronson and I found ourselves in the hotel foyer bar, talking to some giggly girl fans, we were rather less than assured in our otherwise well tried and tested pulling routine. Apart from the perceived threat posed by Tokyo Rose, the staff of the Imperial Hotel appeared to have been forewarned, certainly by our tour promoters we decided, about the possibility of immoral behaviour by their guests from England and America. Our hosts appeared to be guarding the exits from the lobby leading to the lifts and staircases. Were we becoming paranoid? Mick and I suspected that we were being monitored by the hotel staff, and we were about to devise a way of putting our theory to the test when we got the nod from one of the road crew.

The roadie confirmed our suspicion; he had been informed by hotel management that none of our party would be permitted to take any 'guest' upstairs to our rooms, and that this rule would be strictly enforced, at all hotels on our itinerary, for the duration of our stay in Japan. Well, we'd see about that wouldn't we, both Mick and myself resolved to rise above such petty restrictions. Snotty memos about train times were one thing, but setting limits on our social (or anti-social?) behaviour was quite another thing and a bridge too far we decided. We couldn't see David Bowie, for example, going without for two weeks, whether or not Angie, who of course was travelling with us, was involved.

The following day, Saturday April 7th, had been thoughtfully planned as a day off, to allow us to recover from our long journey from the west. I took the opportunity to go for a walk around the city, look at the shops and all that. I was surprised to discover that in 1973, a young white person was something of a rarity in Tokyo. Incredible as it may seem nowadays, very much as when I had been one of very few young, obviously English people in Gothenburg, Sweden in 1965, I was now turning Japanese heads in Tokyo, their capital city. My Spider bangles and UK fashionable clothes may have contributed of course, but I had no idea that my suede jacket and jeans outfit would be considered so unusual in Tokyo. My naturally red-ish (strawberry-blond?) hair was probably the defining difference between me and the rest of Tokyo that afternoon mind you, and within a very short time the Japanese guys would take to dying their hair. I might as well have been Gulliver in Lilliput as I wandered around the city centre. At only five foot seven, or maybe five foot nine-ish in my boot-heels, I was taller than most of the locals. It was a once in a lifetime experience for me, everywhere else that I've ever been I've been a short-arse.

On our very first evening in Tokyo, in order to make minor changes to the set we had played in the USA, the band rehearsed at a studio provided by RCA. In particular, we rehearsed 'Starman' for inclusion in Japan, and I remember it well for Mick Ronson's patient persistence in trying to get me to play the chunky rhythm guitar part to his exact requirements. Mick, though always a very easygoing guy, was also a perfectionist and was as insistent as he had been at our previous rehearsal in New York. I got it right in the end; it's something to do with how you stand.

The following night, our first gig of our tour of Japan was at the Shinjuku Koseinenkin Hall in Tokyo and it was a sensation. David received an uncharacteristically wild reception from the obviously socially repressed and rock-music starved audience. Though the venue was not as big as those that we had played across the USA, the noise produced by the Tokyo audience – predominately made up of young girls – was much louder. It was a shrill, high frequency sound, and it was deafening. On some of our songs I couldn't hear a thing I played, the on-stage monitors in Tokyo were poor (worse than the ones on the USA tour) and almost useless, and I thought of the Beatles' experience at Shea Stadium back in the sixties, not hearing anything and not being heard. It appeared that the crowd could hear David Bowie alright though, and next morning the *Japan Times* reported that: 'Musically, he is the most exciting thing that has happened since the fragmentation of the Beatles, and theatrically he is possibly the most interesting performer ever in the pop music genre'. Both the illustrated pop music magazines, and also the strange hand-drawn 'thriller' magazines that are so popular in Japan, carried spectacular photographs (and drawings) of David Bowie straddling Mick Ronson mid guitar solo. Many of the excellent tour photographs were to be taken by another of David's Japanese acquaintances, the talented Masayoshi Sukita. David had met Sukita in London a year previously, and had asked the photographer to accompany the Japanese tour from start to finish.

Geoff MacCormack had wanted a live action stage photograph to send home to his mum, and so by prior arrangement, mid concert in Tokyo, David leaped up on to the auxiliaries' rostrum between Geoff and me (the only night he ever did that) whilst Sukita took the photograph of the three of us. My mum was to appreciate the picture too.

When the tour-opening Tokyo gig was over we were collected together and returned promptly to the Imperial Hotel, just as the memo from our tour promoters had promised. We were then permitted to sit downstairs in the lobby, and to consume a modest amount of alcohol and chat politely to one or two fans, all of whom had apparently been screened and vetted by the hotel staff before being admitted to their hotel. Mick Ronson and I had been allocated three or four smiling girls to talk to. They were very pleasant, but they were from another world and they were not letting us in. Even in the quite unlikely event that one or two of the girls had been up for some rock and roll debauchery, the hotel minders were not taking their eyes off us. We eventually said our thank-yous and goodnights, we all smiled and bowed, and Mick gallantly paid for taxis to take the young things home to their parents.

David's intuitive decision to wear Japanese designed stage outfits for the Aladdin Sane tours had undoubtedly turned out to be a major factor in the visual impact of our show, and this was to prove doubly so in Japan itself. Designer Kansai Yamomoto had the previous year staged a sensational rock fashion show in Japan, David Bowie had seen a video of the show at home in England and had instantly become a Kansai fan. Many of the designs that Kansai produced for David had borrowed much from the traditional Kabuki theatre, something that David had been fascinated by, along with many other aspects of eastern cultures, including Japanese culture, since childhood. David had worn one or two of Kansai's outfits on the US tour, and he had successfully mixed them in with some of the earlier Freddi Burretti designed Ziggy outfits. When David arrived in Tokyo however, Kansai presented him with half a dozen, even more spectacular costumes. They must have cost a small fortune, but they were invaluable to David's concept, and well worth every yen that RCA paid for them.

The next day, Monday 9th April 1973, was unbelievably another day off and I decided that this tour of Japan was going to be as much a holiday as a gig. Even the saxophone section conceded as much, and most of us just went off and did tourist things. We didn't see David or Angie at all; I guess they were doing family things, as of course David had not seen his baby son Zowie (Duncan Joseph Haywood Jones) for several weeks. I believe that David and his family hung out with Kansai and his family in Tokyo, though I also know that David never stopped working, planning and writing new material. Geoff MacCormack told me that he and David had been to see a performance of Kabuki theatre, had gone backstage after the performance and had met the star of the show, one of Japan's most famous Kabuki stars, Tomasa Boru.

I had walked around the city and looked in the too expensive clothes shops. I had visited the Imperial Gardens at the Emperor's Palace, and had talked to the monster sized goldfish in the pond outside the Imperial Palace. I had also eaten at the perspex-fronted sushi bars and fast food outlets where you could (fortunately for me) order just by pointing at a plastic replica or photograph of what you wanted to eat.

It was not until Geoff MacCormack had met and then introduced me to a spectacularly beautiful girl called Mikki, that I was to get to know some local people and see a little of how they lived. Mikki was a model and was half-Japanese. In fact, the agency she worked for in Tokyo was called appropriately 'The Half Model Agency'. All of the models were just that, half-Japanese, and were all said to be just that little bit more beautiful due to their mixed ancestry. It seemed a bit unusual as a business concept, but the two or three girls from the agency that I met were certainly beautiful creatures.

I was introduced to a lady who turned out to be one of Mikki's bosses at the Half Model Agency, all Japanese and just a little older than the models, she reminded me of Yoko Ono – she was very bright and we got along fine. 'Yoko' took me to a party on our evening off. It was, she said, a very special party to be given in honour of one of Japan's most famous Sumo wrestlers. The venue for the party was at an address in a very expensive area of Tokyo, and the apartment was by Japanese standards a large one. I should explain perhaps that it only gradually dawned on me that, not only did Japan have quite small people, but most of them lived in quite small apartments, and they all drove very small cars along quite narrow roads.

Geoff MacCormack came along to the party with me and the model agency girls, and it turned out that Geoff and I were the only white boys present. We sat on the floor and tried to do and eat what the other guests were doing and eating, but really although everyone else was smiling and bowing at us, only our fellow guests for the evening, the model girls, were talking to Geoff and me. I wondered where the guest of honour had got to, and I wandered into another room where I discovered the huge presence of the special guest, the Sumo wrestler, seated at his own table with several others in attendance. I was quite formally introduced to the wrestler, and I smiled, nodded and bowed. I was getting the hang of that. The Sumo was impassive, but kept looking at me a little uneasily I thought, so I didn't stay in his company too long and went back into the other room. I feared that perhaps my lack of understanding of the rigid and ancient protocols in Japanese culture made me appear disrespectful to the revered Sumo celebrity. Either that or he was about to smoke a joint and couldn't be sure of my discretion.

Yoko and Mikki also took me to a proper Japanese restaurant. It was the sort of place where the Japanese people would eat, not the tourists, nor the bloody stupid businessmen getting legless on sake. These places were not on the main streets in the centre of the city, so I had not, and could not have, stumbled across one. This, my first Japanese restaurant, was in an inner suburban street, a narrow, leafy and well kept little street. It was a small place, a rectangle divided into two halves long ways, one side being a row of solid wooden bench-type tables with bench-type seating, and the other side being the kitchen, totally open and in full view of the customers seated alongside. Chefs and waiters alike wore, with the usual whites, wide red bandannas around their heads and they moved around purposely, making as much noise as possible. This was not a pretentious, money or class conscious sort of place, there were no grovelling or patronising waiters in attendance; this was a good place to eat in. The girls ordered fish for all of us, and Japanese beer, which came in pint bottles. The fish was excellent, as was the beer, which the Japanese have been expertly brewing for centuries, possibly for longer than we in the west. As one beer bottle was emptied, a bandanna'd waiter would appear like magic with a fresh one, its top being quickly removed as the waiter approached our table at speed. The waiter would bang the new full bottle down hard on the table before wheeling away with the empty.

As is the case with all the other countries and cultures that I have seen, the tourist Japan that your dollars, pounds or euros will buy on your holiday is not the Japan that the Japanese live so well in.

April 12th, Thursday, Nagoya

The good gentlemen of TOA Attractions Inc. collected together the sound and lighting crews in the lobby of the Imperial Hotel Tokyo on 12th April 1973 at 9.50am on the dot and took them away in three or four vehicles. Precisely one hour later they returned for everyone else, me and the band, and the Bowies, David, Angie and Zowie.

At Tokyo's Yaesu railway station, we, that is the TOA Attractions tour staff, the MainMan tour staff, the hairdresser, the wardrobe girl, the eight musicians and David Bowie with his bodyguard and family, all climbed aboard our first Bullet Train. Our train was called the *Hikari No. 67* and it duly departed Tokyo railway station at 10.30am precisely. The Bullet Train is a beautiful piece of engineering, as sleek as an aircraft, inside and out. They are very fast and very comfortable, and *Hikari No. 67* appeared to be brand new.

David Bowie and his family took their seats in the same carriage as the other Spiders and me, as there didn't appear to be any 'class' system in place on the transport system in Japan. David always dressed up for travelling, he was in a way still 'on-stage' when in public, and most of the rest of us would try to play our part – only the saxophone section could pass as civilians. Some like Mick Ronson were as glittery, bleached and bangled as David himself and the group as a whole had (as we had intended) attracted a lot of attention at the railway station. On the train however we had two whole carriages to ourselves, we had our privacy and were able to move around and socialise, read, sleep or watch the amazing view from the carriage windows. It was a great way to see the country, we were travelling at high speed, but we saw the people working in the rice fields, we saw their farms, their rivers, their bridges, and behind the expanse of greenery we saw volcanic Mount Fujiyama, the iconic symbol of Japan. It seemed as though Mount Fujiyama was in view for much of our journey time, though we must have just passed it twice, once heading north and once coming south again.

David and Angie appeared to be relaxed and happy, and I even chatted a little with them on the train journey. This was quite unusual, as David was still really only keeping company with Geoff MacCormack, whilst I would generally hang out with Mick Ronson after gigs. David and I were still old friends of course, we never had any disagreements, but I was now a friend who was more importantly an employee on the tour, and I had learned to live with that. It was a different kind of friendship now.

Zowie Bowie, at two years old, was a year younger than my second son Jesse, but was very much like him with lots of blond hair and lots of energy. I sat Zowie on my knee and tried in vain to interest him in the sights of Japan passing by the carriage window.

There have been several photographs published of David and me with my elder son Christian, taken when he was about two years old too, and many people have been given the false impression that it was Zowie in those pictures. Ken Pitt in fact took those photographs at David's flat in Clareville Grove in 1969, and Christian Hutchinson is actually four years older than David's son Duncan Joseph Haywood Jones, or rather Duncan Jones, the extremely talented and very famous film director as he is these days. They say that David calls him Joe.

Another regular misconception that I have noted in some biographies concerns the identity of the drummer for the 1973 tour of Japan. More than one account that I have seen has Aynsley Dunbar as our drummer for the tour, yet although I have of course heard of him by reputation, I have never met Aynsley and he was certainly not with us in Japan. Woody was on the tour, and he was working on his Scientology for the whole of the three weeks.

Nagoya went smoothly and strictly in accordance with the TOA Attractions Inc. published plan of action. We were collected and transported as decreed, and the gig was another sensation. The next day was a travelling day and it was to be approximately a five hour journey to Hiroshima. In fact, there was nothing approximate about it – it was to be exactly a forty-eight minute car journey to the station, and exactly a four hours and thirty-seven minute train ride to Hiroshima. We have the itinerary memo to prove it don't we?

April 13th & 14th, Friday & Saturday, Hiroshima

Hiroshima – the name of the city will forever be synonymous with apocalypse. The cine-footage of the American bomb that flattened the old city and put the Japanese out of the Second World War is ingrained on the memories of my generation, as clearly as are the television pictures of New York, September 11th 2000.

The place did have a sort of Milton Keynes feel about it, as we might have expected, but the total rebuild had allowed for a huge open space, a 'peace park', around the area where the bomb had hit the earth. In the centre of the park is a museum of tangled metal remnants and horrific photographs, lest we forget. We had a day free in Hiroshima and I just had to go to the Peace Museum and have a look, and I will not forget.

I will probably not forget either the strange sight of dozens of Japanese workers lined up on the roofs of their office buildings at dawn each day, dressed identically in white shirts and ties, working their way through a programme of regimented physical exercises. This was followed by some sort of chant, or rallying call, presumably in praise of the company and how good it was to work there. I had done the straight-job routine myself, but this was too much I thought. All this would be going on as I drew the blinds before retiring to bed, drunk as a skunk and all alone as the sun came up on the land of the rising sun.

The kids in Hiroshima were no different to kids anywhere else, and they went wild for David Bowie and the Spiders from Mars at the 'Yubin Chokin' Hall. I sometimes wondered if the translators ever had hysterics during their working days. Some Japanese names were just hysterically funny, while others were censurable.

David Bowie's on-stage performances had become better than ever in Japan, David obviously relished the other-worldliness of the place and his response could be seen in the developing theatrics of his show. I rarely saw David while we were in Japan, other than when we were all travelling by train, and obviously for the duration of the stage show each evening. At a typical sound check, we, the eight musicians comprising the Spiders from Mars, stars and auxiliaries alike, would take up our positions on-stage and after individually testing microphones, guitar amplifiers and drum kit, we would run through just one of David's songs with Mick Ronson standing in for David on vocals. If we were waiting for something, or someone, we might jam a bit, with Mike Garson generally taking the lead with some jazz-style riff. I would enjoy the short jam, but I don't really know that any of the crew, or any of my band mates other than Mike Garson I think, noticed that my natural style is a kind of jazzy blues. It might be hard to believe but nobody (apart from a few conversations I would have with Mick Ronson) ever really talked about music on tour. I would really have enjoyed more time playing some jazzy stuff with Mike Garson – quite apart from the Aladdin Sane tour repertoire where I had only backup rhythm-guitar or 12-string parts to play.

Certainly the crew took notice at just one rehearsal when I picked up Mick Ronson's guitar and played, very loud, through Mick's amplifier set-up. One of the crew told me that it sounded just like Mick was there – not that I play anything like Mick of course. I had just been fooling about, filling in time, but it goes to show what a big part an equipment set-up plays in any musician's individual sound identity. Anyway that was only a few bars of music that I had played, and nobody played like Mick Ronson. Mick had taken his inspiration from his hero Jeff Beck, but he had, through his collaboration with David Bowie, carved out his own very passionate and individual style as a guitarist.

David himself would briefly sound check, but only after Mick was satisfied with everything. David would sometimes just stroll on to the stage, nod at one or two of us, then do just a part of one song, and stroll off the stage again. He was a professional, just like the rest of us, but David Bowie was maybe playing just a little more of the prima donna in Japan. It was bound to happen, we were all in fantasyland, but David had more to deal with, for he had devised the fantasy, all by himself.

April 15th & 16th, Sunday & Monday, Kobe

Kobe, the old capital of Japan and still its spiritual centre, was an impressive place and probably the prettiest city in Japan. I played tourist again, and the Monday night gig at the Kobe Kokusai Kaikan theatre was another near riot of teenage frustration; identical behaviour to the previous concerts.

David was working hard at his performances, enjoying himself, but pushing himself to the limit. He had contracted what he described as an 'Asian Flu' but he did not let it stop him, he would not cancel or postpone a single show. He was also now in the habit of climbing all over the PA speakers at the sides of the stage, and even up to the theatre balconies if he could get there. The spotlights would follow him on his climbs, and the audiences loved it. One night David made an impossible leap, from the top of a speaker on to the stage-floor, and he twisted his ankle badly. He continued with the song and finished the gig, much of it sitting on a chair, and we didn't know how bad his injury was until the following evening, when David used chairs and microphone stands as supports throughout the gig. David was always the totally committed professional, and even in the old days with David Bowie and The Buzz he had put his performance before any other consideration. He was always a hard worker, and the show went on.

For myself, I was just the rhythm and 12-string guitarist and I had no big musical or on-stage performance responsibilities, and so perhaps in consequence I felt that there was beginning to be something strangely impersonal about the gigs while we were in Japan, for the whole band, not just me. Just being in the country was a fantastic experience of course, and the audiences were enjoying the concerts for sure, but the band, well, we were just dressing up, going through the motions then going back to the hotel. We would eat, sleep, then travel, go to the gig, and do it all over again. We couldn't even get laid.

April 17ᵗʰ, Tuesday, Osaka

We travelled, this time by road, to the Osaka Koseinenkin Kiakan Theatre. The concert was a near riot, we went back to the hotel, ate and slept again.

April 18ᵗʰ, Wednesday, Tokyo

I now thought of Tokyo as home, and was glad when our final Bullet Train, *Hikari No.60* dropped us back in Tokyo at 1.35pm exactly – as promised in our faultless itinerary memo.

We were to play a new Tokyo gig, the Shibuya Kokaido twice before we were finished with our tour in Japan, the first on the Wednesday, and then a final 'farewell to Ziggy gig' on Friday.

The Wednesday gig went as expected. Yes, you guessed it, it was a near riot, we went back to the hotel, ate and slept etc.

At least I had some friends in this city and I could escape the suffocating protectorate of TOA Attractions Inc.'s bloody itinerary, which had only just stopped short of specifying the times that we could go to the toilet. I went with 'Yoko' to eat in a proper restaurant for a start. Whilst travelling around in Japan we had been more or less obliged to use the hotel restaurants, and on the one occasion when we did go outside to eat, we had been obliged to visit a city centre businessman/tourist restaurant. As we had climbed the stairs to this exclusive and presumably quite expensive place, they were carrying small businessmen out, down the staircase. The idea was apparently to drink as much sake as possible before passing out. The small businessmen had come out straight from work, they lived in their suits and ties, and they were having their kind of a good time. Bless 'em.

Back in the good old Imperial Hotel, I couldn't help but notice a very pretty and unusually smiley girl who seemed to have duties all over the hotel, even though I never saw her behind the reception desk. When Geoff MacCormack and I inevitably passed her in the corridor as we were leaving the lift, Geoff said, "You don't know who she is? Man she's the hotel prostitute!" The smiling girl was apparently the hotel's one small, though unofficial, concession to the sexual needs of its guests. She must have been a busy girl, and probably was an expense account item. She was no good to me, nor to Geoff, she might have been Tokyo Rose herself for all we knew, and anyway we had friends in the city.

Geoff MacCormack and I knew the same people in Tokyo, and when Geoff left for home with David Bowie a couple of days before my own flight back to London, Geoff's friend Mikki and I went out in the city together a couple of times. David, with Geoff along for company, was to leave the Imperial Hotel at 9.00am on Saturday 21st April 1973, the morning after our farewell Tokyo gig. That afternoon Mikki took me on a rickshaw ride through part of the city, and through the gardens of the Imperial Palace. We went shopping, and I bought kimonos for my mum and the kids. I already had some souvenirs. The hotel pyjamas, at more than one top place, were good quality kimono sort of things, and so along with many of the others on the tour I left with those in my suitcase too. They are the best souvenirs aren't they? The ones with the hotel name on them.

Half Model Mikki was as much a mystery to me as she had been to Geoff MacCormack. Geoff had confided to me that he couldn't be certain because Mikki spoke so very little English, but he suspected that although she was very sweet indeed, she might just be a bit on the dim side. Personally, I was of the opinion that Mikki was just very sweet, very young and far too nice for old Geoff.

It did occur to me that perhaps Mikki was under the misapprehension that both Geoff and I were very rich rock stars. Geoff certainly looked and acted the part in his St. Laurent trouser suits and all, and maybe even my own well-worn suede jacket and jeans outfit would not have been unusual for a real, rich rock guitarist after all, so why shouldn't she presume that we were wealthy and famous lads? We were in the company of David Bowie after all, and we lived in the best hotel in Tokyo. I tried to explain to Mikki that I was just an ordinary bloke, along for the ride with David and the Spiders from Mars. I don't think she believed me, even if she understood.

Some months later, Geoff was to tell me that he had learned that Mikki had turned up in London, presumably looking for him. As fate would have it both Geoff and I were out of town, somewhere on the road. Tokyo is just too far away, and I will never know why Mikki flew to England, or what or who she hoped to find. Neither Geoff nor I were really at fault, but in this case, as with probably several other instances on our tours, we surely left some stuff behind us. I don't know about broken hearts, but certainly 'stuff', and we all carry our guilt with us, for as long as we have a memory.

The final gig in Tokyo, on Friday 20th April at Shibuya Kokaido Hall, was a riot. No, really, I mean it *was a riot*. In the estimation of the attendant Tokyo police it was anyway.

The gig had certainly, almost predictably, been a triumphant end to the Japanese tour. David unusually took three encores, and the very last one, which was some old rock and roll song, most probably Chuck Berry's 'Round and Round' because it was a favourite of David's, was delayed for fifteen minutes whilst the crowd went even wilder. The kids rushed the stage before we had finished the song. Mick Ronson yelled at me, Geoff and the saxophone section, "Fuckin' run for it!" as he made for the exit stage-right at a gallop in his high heels. I was right behind Mick, we had no time to unplug our guitars, and amplifiers crashed over behind us on-stage as guitar leads were torn out of jack sockets. The 'wings' of the stage very luckily for us had solid hinged doors, and everyone in the band got safely behind them without any injury, but it had been a close thing. The theatre was in pandemonium, policemen grappled with screaming girls on the stage and in the auditorium. The road crew struggled to extricate kids, frozen by panic, from the crush, and Angie Bowie, who had been out front and enjoying the frenzy, was now caught up in the fracas, and was helping youngsters who had become trapped under their seats which had toppled over, row after row like dominoes.

The Police were furious, and there were claims that some 'westerners' in the crowd, allegedly Angie Bowie and Tony Zanetta, had incited the near riot by swinging some chairs around their heads when they had decided that the show was a little dull and needed a boost. Tony and Angie had in fact encouraged the kids to rush to the front to make for a better finale, as Leee Black Childers, who was with the guilty pair in the audience, was to admit later. The Tokyo Police complained to the RCA office in Tokyo and demanded that RCA identify and hand over for questioning the people who had incited the riot. The next morning, believing that warrants had already been issued for their arrest, Leee rushed Zee and Angie, along with little Zowie, to Tokyo Airport. There Leee discovered that the Tokyo Police were watching all departures for London and San Francisco, ready with warrants for the arrest of Zee and Angie. Improvising with commendable speed and ingenuity Leee bought new tickets and put the fugitives on the next flight to Honolulu. Nobody said a word to the band about the dramatic escape and I knew nothing of this story at the time. I'm glad that I didn't know, it might have spoilt my last couple of days in Tokyo if I'd known that the local Police were so intent on enforcing their rigid Japanese moral standards on our glittery and obviously debauched little tour party.

David Bowie, who still would not fly of course, had decided before accepting the Japanese tour that he would return to England by the land route, the long way home across Siberia. David had chosen Geoff MacCormack and Leee Black Childers as his travelling companions. Leee was intelligent, well travelled and resourceful, and Geoff was good for laugh, up for anything and good company.

Secure in the knowledge that Angie and Zowie, in the company of Tony Zannetta, had escaped the Tokyo police net and made it safely to Honolulu, David, Geoff and Leee left Japan on Saturday April 21st 1973, sailing from the port of Yokohama aboard the *Felix Nzerjinski*. The ferry would take them around the tip of Honshu, Japan's main island, and 600 miles across the Sea of Japan to the port of Nakhodka on the south-easternmost coast of Russia. The voyage was a long one, and David was able to relax and rest on the boat. Geoff told me that David even played a cabaret of a few songs, including 'Port of Amsterdam' and 'Space Oddity' to his fellow passengers. A train from Nakhodka took the travellers to Vladivostok, where they boarded the Trans-Siberian Express bound for Moscow, which at almost 6,000 miles and taking a week to complete, is the longest train journey on earth.

Also boarding the famous train, having decided to accompany David as soon as he had heard of the rock star's plan, was a hard-boiled US newspaper writer called Bob Musel. Bob was a veteran Second World War journalist and was currently employed as Moscow correspondent by UPI, the American news agency. The agency's idea was to cover the extraordinary journey, which began with a 2,000 mile stretch of frozen Siberian landscape, and Bob's close observation of David Bowie on the journey was to be an added bonus for the trip. Bob Musel had been a songwriter himself, his biggest success being the 1950's hit 'Poppa Picolino', and he was to enjoy hearing David writing and playing his own songs during the long cold journey.

On one occasion David played all through the night to a group of passengers until the Siberian dawn came up through the frozen fir trees and broke the spell. The journey was, as advertised, to take a week and included almost one hundred stops, at which all the western passengers, including David Bowie, Geoff, Leee and Bob Musel, would disembark to buy roast potatoes, boiled eggs and jars of fresh yoghurt from the vendors on the platforms. Their appetites needed the stimulation they found on the platform, as the diet provided on the train was Spartan, even for first class travellers (or soft-class as the Russians call it) and the choice of schnitzel or boiled chicken did not vary.

Whether on the train, or during the short stopover in Moscow, David, now that Angie had left, must obviously have gone on the pull again, for Bob was to report of David later that, 'He fucked everything that moved and quite a lot that didn't'. It can't have been that cold then.

David, Geoff and Leee completed their mammoth journey aboard the Orient Express, which had taken them in some style from Moscow to Paris, and David met up with Angie again in Paris, on May 3rd 1973. There they were to meet and be entertained by one of David's heroes, the mysterious Jacques Brel whose songs David and I had devoured, worked on and performed just a few years back with Feathers. Next morning, after spending the night at the George V Hotel in Paris, David and Angie missed their boat-train from Gare du Nord to Victoria. After much deliberation, they settled for a hovercraft from Boulogne, even though David was not at all happy about it. It seems that this unique and quite new form of transport (remember I had seen the prototype operating in Montreal just six years earlier) travelling just two feet above the waves was too close to flying for comfort, even if it was bringing David back to England for the first time in many months.

Now we would tour the United Kingdom. I wondered, as no doubt did David Bowie and the entire entourage for that matter, what folks at home would make of us. We were back from other worlds, we were ready for the United Kingdom and we just hoped that it was ready for us.

1973 Japan; Hutch, Bowie & Geoff © Masayoshi Sukita

Chapter Twelve - The Fall of Ziggy Stardust

Upon landing at Heathrow the Spiders from Mars, auxiliaries and road crew all became individuals again, and again none of us would be required for tour duty by David Bowie and MainMan Management Inc. for at least two weeks. This second fully paid break was again entirely down to David Bowie's avoidance of air travel, and we appreciated the holiday just as David would enjoy his Trans-Siberian rail journey home. I made my way to Kings Cross Station and bought a ticket back to Scarborough. It was great to be back in England, and to be free again.

Peter Adams, the owner of The Penthouse, a well misnamed establishment and Scarborough's only proper rock music venue, had become a friend and he very generously offered me the use of one of his properties, a small flat near the seafront on the South Bay, for a couple of weeks while I was to be in Scarborough.

From my perspective at least, Peter Adams had been born with a silver spoon in his mouth, and he had invested his inheritance into making a success of his Penthouse club. David Bowie and The Hype had played there of course, but so had Derek and the Dominoes, Manfred Mann, Free, Vinegar Joe, John Martyn and many other class acts, as generally Peter endeavoured to engage them just before they became too big and too expensive to book. Even the Sex Pistols played at The Penthouse. The conservative seaside town hardly deserved such a magnificent venue in the early seventies, and never before or since the club closed down has Scarborough seen the like of Peter Adams' Penthouse.

The name of the club, its neon sign and its naff red-plush décor, all came with the lease, as the place had been designed and opened initially by a member of one of the town's amusement arcade families. When the scampi-in-a–basket, poor man's Penthouse cabaret-joint era was thankfully over, the Penthouse rock music venue was opened. Peter had most probably wanted to call it 'Middle Earth' or 'Gandalf's Garden' or something along those lines, but the corny old 'Penthouse' name stuck, and somehow it came to suit the place. Peter Adams was a rich hippy, an early prototype of that rare creature, and though we were friends, he could never understand why I would insist on working for a living, for at least some of the time, when I was not being a rock-star guitarist. Peter would have made a success of anything he wanted to try, but he loved the music world, and in particular the emerging 'underground' music world of love, peace and soft drugs.

Peter Adams' own love of the peaceful soft drug cannabis was to land him in court, charged with the crime of not just possession of the deadly substance but with the actual supply of cannabis because he had allegedly permitted other people to smoke the drug in his house – at a party. He had used his house in Whitby as a drugs den they said. That was how it was in the provinces in those days, and it wasn't at all funny. To make matters worse Peter had taken a leaf out of a Rolling Stone or a Beatle's book and had driven up to the county courthouse in Northallerton (my birthplace incidentally) in his Rolls Royce, dressed to kill in Afghan coat, feathers and beads. This, quite predictably I would have said (had Peter asked me), was bound to wind the county court magistrate up. And it did, Peter was handed a nine month custodial sentence and was 'taken down forthwith' as instructed by the old buffer running the show. I don't know who drove the Roller back to Whitby.

The sentence was ridiculous of course, but it must have been pretty sensational in court that day. Peter was released quite soon, within a matter of days if I remember correctly, pending appeal, and the sentence was eventually reduced to the appropriate fine and a suspended sentence. Peter no doubt put it down to experience, but the case highlighted the gulf between the Law's attitude to soft drugs in the North of England, and that in the South. Nothing has changed much in that regard, everybody pleases themselves in Brixton (for example) these days, and after dinner joints are commonplace in Knightsbridge and the country houses, and yet drug squad persecution of gentle old hippies like Peter still persists in many little towns north of Watford.

Incidentally Peter Adams' follow-up venture in the later seventies would be another nightspot, but this time it was not an inherited former cabaret joint and he would name it himself. Peter would call the new place 'Middle Earth' and it became a hippie heaven, not the rock and roll palace that The Penthouse had been, no matter how naff the name it had carried proudly. For a year or two, after leaving the Bowie caravan in 1973, I regularly played as resident support act on Peter's weekly Sunday evening 'folk nights' at The Penthouse; I acted as host as well as playing my own set, and our guests included John Martyn, Ralph McTell, Mike Absolom, my old mate Michael Chapman and the wonderful Gas Works.

Peter Adams' characteristic generosity allowed me to live for a few days in comparative peace and quiet in my home town between the Japan and UK tours in 1973. The flat had a wonderful view of the sea, and I could stroll down to the beach where I had played football as a schoolboy, when the proper pitches up on Oliver's Mount above the town were too waterlogged to play on. Mostly though I took up my position in Liggers Corner at The Penthouse every evening, drank quite a lot and bathed in the reflected glory of David Bowie. My current almost celebrity status in the local pop world made pulling 'chicks' comparatively easy. I was between world tours and looking forward to several more months, or even a year or two, of star treatment in the UK, Europe and the USA again, and reality – the hard truths of a temporary rock and roll existence – did not really enter my head.

It was during that first week back in Scarborough that I saw a ghost. I had never seen one before, I did not particularly believe in ghosts, and I have never seen one since, but I saw one in Peter Adams' flat one night. I had been sleeping soundly, but I awoke with an uneasy sort of cold feeling and I sat up in bed. A ghostly white transparent figure came out through the front of Peter Adams' wardrobe, moved across the small room and went out through the wall behind me, oblivious to my presence in the room. I was sure that the apparition was male, he was totally expressionless and did not make any sound. I felt that I was looking at the past – the thing was not of the present. The cold feeling that had woken me turned into a shiver. I had seen it, but still could not believe it; I shook my head to make sure that I was wide awake then went and made a cup of coffee. If there had been alcohol or any kind of drugs in the flat, I would have taken them all. Next morning I could not bring myself to tell anybody for fear of ridicule, and it was to be several days before I carefully selected someone to confide in. I don't think they believed me, they most probably thought I must have smoked one joint too many. Heightened awareness may have contributed perhaps, but I did see the ghost of Museum Terrace, just once.

I had enjoyed my short break in Scarborough, I had seen a little more of my two sons and I had stretched my ego around my home town again, but I was ready to resume touring and quite happy to catch the train south again. The UK tour was going to be a long one; we were scheduled to play 37 towns and cities in 45 days. The prospect of then going on to visit all the best European cities, to include Paris and even my old home town Gothenburg before returning to the USA, would keep me going for sure. As David Bowie had told me would be the case, I didn't want the touring to stop. Not at that stage anyway.

David Bowie and Mick Ronson had called a rehearsal in order to sharpen a few things up after our fairly long holiday, and in David's case, his very long train ride across Siberia and Europe on the way back from Japan. The rehearsal room turned out to be a large former cinema in South London and it was draped to the floor, from the ceiling and the balcony, with parachutes, presumably intended to improve the cinema's acoustic qualities – a technique that was beyond my understanding – but anyway the place had been borrowed or rented for the day from its famous owners, Led Zeppelin.

We had rehearsed for maybe half an hour when we saw that two people had walked into the back of the auditorium. David stopped the song in mid-stream as Paul and Linda McCartney walked up the steps and on to the stage. Paul nodded at everyone and said, "Alright lads?" then surprised me by walking over to me, while Linda talked to David. Paul asked me what I thought of the Harptone 12-string guitar that I was playing, as he had one himself, as did 'George'. Both Beatles apparently rated the Harptone guitars very highly and so did Bob Dylan – Paul told me. I felt, for perhaps the only time in my life that I was talking to some kind of fictional character – even a comic strip superhero – or that maybe I was dreaming. Now this is hardly fair on Paul McCartney, for he seemed to me to be an extremely nice and down to earth guy, but bloody hell it was Paul McbloodyCartney! In Person! And talking to me about my guitar! I managed, I hope, to hide my amazement and to act as cool as a Spider from Mars (even an auxiliary one) should act in those circumstances, and I told Paul that it was in fact David's guitar, but I hoped to get another one for myself when we returned to America later in the year. Linda walked away from David and called Paul over; it was time for them to leave us to rehearse, so Paul said to me, "Okay mate, go ahead, just show-off." That is sound advice for any performer to take on board actually, and I have always remembered it. The customers in one way or another are paying to be musically entertained, and Paul's point certainly was that we should give 'em all we've got. It is funny though, no other famous face has ever had quite that peculiar effect on me, even

261

though I have met many famous faces. I guess the Beatles really were something special to all of us.

Before the start of our UK tour proper, set to start in Aberdeen on Tuesday 16th May 1973, we were to play a one-off concert at London's famous Earl's Court. I had looked forward to this one, it seemed to me that this was a very prestigious venue, even though I knew that Earl's Court was actually a large exhibition venue and I had never heard of a rock concert being held there before. Tony Defries, ever ambitious, had let the prospect of a good payday overrule any misgivings anyone may have had about the size and suitability of the venue for a rock and roll event. With a seating capacity of 18,000 the receipts would yield a big profit for the one evening's work.

The gig was a disaster. The PA system, which Robin Mayhew and his Sound Control team had controlled reasonably successfully (apart from my stage monitors as you know) for both the US and Japanese tours, just could not cope with the cavernous acoustics of the huge exhibition hall. The lighting crew had a similar problem in that they just didn't have enough gear, or enough power even if they had, to light the stage adequately in the huge gloomy space that was Earl's Court.

It transpired that in fact no rock concert had ever before been held at the venue. David Bowie and the Spiders from Mars were the first, the guinea pigs, and the nine of us on-stage, plus the harassed sound, lighting and road crews were to pay the price for Tony Defries's overambitious gamble.

The band knew right away, at the sound check, that we were in big trouble. The on-stage monitors were useless to me as usual, but whereas I would normally hear something of the overall sound in the auditorium, at Earl's Court all I heard was a cacophony of slap-back echoes, criss-crossing and colliding. We were all experienced musicians and the others had certainly encountered poor acoustics in town halls and church buildings in the past, just as I had myself, so we resolved to make the best of it and the gig started as planned to a roar of welcome from 18,000 enthusiastic Londoners.

Several thousand people towards the back of the hall quickly realised that they were unable to see or hear anything of the show that they had paid good money to see and hear. Shouts of protest from the disgruntled people at the back led to scuffles between fans, and between fans and security men. Some drunken members of the audience took their opportunity to misbehave badly, and they danced naked and even urinated in the aisles – so we were told later anyway. Twice David was forced to stop the show, and he appealed in vain for order to be restored.

From my own, very personal point of view, the pièce-de-résistance was to come at the very end of the show, and it concerned the start of our barely deserved encore. The planned encore song was as always 'Rock 'n' Roll Suicide', which began with the very well known solo 12-string guitar strum across the chords of C major and G seventh – played solo by me on-stage of course. My brief was, from Mick Ronson as always, to wait for the applause for David's 'final' song (usually that was 'Suffragette City') to die away, make sure that David was centre stage and in an obviously 'ready' pose before I started the intro to 'Rock 'n' Roll Suicide'.

I started the guitar part, then immediately realised, as the other members of the band all stared across the stage at me, that no one on-stage could hear me playing as I was not in anyone's monitor mix. I suspected that my guitar was not being heard either by the audience through the main PA, and when I heard Mick Ronson shout something unintelligible to me, I moved towards him, in the direction of my guitar amplifier, in order to at least check that my own gear was working.

When the lighting crew realised that something was wrong, and that nobody appeared to be able to hear my intro, they for some reason turned the rest of the already poor stage lights off altogether. As I tried to move a couple of feet to my right in the darkness, I fell off the rostrum, full length on to the stage floor, still hanging on to my acoustic 12-string guitar for dear life. No one saw me fall over except the sax players, who thought it was hilarious of course, and both Geoff MacCormack and Mick Ronson, as they were standing alongside me in the gloom. The people in the front rows certainly must have heard the crash, as did David Bowie himself, who must have wondered what I was playing at. I had at least managed not to land on my guitar, and it was still more or less in tune, so I climbed back on to the rostrum and began the song again. Mick Ronson, ever the professional, played along with me this time, to reinforce the weak sound of my 12-string coming out of the PA system, though it was still not to be heard at all through the on-stage monitors. I got a funny look from David as he started his vocal, and another from Mick, but my own small disaster was destined to be forgotten in the aftermath of the overall concert disaster. Nobody after the gig was particularly interested in my explanation for the balls-up, or interested in listening to my complaints about my individual on-stage sound and lighting problems, and the post-mortem appeared to be concerned exclusively with the poor choice of venue.

The music press was scathing about the Earl's Court concert, but at least it did make front page headlines. The *New Musical Express* headline was 'Bowie Fiasco', and asked 'What went wrong?', while the *Melody Maker* simply headlined 'Bowie blows it'.

A second show scheduled for 30th May 1973 which had also sold out in record time, was cancelled. To their credit, Tony Defries and the MainMan team did not make too much fuss about where improvements could have been made to combat the characteristics of Earl's Court, and David himself very professionally behaved as if the debacle had just never happened. Strangely enough, the evening was to have no effect whatsoever on the success of the coming tour, or on the rapidly accelerating runaway success of the brand new pop phenomenon Ziggy Stardust – or should I say David Bowie. In fact, Ziggy Stardust and David Bowie were perceived to be the same individual, by press and public alike, and possibly only David himself needed to keep the two identities apart, as he, David Jones, had created them both.

The music press soon forgot about Earl's Court, and David Bowie stayed on their front pages. The Spiders from Mars did not worry about the disastrous gig afterwards, we just had a few drinks and looked forward to the thirty-seven proper theatres that we were about to visit. When you have cut your teeth playing the northern clubs, village halls, ballrooms and pubs, the odd crap night, the odd disaster even, is something that you just take in your stride.

May 16ᵗʰ, Tuesday, Aberdeen

We played: The Music Hall
We stayed at: The Imperial Hotel

We were to travel north to Aberdeen, way up in the north-east of Scotland, as we had recently travelled all over Japan, and in David and Geoff's case right across Siberia, by express train, departing from London Kings Cross on the morning of Monday 15th May 1973. Kings Cross railway station was buzzing like an airport when our tour group, including the now very famous David Bowie, arrived in long shiny black limousines and took first class seats in especially reserved carriages. David was still dressing up for travelling, for maximum impact, as was Mick Ronson. Often both David and Mick would wear eye make-up and the like for the benefit of the watching public, and perhaps carry a shoulder bag, and their travelling outfits were designed to be noticed. David might wear a floppy hat and a loud, colourfully striped suit, whilst Mick's off-stage gear was often a sort of schoolboy blazer, white shirt and school tie, worn with either black or yellow Lee Cooper jeans – which incidentally Mick would always buy from Harrods. I still had not bought too many clothes, as we had become used to living out of just one suitcase – all we were permitted to carry on tour – and the other Spiders, apart from Mick, did not try too hard either. All the same, we made for a gaudy little group in comparison with our fellow passengers on our train ride northward.

The journey to Aberdeen from London is a long one by road or rail, and we were more or less ready for our beds when we finally reached the Imperial Hotel in Union Street, Aberdeen (the hotel is gone now, long since replaced by a shopping centre – across from the top of Market Street).

I would have time during the following morning to have a look at some of the city centre, little knowing that some ten years later I would be working in the city as a contract designer-draughtsman in the oil industry.

In spite of the remote location and the long cold winters, I would eventually grow to love Aberdeenshire. I was to make some firm and lasting friendships there when I lived with my family in a country croft some thirty miles north of the city throughout the eighties. I would play almost every Saturday night at a pub called The Northern Lights in the little village of Hatton of Fintray, not far from the prosperous market town of Inverurie. The resident band was called Special Branch and it had been put together by our irrepressible and musically enthusiastic pub landlord, BBC radio producer and bandleader Kenny Mutch who sang and played rhythm guitar. Kenny had been busy enough as a BBC producer but he wanted to sing in a pub and so he bought one. The trio was completed by me on lead guitar (and a couple of songs now and then) and the late, great and irreplaceable Paddy Byrne, one of Dublin's finest exports and probably my best real friend ever, on vocals and bass. My Saturday nights playing rough and ready Scots, Irish, Country and Rock and Roll music, all taken with a lot of drink, were my escape, my relief valve, and were to keep me more or less sane for almost ten years, and my Saturdays at The Northern Lights would compensate for my commitment to the fifty or sixty hour weeks of long hard working days in the oil industry design offices in Aberdeen, not to mention the regular and sometimes a little hair-raising offshore visits to the oil platforms themselves.

On that first visit to Aberdeen in the spring of 1973 however, with David Bowie and the Spiders from Mars, I thought we had come to the far northern extremities of the British Empire and I wondered why on earth anybody would want to live all the way up there.

The Aberdeen gigs, the first concerts of our UK 1973 tour, were a resounding success, and they banished all memories of the 'Earl's Court Performing Disaster'. We played both a matinee and an evening show at the Music Hall, Aberdeen – the grand old theatre which was just walking distance along the road from our hotel in Union Street. Not that we could walk about much, the street was packed with fans and we waved like rock royalty down to them from our hotel windows above. It was no night to think of a party anyway, we had made a long train journey and played two shows, and I slept like a log (woke up in the fireplace) in spite of the crowd outside and the rattling pipes and plumbing noises that are a feature of most grand old hotels that are well past their glory days.

May 17th, Wednesday, Dundee

We played: The Caird Hall, Dundee
We stayed at: The Angus Hotel, Dundee

I have observed Dundee to be a hard-bitten kind of place in general, although having said that I have met some great characters from that city over the years, not the least of whom would be the unique Alexander 'Sandy' Kidd.

Sandy was, like me, an Instrumentation Draughtsman who worked at the drawing board (we had no Computer Aided Design yet in those days) directly behind me in an oil service company engineering office in Aberdeen in the early eighties, and he had designed and built a small prototype of a mechanical device, based on a pair of gyroscopes, that would in theory defy gravity. That is, it would lose weight, and have the potential to hover and to fly. It was the stuff of science fiction all right, and yet we were surrounded every day by the very real world of the North Sea Oil and Gas business.

Sandy had a milling machine and a Colchester lathe in his garage at home, and would bring in to work some of the tiny and intricate parts that he had worked on during the previous evening, often into the wee small hours. I was sceptical about the truth of Sandy's claims for his gravity defying invention, as you would expect, but somehow our boss Jack Campbell seemed to believe in Sandy Kidd and would, to an extent at least, tolerate his obsession. I would listen myself to Sandy's softly mumbled explanations of how he was intent on achieving the impossible. Impossible according to Albert Einstein and quite a lot of other very clever people anyway.

Sandy explained to me that whilst he had been serving in the Royal Air Force many years earlier, he had one day been carrying a standard navigation device, some sort of aircraft compass encased in a wooden box, out of an aircraft. He had been halfway down the steps from the plane when some incredible force, emanating from the wooden box that he was carrying, threw Sandy from the steps, several feet on to the ground. The navigation device used a system containing a gyroscope, itself a bizarre and barely explainable invention. A germ of an idea came to Sandy Kidd, and he was hooked.

The device that Sandy designed and built was based on a system involving a pair of gyroscopes, rotating in opposite directions, and he made it work. He powered the prototype from a pedestal drill, and when he switched it on, the device effectively lost weight. It just lifted off and travelled vertically up a spindle attached to the pedestal drill. It would fly, said Sandy, when a suitable power source, yet to be discovered or invented, eventually came along. His basic principle would eventually drive a flying saucer, of that Sandy had no doubt. It transpired that the basic idea was not entirely new, and not unique to Sandy Kidd, as the Japanese government were said to be experimenting secretly with quite large gyroscopes, and presumably trying to make them fly. Sandy was way ahead of the Japanese government's research in his own opinion, and he had built his prototype machine in his garage at home in his spare time. The Japanese government's budget for their own similar research must have been zillions of Yen.

The BBC eventually got to hear about the device and made a documentary about Sandy Kidd and his flying machine, Terry Wogan even interviewed Sandy on his national TV chat show and the national papers had a good laugh, but some university men took it very seriously indeed, particularly one professor at Dundee University. We used to joke about the danger of Sandy being kidnapped by the Russians, or by the CIA, because he knew too much. I was told that an Australian millionaire eventually took Sandy under his wing, and then I heard that he had moved his experiments to California, but that it was all very hush-hush. Sandy Kidd I hope that you are still well, alive and kicking, and hopefully still pushing the boundaries of belief and of gyroscopic assisted space flight, in your own time, be it back in your garage in Dundee or in some space lab in California.

The second gig on our 1973 UK tour, on May 17th at Caird Hall, Dundee was another stormer, and David Bowie came very close to being injured after the gig, when leaving the venue by the stage door. Bodyguard Stuey George earned his wages again that evening in Dundee when he pulled David clear of the hysterical fans. We all went back to the Angus Hotel and had a late evening in the bar, and Mick Ronson and I drank several Irish Coffees.

May 18th, Thursday, Glasgow

We played: Greens Playhouse Glasgow
We stayed at: The Excelsior Hotel

David Bowie and the Spiders from Mars' Aladdin Sane tour had finally arrived at Green's Playhouse, Glasgow (the venue was of course later to be renamed the Apollo); it was certainly Scotland's premier rock venue and we were happy to be playing there. David himself had become something of a remote figure to me again; now that the UK tour was rolling he was just taking care of business, keeping himself to himself as the saying goes. We might nod to each other at the sound check but I never saw him after the gig as only Geoff MacCormack would be admitted to his inner circle. These days I think perhaps I could have tried a little harder, after all David might have thought that I was not being sociable – but I didn't want to be seen as a hanger-on, just along for the ride.

At Green's Playhouse Tony Defries again added a matinee, and both shows went very well, except for a little Glasgow crowd violence involving some demolition of seating.

The band had begun to notice, around the time of the Glasgow gig, that the usual practice of staying in the very best and most expensive of city centre hotels had been discontinued by our management. Though no cost-cutting memo was ever issued, it was to be that way with most of our accommodation throughout the UK tour in 1973. Following the Green's Playhouse gig we were to stay at the Excelsior – it was just a typical travel lodge on the outskirts of Glasgow. The travel lodges would of course quickly become just a little boring, and I was beginning to learn to like Scotch whisky. There was little else to do but drink, out of town hotels were not likely to be buzzing with fans, or groupies, unless our location was made public knowledge, and the management would have never allowed that.

It was Suzi Fussey who came up with an inspired solution to our unaccustomed après-gig isolation on the UK tour, although it is more than likely that Suzi had some help with the idea from Jamie Andrews or Tony Zanetta. David Bowie would, as befitting a major rock star, travel from city to city and from hotel to gig in the UK exclusively by limousine, but all his musicians, stars and auxiliaries alike, would take a bus. We had our very own bus for the tour, but these were the days before big custom band buses were available outside of the USA, and so ours was a luxury pensioners holidays kind of a coach with card tables and little table lamps and chintzy curtains. We also had the luxury of an 'eight track' player for our entertainment on the road. This eight track device was a type of large clunky cassette player that never really caught on, and for which in any case we had only two eight track cassettes. Nobody was going shopping to try and find any more of the fast going out of style clunky big cassettes, so our choice of music on the coach for the duration of the entire tour was either The Album by The Buddy Rich Orchestra, or The Album by The Stylistics. Both albums are still sonically etched on my memory, and I still prefer the Buddy Rich I think.

Suzi's inspired solution to our lonely nights was simple; she would invite a few guests back to the hotel after the gigs, and just take them back on the bus with us. This procedure would ultimately put a certain amount of pressure on Suzi, as she would generally be the one who would have to do the pimping. Sorry Suzi, I mean make the invitations. Generally, a few likely looking girls (and boys) would be selected by Suzi from the thousands that attended the gig, or more accurately from the hundreds who most looked as though they would have been up for it. The girls at the front of the stage would be favourites as they may well have been ogling some guitarist or other during the gig. This kind of 'getting off with a pop star' behaviour was nothing new of course, it happened with all bands on the road and I can confirm, having checked with some of the younger guys, that the sport is still widely popular to this day

David Bowie would always be first choice for any would-be groupie to go for, with Mick Ronson a close second, but I did okay, considering. I would often climb up into the bus to find it half filled with girls, most of whom would fail to recognise me as the 12-string guitarist and backing singer that they had been watching at the concert. I always took it that our guests presumed me to be a roadie or something, probably due to the state of my old jeans and Mick's old jacket and second-hand boots, and I would generally play along with that misconception until I was aware of all the options or choices available. I did not perhaps approve of the bus groupie selection game that had been devised on our behalf, but I hypocritically went along with it just the same. What else was I going to do, watch TV and drink whisky or read a book? I was reading enough books on the bus rides between cities.

May 19th, Saturday, Edinburgh

We played: The Empire Theatre
We stayed at: The Post House (no surprise)

Tony Defries was getting his money's worth from the tour party; a matinee show was again added for the Empire Theatre in Edinburgh. No one was paid overtime on this trip, and we just did as we were told; two shows a day for the price of one was fine by us.

The gig was another good one; it seemed to be that they were all good ones these days. David and the band, and the road crew, were now a well oiled little machine and the Aladdin Sane tour was the talk of the United Kingdom.

Back at the Post House in Edinburgh, Jamie Andrews, who had more or less taken over from Tony Zanetta as chief roustabout for the band, called a meeting. Jamie explained that there was a bit of a problem with our luggage. For some reason there was not enough room on our coach for all the suitcases and bags going south, so Jamie was asking for two volunteers to drive a 'station wagon' – he meant a Ford estate car – full of suitcases from Edinburgh to Norwich early the next day. When we heard what MainMan were prepared to pay the two drivers, Ken Fordham and I volunteered for the job. It was after all just a gig wasn't it? And we were there for the money, weren't we?

May 20th, Sunday, travelling

May 21st, Monday, Norwich

We played: The Theatre Royal
We stayed at: The Post House (same room, different town)

Ken and I set off comparatively early on our travelling Sunday, well before the roundup of Spiders had started in Edinburgh later on that morning; in fact it was well before they were out of bed, as Jamie Andrews had sensibly collected everyone's suitcase the night before. Ken and I were both well used to long drives all over the United

Kingdom, musicians do it all the time, but it felt a little strange leaving the confines of the tour party for the journey south. We took turns behind the wheel, a couple of hours or so each, but the 400 mile trip was a long day on the road. Ken and I checked into our Post House, our familiar home from home (these motels are of course pretty much identical all over the country) well ahead of the arrival of the coach, and we were ready for an early night ahead of the big Ziggy Stardust and the Spiders from Mars concert in Norwich.

Ken Fordham was a down to earth character; he was a good musician and no fool. Ken knew as well as I did that David Bowie and MainMan would dispense with our services whenever it suited them, and we might just as well enjoy the ride with the Spiders from Mars while it lasted. We knew the day would come soon enough when we would be looking for our next gig, though we still had no idea that the day of reckoning was actually not so far ahead.

Ken Fordham was to provide a special on-stage moment, one of the funniest memories of all on the 1973 tours. The generally gloomy stage lighting up on the rostrum at the back of the stage would enable Ken or Brian, Geoff MacCormack or me to slip more or less unnoticed off-stage during Mick and Trevor's guitar battle, and also for the duration of some three-piece band numbers like 'Jean Genie'. In addition, either of the sax players could, if absolutely necessary, nip off for a pee when not required for backing riffs or a solo. Ken Fordham had played a memorable solo in the studio on one of the Aladdin Sane album tracks and would nightly repeat the solo on tour, note for note, perfect every time. The special moment came when that instrumental solo break in that song came along, and as usual a small and brilliant white spotlight picked out Ken's place on our rostrum. But this time our Ken was not there, the spotlight was empty. David did a double take, Mick Ronson must have thought for a split second about an impromptu guitar break, but within half

274

a bar, Mike Garson was playing a beautifully crafted piano version of Ken Fordham's missing saxophone solo. It was priceless; Ken had popped off-stage for a pee, it had taken longer than usual and he had missed his cue. The attending thousands of people were deprived of Ken's solo that evening, though most of them probably hadn't even noticed as Mike Garson's solo had seamlessly covered the gap. As Mike was playing his solo, Ken reappeared on our rostrum looking sheepish, and he duly received one of David's more withering looks. David would not have pursued the matter any further after the gig, the incident was over, and Ken would be careful to time his run better in future. Ken was an old pro, and although this was just another gig he would always do it justice.

I had never been to Norwich myself before, but I guessed that it would be very much like so many other rural English towns – or cities as they are sometimes allowed to call themselves when they have a large cathedral in their town. Sorry, city. Well it was indeed a very nice, quiet kind of place, and on Monday 21st May 1973 the Theatre Royal Norwich was filled with a lot of a very nice, quiet kind of people. David Bowie was both amused and perplexed, along with the rest of us, we hadn't seen anything like the Norwich audience anywhere. The crowd enthusiastically applauded David's opening songs, but nobody seemed to be getting overexcited about the show, and they all remained in their seats. These people were all more like me really, I wouldn't have been leaping up and down either, given that someone would have had to buy me a ticket and insist that I attend, but this sort of behavior was most unusual on our tour.

David had obviously decided to prove that point, for suddenly in mid-song he dropped over the front of the stage and down into the centre aisle of the Theatre Royal Norwich. Stuey George was obviously considering grabbing David and carrying him back on-stage, but Stuey managed to restrain himself and instead prowled along in a crouch behind David as he made his way up the aisle, still singing. It was one of the most bizarre scenes that we were to witness on our travels, David Bowie aka Ziggy Stardust then just sat down on the floor, legs crossed, half-way up the aisle in the centre of the auditorium and waved back at the band on stage. David did receive a tremendous ovation for his move, but at any of our previous gigs, in any other city, he would have been risking having his clothes torn to pieces. Norwich simply did not do rock and roll hysteria that evening, it was just a pleasant gig and we all had a quiet night.

May 22nd, Tuesday, Romford

We played: The Odeon
We stayed at: The Bell Post House, Epping

We were back in the Home Counties for a few gigs and we felt happier about it, though we were still staying in an almost identical bloody Post House and this time it was near Epping.

Although unremarkable, our gig at the Romford Odeon was a great success as had been expected, and the bus came back to the Post House full of pretty young things ready to party and life was not so bad again.

May 23rd, Wednesday, Brighton

We played: The Dome
We stayed at: The Bedford Hotel (these days it is called Holiday Inn Brighton)

A matinee was added at The Dome in Brighton, but our hotel for a change seemed to be a good one, it was The Bedford and it was right on the seafront, so I felt right at home and went for a walk on the beach and had a paddle in the sea.

The evening show at The Dome was a particularly lively one, a film crew was at work and that added to the excitement, and we were all up for it in Brighton, both on-stage and off. There was again apparently some damage to seating at the gig, the crowd was just a little too wild for the management of The Dome, and they announced immediately after the gig had ended that David Bowie was henceforth banned from ever appearing at the venue again.

David and his MainMan management team would have been delighted at the press publicity that the ban generated, and certainly David himself did not appear in the least concerned. David could not have told us, but he had obviously already decided that he would very soon be breaking up the band and would not be looking for gigs on the UK circuit again in any case – for some time to come.

Generally the band, me included, saw very little of David Bowie at this time, apart from briefly at the sound checks and on-stage at the concerts themselves. David of course always had his own dressing room to himself, while the rest of us would share, and as with most bands on the road we would have a few laughs. Geoff MacCormack, as his resident pal, would have automatic access to David's dressing room, as would Mick Ronson as bandleader, but the rest of us were generally kept in our place by Stuey George and Suzi Fussey.

Our Spiders from Mars dressing room would be filled with our 'rider', plenty of wine and bottles of beer, as well as chicken wings, rolls and dips and the like, so that we rarely needed to nip out to eat before a concert. The system had been designed to keep us cooped up together in the theatre and to not go wandering around outside on the loose prior to performance time.

Mick Ronson had always followed David's example and would take great care in making himself up for the stage. He experimented with eye-liner and eye-shadow, and would sometimes fake-tan his chest, to go with an open to the waist shirt. Trevor Bolder, who had been persuaded by David to adopt the spiky hairstyle, had cultivated very long sideburns, and had taken to spraying them silver, and Woody was by now peroxide blond, so both Trevor and Woody were easily persuaded to 'make-up' for more star-Spider impact. The scene in the dressing room was often bizarre at make-up time, and I can still laugh at the memory of Mick shouting across the room, "Ey, Trev, 'ave you got my bloody mascara down there? You thieving get!"

Apart from just one night that I can remember, when I applied some eye make-up for a laugh, the rest of us in the band were not required to, nor prepared to, go as far as Mick, Trevor and Woody. There was no need, as I have mentioned before we were often in semi-darkness at the back of the stage, and anyway the Freddi Burretti stage suits were enough to put up with, for although the outfits were dry-cleaned between tours, we had only the one stage outfit each. Geoff and I wore green lurex and satin, and the sax players wore a black and white version, and as we had no time off, the ensemble would not be cleaned for the entire forty-five days of the UK tour. By the end of the tour they stood up on their own. At the end of the tour I would leave mine standing, I didn't want it.

On-stage David would occasionally run across to me and 'borrow' his Harptone 12-string guitar back in order to perform one or two solo-acoustic songs in the middle of the gig, usually just before the intermission. Now and then, just before we were due to go on-stage David would ask if I could remember some old song lyric, such as the words that started the second verse to one or other of his favourite Jaques Brel songs, the songs we had played together in our Feathers and Bowie and Hutch days. David never once asked me to sing our old favourite Space Oddity with him on-stage of course – there were no management plans to make a star out of me!

May 24th, Thursday, Lewisham

We played: The Odeon, Lewisham
We stayed at: The Hertford Hotel

Lewisham was another successful gig, though I remember nothing much of it.

May 25th, Friday, Bournemouth

We played: The Winter Gardens
We stayed at: The Norfolk Hotel

And Bournemouth was yet another successful gig.
And maybe it was getting a bit boring.

May 26th, Saturday, Bournemouth

A day off
We stayed at: The Norfolk Hotel

Funny, I don't remember a thing about the day off in Bournemouth.

May 27th, Sunday, Guildford

We played: The Civic Hall
We stayed at: The Whitehorse, Dorking

Two shows, both good ones; I saw folk singer Mike Absalom at the gig, and he had brought his girlfriend along with him to say hello. Coincidentally Mike had been a friend of both David's in London, and mine in Scarborough. It's a small world, the music world. Have I said that before...?

May 28ᵗʰ, Monday, Wolverhampton

We played: The Civic Hall, Wolverhampton
We stayed at: The Post House, Birmingham

It was a successful gig in The Midlands. I can't be sure now that Hamptons were actually Wolvered but certainly the after show routine had become quite boring. The terrible 'Hamptons' joke has to be credited to Dave Grohl.

May 29ᵗʰ, Tuesday, Hanley

We played: The Victoria Hall
We stayed at: The North Stafford Hotel, Stoke on Trent

Er, ummm, well nothing out of the ordinary happened, I guess.

May 30ᵗʰ, Wednesday, Blackburn

A day off
We stayed at: The Excelsior Motor Lodge, Charnock Richard

A day off in a Motor Lodge somewhere outside of Blackburn, Lancashire. Great.

May 31st, Thursday, Blackburn

We played: King George's Hall
We stayed at: The Excelsior Motor Lodge, Charnock Richard

It was the same kind of hall again, and the same kind of hotel again. Give us a break. Still there was always the USA tour to look forward to.

June 1st, Friday, Bradford

We played: St. George's Hall
We stayed at: The Leeds Bradford Post House, Bramhope

The Bradford gig was fine; it was good to be back in Yorkshire. The following night's stay at the The Leeds Bradford Post House Hotel on the outskirts of Leeds was to prove interesting – though not at all in a good way.

June 2nd, Saturday, Leeds

We should have played: Leeds University, but it was CANCELLED so we had the night off.
We stayed at: The Leeds Bradford Post House, Bramhope

At around midday, just six hours before our matinee concert at Leeds University was due to start, the MainMan tour managers Zee and Jamie, having consulted Tony Defries by telephone, abruptly cancelled both of the sold-out shows. We had turned up for the sound check, David Bowie had arrived, and then suddenly the gig was cancelled. The problem was that the University venue was not a theatre as such, the stage was just a temporary structure and the dressing room facilities, such as they were, were at the back of the hall. The band would have had to troupe through the hall to access the stage, not such a problem for backing musicians perhaps, but for David Bowie the security risk was too great. David, and potentially the rest of us too for that matter, could have been seriously injured at the end of the concert, with near riot conditions being quite possible in spite of the university setting, with no safe way off the stage and out of the hall for us. The road crew had set up many tons of lights and sound equipment, and they just had to take it all down again and put it back in the trailers.

It may have been a bad night for business, and a big disappointment for the fans in Leeds, but suddenly I had a bonus night off. Our very few nights off on this tour had so far just all been in the wrong towns, and I was not going to waste a Saturday night in a Post House hotel bar several miles outside of Leeds city centre. I promised Jamie Andrews, on my life, that I would be back before the tour bus set off for Coventry in the morning and he said okay. I hired a rent-a-car at the hotel desk, supplied by probably the biggest car-hire operator in the world, and drove the seventy or so miles to good old Scarborough. It felt great to be free again, even if it was just for a few hours. By that stage I could feel very strongly how claustrophobic the confines of the UK tour had become. Many of my band mates, with possibly David Bowie included, appeared to be quite happy to be cocooned in the hotels and venues whilst on tour, and they apparently had no thoughts of rejoining the real world outside until the tour was over. Maybe the tour *was* their real world, but it was not so for me.

I made my way to Ligger's Corner in the Penthouse and played superstar to the regulars, those that had not travelled to Leeds to see David Bowie and me play anyway. The good people of Scarborough were of course surprised to see me, and everybody wished me well. I didn't drink alcohol, only orange juice all evening, but I talked to friends and I enjoyed my escape from the tour routine immensely. I eventually drove back to the Leeds Bradford Post House in the early hours, just as I had promised Jamie Andrews.

I handed the hire car keys to the night clerk, as I had been instructed when I had collected the car. I had pre-paid for the 24-

hour hire period earlier, when I collected the car keys, and so I went straight to bed.

Almost a year later, I had finished with all the David Bowie guitarist stuff and was working in a 'proper job' as a draughtsman again, this time for a well respected sound-level meter manufacturer who was based in Scarborough. I had arrived back in Scarborough at just the right time to drop into the job and I got along well with the directors, who would utilise my musical talents to publicise and demonstrate some of their products on a couple of TV features, as well as have me produce all their manufacturing drawings, both mechanical and electrical.

Then out of the blue one morning, a bill arrived from the big international car hire company asking for several thousand pounds for the hire of the car that I had hired and used for just one night, to go from Leeds to Scarborough and back. The bill said that I now had several hundred miles on the clock; they had recently examined it at the Leeds and Bradford Post House Hotel, and the hire firm was asking me if they might also have their car back. David Gregg, one of the sales directors at the sound-meter company, was a good talker of course as sales guys need to be, and he very kindly offered to call the hire firm on my behalf. Our director was able to convince the hire firm that a mistake had been made at the hotel, probably by the Leeds and Bradford Post House Hotel receptionist who had not properly finalised the paperwork when I returned the car, and that I had used the car for only a few hours and had driven no more than a hundred miles or so, from Leeds to Scarborough and back. I was too angry to call the hire firm myself, the bill had been too much of a shock and I wasn't ready to be reasonable.

It was to be more than just a few years later (did I warn you it was going to be a very long story?) when I finally got to the bottom of the car hire fiasco. I was in a pub in York talking to a chap about my days with David Bowie – a subject I often had to talk about whether I wanted to or not in those days – when his girlfriend said, "Oh, David Bowie stayed at the Post House at Leeds in 1973 when I worked there." I told the lady that the evening the Bowie tour had stayed at her Post House would be unforgettable because of my bit of trouble with the car hire. The lady was amazed at my story, she told me that many of the staff at her hotel had used a hire car for several months to run errands into town and the like, and that nobody at the hotel seemed to know (or care) who had arranged for the car to be there in the first place!

The night clerk that I had handed my keys to in the early hours of that Sunday morning had not correctly returned the keys and paperwork to the hire company, and the company must have presumed somehow that I had changed my plans and kept the car. Both the hotel and the car hire company were at fault, and I have subsequently ever since been extra careful in my dealings with all hotels and with all car hire companies. We live and learn.

June 3rd, Sunday, Coventry

We played: The New Theatre.
We stayed at: The Post House of course.

Okay, I don't remember Coventry. I mean, I may remember it, but by this time, I would not necessarily know which town or city we were in. We had played perhaps twenty more or less identical gigs (including matinees) and stayed in maybe sixteen almost identical Post House hotels so far, with another twenty or so yet to come, so there was the problem. The routine was incessant, though somehow we all still enjoyed the gigs, and we continued to make the best of the fringe benefits of touring with a world famous rock band.

I had met a few ladies on the road. Some of the girls were very nice, though at the time it could be no more than just another one-night stand with a groupie. Some regrets did come along many years later, when I had grown up a bit.

There was though one very weird and unusual evening midway through the tour when we all, David Bowie included, strangely encountered an almost total drought of female company after our gig. I don't know how it happened, and I don't remember which particular Post House, or even which town we were in when it happened, although I think it must have been south of Watford. Maybe it's just as well that we all have selective amnesia from time to time. It was unusual for David Bowie to be drinking in the bar with the rest of us for one thing, and even more unusual for Suzi's regular girl-supply system to have not been working properly that evening. David was giving me some funny looks across the bar, as I had somehow managed to pull, despite the acute shortages, but I thought nothing of it. When David left the bar, he made a point of walking past my table and having a good look at my lady friend whilst wishing us both a good night. A little later, as my friend and I were making our way along the familiar and featureless corridor to my room, one of the room doors opened very quickly. In a flash, David Bowie leaned out, grinning wildly, and grabbed my girl by the wrist, pulling her into his room, slamming the door on me and leaving me in the corridor! I banged on David's door in vain, shouted my protests but without any response. I knew that the girl would probably regard the kidnapping as a kind of promotion and would be in little more danger with David than she would have been with me, so I left them to it. I was not that bothered, it was all a game after all and this was just another variation that had not happened before, not to me anyway.

Geoff MacCormack was in his pyjamas, home for the night in our shared room. He had no other commitments either and I had forgotten that he might be in, so we just had a laugh at our old friend's bloody cheek, or possibly his desperation, and climbed into our beds. We had no sooner turned out the light when there was a knock at the door. It was the kidnapped girl, and she was looking embarrassed. I asked her why she hadn't stayed with David and she said she didn't know, so I suggested that she go back to his room or just take a taxi home, and not to worry as Geoff and I were going to bed. The girl apparently did not take the taxi, I bumped into her in the morning in the hotel café-bar and so we had breakfast together. The girl was still looking sheepish, so I assured her the happenings of the night before were not at all unusual, these things happened all the time in our crazy world and it didn't matter in the least. What a funny old game it was. I don't think David and I even discussed the kidnapping, I had forgotten about it within a day or so, and it would have troubled him for less than that I believe. I did make a short note in my diary though, and I found it many years later. The note said, 'David stole my horse'.

June 4ᵗʰ, Monday, Worcester

We played: The Gaumont.
We stayed at: The Giffard Hotel

The auto-pilot was engaged again.

June 5ᵗʰ, Tuesday

A travelling day. The Stylistics and Buddy Rich played on, and on, and on.

June 6ᵗʰ, Wednesday, Sheffield

We played: Sheffield City Hall
We stayed at: Hallam Tower

The concert went very well as usual, but I was on auto-pilot for this one too. The after-gig party back at the hotel was very entertaining though, and it was a very special evening all round. Both Labi Siffre and Lulu had coincidentally both been performing somewhere in the West Yorkshire area, at separate gigs of course, and they too were both booked in to the Hallam Tower Hotel for the night.

Both Labi and Lulu joined us for drinks in the hotel bar, and the bar happened to have a decent piano in it. I never, ever carried a camera with me on any of our tours, and ever since very often I have wished that I had done so. Some sort of movie camera, whatever might have been available in 1973, would have been even better. The image of David Bowie, Lulu and Labi Siffre grouped around the hotel bar piano (I think Labi played the piano) singing 'My Funny Valentine' would have been priceless now I think. Well, maybe not priceless, but valuable enough.

Much later that night, long after I had fallen asleep, there came a knock on my door. This was not unusual, it could have been anybody, it happened all the time and sometimes it would even be David, come to borrow the acoustic guitar that I still carried around, so that he could write another song in the middle of the night. It was neither groupie nor David Bowie at my door, it was Angie, and she was looking for David, and for Lulu. I have no idea why she came to my room, but most likely she was looking for Geoff, who would most probably have known the whereabouts of her missing husband. I didn't know what was happening, your guess would have been as good as mine, but following that first meeting in the Hallam Tower Hotel, I do know that David, Lulu and Angie eventually all became good friends.

Lulu is a very nice lady indeed, as well as a great singer. I was to meet her again some years later in Scarborough at some awful showbiz party, and she told me I could have joined her band for the summer if she had known that I was around. I used to think that

Lulu probably thought that I would know something about the Hallam Tower Hotel shenanigans, but that I could probably keep a secret. Then Lulu wrote her autobiography and it was a secret no longer. So David did shag Lulu. I don't know about Angie, I still have not read Lulu's account yet, nor have I read Angie's book, but even if they kissed they probably don't tell.

June 7th, Thursday, Manchester

We played: Manchester Free Trade Hall
We stayed at: The Excelsior

The two shows in that which I have always (sorry Birmingham) considered to be our nation's second city went without a hitch, and David Bowie was happy enough. We could play our set backwards in our sleep by now.

It was to be in Manchester, at the MEN, where many years later I was to arrange to meet backstage with David, during his 'Reality' tour; the one that quite possibly was to be his last tour ever. I will tell more of that story later, in my own final chapter about Bowie and Hutch.

June 8th Friday, Newcastle

We played: Newcastle City Hall
We stayed at: The Gosforth Park Hotel
I have always felt entirely at home in Newcastle-upon-Tyne, and the City Hall is perhaps my idea of the perfect venue. It is stylish and old-fashioned and not too big for its boots. It's a bit like me?

Many years later I would find myself living in the west end of the city, before moving even further westwards to a country cottage at Haydon Bridge on the banks of the North Tyne. My daughter

Hayley would be born at nearby Hexham, and I was to spend an idyllic few years living in the countryside and playing gigs around the North-East.

I played solo supports to Lindisfarne, the local boys made good, at the City Hall, I appeared occasionally on local TV and Radio and I had a Dave Lee Travis BBC Radio 1 'Record of the Week' in 1979 with an up-tempo Gram Parsons song called 'Ooh Las Vegas' with my excellent Geordie country band American Echoes.

The Gosforth Park Hotel, our digs for the Friday evening on 8th June 1973, was also to be the place where I was to see David Bowie again, very briefly in passing, in June 1978. I was living at the time just off Newcastle's West Road, in the terraced street next to the one where Hank Marvin had grown up, when I leaned that David was to play the City Hall. It was five years almost to the day since I had played the venue with the Aladdin Sane tour in 1973 and I guessed that David, with his 'Low and Heroes' tour party, would again stay at the Gosforth Park Hotel. It is a very conveniently situated and well organised hotel and they know all about rock and roll bands. In spite of an insistent toothache on the afternoon of Wednesday 14th June 1978, I drove out to the Gosforth Park, full of anticipation at the prospect of seeing my old friend again, and I walked into the hotel foyer looking for any familiar faces.

I immediately recognised the only black face in the hotel, the only black face in Gosforth probably, and it was the grinning face of Stuey George, David's faithful bodyguard who had stayed with his boss since 1973. Stuey appeared to be delighted to see me, we had always got along fine, and he persuaded me to take him into Newcastle so that he could do a bit of shopping. Stuey told me that David was still in bed, so 'no problem mate' I would see him later. On the way out of the hotel foyer with Stuey I recognised one of David's musicians, the violinist Simon House. I doubted that he would remember me. I had last seen Simon only very briefly, and worse for wear at that, at ex-Turquoise guitarist Tony Hill's London flat in 1968. I did not speak to Simon, but then I bumped into Sean Mayes, who had played piano for Fumble, our support band on the USA tour in 1973. The talented Sean had been recruited by David to play the 'Low and Heroes' tour with him, and they were to remain friends until Sean sadly passed away, at far too young an age.

When Stuey and I had returned from our shopping trip, we waited around in Stuey's hotel room, which was, as it had always been in 1973, located right next door to David's. From Stuey's room, where he had the obligatory tour hotel contact sheet, I telephoned David's personal assistant Corrine 'Coco' Schwab's room, and I asked her if she thought I could get to see David that afternoon. Coco very kindly came over to Stuey's room to say hello to me, and to say that she was sorry, but it seemed that David was not available until later on as he had to go to the City Hall for the sound check quite soon. Coco gave me a couple of tickets for the gig that evening and told me that of course I would see David later. Stuey would be required to go to work quite soon too so I went downstairs and sat in the lobby, thinking that I might possibly catch David briefly before he left for the sound check. Just in case nobody had bothered to tell him that I was around, you know.

I had not been waiting for very long when the lift doors opened, and David Bowie, surrounded by a small crowd of protective bodies including Stuey George, emerged from the lift and rushed through the hotel foyer at some speed, into a waiting limousine and away.

I was a little taken aback; I had more or less forgotten the strange ways of the rock star business and had not anticipated any need for this kind of security-conscious behaviour in a suburban hotel that was only just half full of totally oblivious reps and businessmen. There were no crowds of media at the Gosforth Park that day. Maybe it was Stuey George's daft idea; it couldn't be just that David Bowie was avoiding little 'ol me – could it?

I was about to leave the hotel myself when a young couple, a boy and a girl dressed in the all-black outfits favoured by the 'Goths', came out of the lift. It appeared that the young Goths had been keeping David Bowie company throughout the day, and this prior commitment had prevented David from making time for a reunion with me. Or maybe neither Coco nor Stuey had told David that I was around. I may have got it all wrong but it seemed to me that Sex, Drugs, and Rock and Roll were still David Bowie's driving forces, and I reckoned that at least two of those diversions could have been taking up his time that afternoon. Of course it is equally possible that David and the Gosforth Goths were playing guitars and talking about artwork all day.

I went back to my flat in the town, full of toothache and disappointment, and told my girlfriend Susie (later to become my soul mate and wife no.2) that we were going to the Newcastle City Hall that evening to see my old pal David Bowie in concert.

We went out a little earlier than necessary as I still had an idea that I might get in through the stage door to see David before the gig, after all I knew some of the City Hall staff as I had played there myself a couple of times. In any case, Newcastle was a small town, musically speaking, and everybody knew everyone else.

It didn't work, I couldn't get past security even though I knew the guy on the stage door, so Susie and I went to a nearby pub, The Haymarket, as my toothache needed a whisky or two and there was an hour or so to spare before gig time. The pub was full of people that Susie and I knew, and I had to hide my disappointment, embarrassment and maybe some anger over my failed attempts to get to see my old friend and famous pop star David Bowie.

After I'd downed two or three whiskies to help relieve my toothache, my anger got the better of my previous determination to get past David's impenetrable security barriers. I just did not fancy joining the usual crowd of liggers trying to gain access to their hero after the concert was over. This guy was my friend, not my idol, I wanted his friendship, not his celebrity, and I did not enjoy being somehow caught up with people who were only in pursuit of David's reflected glory. I knew it was not his fault and I'd seen it all before but that did not help.

I had only to ask once in The Haymarket if anyone wanted two tickets for the David Bowie concert which was about to start in ten minutes along the road at the City Hall. I sold the tickets for their face value, not at tout prices, and with the proceeds Susie and I stayed in the pub where I drowned my sorrow at the sad state of affairs, and reflected upon how things had changed in just five years. Five years, stuck on my eyes, indeed. On that day in 1978 I thought that it would most probably be the last time that I would see David Bowie. I believed that my last memory of David would have to be of him running like some sort of paranoid Greta Garbo through the almost empty lobby of the Gosforth Park Hotel with a cloak of hangers-on wrapped around him.

Back in June 1973, living it up as part of David Bowie's entourage at the Gosforth Park Hotel, I would not have believed that David and I could totally lose touch so easily and so quickly. I still felt that I was close enough to David under the circumstances imposed by the tour. I very occasionally would eat dinner at his table in a restaurant, we still would nod to each other on-stage, and David would still come to my room to borrow my travel guitar to write his million-selling songs on. I just figured that maybe we would see a little more of each other and catch up a little when all the touring in 1973 was over.

Mick Ronson and I had already discussed the possibility of working out some twin-guitar parts together for some of David's work-in-progress, some unfinished fragments that he had played to Mick. The twin guitars thing was Mick's idea, but I believed then that I might yet get the opportunity to show what I could do musically as a creative guitarist, and so contribute more to David's current musical output. More creative anyway than I had been able to be so far in my role as the added-on 12-string guitarist, rhythm guitarist and wobbly falsetto backing vocalist with The Spiders from Mars auxiliaries. Of course both David and Mick already knew that the current state of affairs, including The Spiders as a band, would very soon be over, so I would never get to know what Mick really had in mind for the twin lead guitars idea.

June 9th, Saturday, Preston

We played: The Guildhall
We stayed at: The Excelsior Motor Lodge, Charnock Richard, again. Home sweet Home.

We pressed on.

June 10th, Sunday, Liverpool

We played: The Liverpool Empire
We stayed at: St. Georges Hotel

Liverpool is a lively city, it was a good gig. Everyone is a comedian, just try asking directions.

June 11th, Monday, Leicester

We played: The De Montfort Hall
We stayed at: Another Bloody Post House

June 12th, Tuesday, Chatham

We played: Central Hall
We stayed at: I don't remember

<u>*June 13th, Wednesday, Kilburn*</u>

We played: The Gaumont
We stayed at: The Grosvenor House Hotel, Park Lane, London

Wow, we were back in a top hotel, and in the posh part of London. Things were looking up. We were easily pleased.

<u>*June 14th, Thursday, Salisbury*</u>

We played: The City Hall
We stayed at: The White Hart Hotel

At the majority of UK venues, after we had finished our sound check, which would usually be in the late afternoon, the band would have no choice but to hang around the venue until show time. These few hours would sometimes be brightened up by a visit from some old friends, or from fellow musicians, other bands presently in the area who just wanted to say hello.

I was surprised though when we were visited by Dozy, Beaky, Mick and Tich, the whole band apart from Dave Dee their energetic frontman. I remembered these guys from the *Ready Steady Go!* TV show that David and I had done with The Buzz in 1966, so I went out to chat with them when I heard that security at the venue would not let them in. In any case I doubted that David would have given them any time, in spite of their considerable pop star status. Dozy and Co. were all nice guys, and of course they were just like us – instead of sticking with a job in an office or on a building site they had become rock musicians.

The same thing happened more than once. Wayne Fontana, who had been a huge star in the sixties and had had one of the best bands in The Mindbenders, came to visit David when we were in Manchester, but he too was given short shrift and had been told that we were all busy.

David kept his dressing room to himself and he very rarely let old friends and well-wishers in. On the odd occasion that David did let them in, it was usually just a brief and embarrassing audience with the star, never the hoped for reunion, and in my opinion the visitors would have been better staying away. I resolved that I would never resort to a dressing room visit myself in the future, be it in the immediate or very distant future, following my next inevitable departure from David's latest band. I had good intentions anyway.

June 15th, Friday, Taunton

We played: The Odeon.
We stayed at: The County Hotel, Taunton

We were now in holiday country, it was a beautiful June in 1973 and we were in Devon where my mum and dad would take me for a week every year when I was a little lad. We had always made good use of the holiday rail passes that were issued to my dad because he was an employee of British Railways. Frank Hutchinson, my dad, had progressed rapidly – due as he would tell me, to his organisational skills and his ability to get on with people – to the rank of Major in the British Army in India during the Second World War. When he was demobilized at the end of the war my dad joined 'The Railways' which was a plum job in those days – thought to be a much better career proposition than banking or insurance and the rest. Frank worked his way up from a position as a clerk in Thirsk and Northallerton to become the British North Eastern Railways 'Goods Agent', the goods traffic equivalent of Station Master, at Scarborough and later on in York. They did not have too many university graduates around in those days, and a chap would get ahead on a day to day basis by virtue of his efforts and his abilities. The driving forces, the ambitions and the ladder to higher social status in the 1950s had been exactly the same for my parents Frank and Rene Hutchinson in Yorkshire as they had been for the young David Jones's parents John and Peggy in Kent.

June 16th, Saturday, Torquay

We played: The Town Hall.
We stayed at: The Imperial Hotel

This is the life, I thought to myself as I took in the view down from the hotel to the sea. The Imperial Hotel, Torquay is situated right above the waves, up on the cliff top, and it has an outdoor swimming pool overlooking the bay. The weather was glorious and the entire tour party, road crew and band, with the notable exception of David Bowie himself, all took time out by the pool. It was said that David was avoiding sunlight as he did not want a suntan to spoil his appearance in his role as Ziggy. And there was the odd Dracula joke.

David was most likely exhausted, we were all tired by now but he took all the strain, he knew that there were problems with the forthcoming USA tour arrangements, whilst we, the band and most other tour employees were blissfully oblivious of all the trouble that had been brewing for several weeks.

The gig was good, and I met another pretty girl, a nice Devonshire girl who I would have liked to see again, outside the tour bubble, if it had been possible.

June 17th, Sunday, Torquay

We had a full day off in Torquay, and the night off too, and in summer holiday country. MainMan Management Inc. was giving us a break and we all, David Bowie included, were ready for it. We appreciated the thoughtful planning by Tony Defries or whoever had arranged the holiday.

Our tour promoters were the up and coming Mel Bush Organisation, and Mel himself was with us in person for much of the tour, not least in order to collect and count all the gate receipts himself. Mel would tote the huge amount of cash away from the theatres and town halls in a large leather shoulder bag – he was a big bloke and well capable of looking after both himself and the money. I had become quite friendly with Mel and also his sister who was sometimes around, and when I mentioned in conversation that I would have loved to drive over to see the girl that I had met the previous night, Mel just gave me the keys to his car. I was flabbergasted at Mel's generosity, but could not refuse and so I set off in the sunshine with the top down in Mel's Rover, a shiny new big automatic convertible.

I don't know much about cars, but this was an expensive one, and I was playing the pop star when I stopped to pick up a pretty blonde hitch-hiker. The girl was German, and she was immediately impressed with my apparent pop star status, car and all. It was fifty-fifty, very much 'touch and go' whether I made it over to the Devonshire girl's house or went with the new hitch-hiker option. I stayed with my original plan in the end, but there had been an embarrassment of riches down there in glorious Devon.

June 18th, Monday, Bristol

We played: The Colston Hall.

We stayed at: The Unicorn Hotel

I just wanted to go back to Devon.

June 19th, Tuesday, Southampton

We played: The Guild Hall.
We stayed at: Post House!

Well, I woke up this mornin',
I found I got those Post House blues...

June 20th, Wednesday, travelling day

Well, man we done some hard travellin'
And the more time you got, the more you got to lose.

June 21st and 22nd, Thursday and Friday, Birmingham

We played: Birmingham Town Hall
We stayed at: The Excelsior Motor Lodge, Charnock Richard – again.
Home sweet Home.

We played four shows in two nights in Birmingham, and the well-oiled machine just kept on rolling, and we continued to stay as well-oiled as possible as we rolled.

The Spiders from Mars were no different to any other band on tour, in that we drank too much, we shagged groupies and we became bored with the routine. We met other acts on tour who suffered the same terrible hardships as we did, both in the UK and in the USA. In the States we had found ourselves sharing hotels with the likes of the band Chicago, the Mark III version of Fleetwood

Mac, and the London Philharmonic Orchestra. In the UK we had shared a hotel with Lulu and Labi Siffre as you already know, but also more than once we shared hotels with high flyers Slade whose tour was also being promoted by our promoter Mel Bush, in parallel with our own.

Slade were being managed by ex-Animals bass player Chas Chandler, the man who had been responsible for bringing Jimi Hendrix to England and promoting the groundbreaking guitarist into the limelight. Chas was around the hotel and in the bar, but I never had the opportunity to talk to him. He was another lad from Newcastle and I knew people up there who knew him (it's a small world). I never saw Noddy Holder or the other boys in his band at all, not even once in passing, but Mel Bush did give Mick Ronson and me some tickets to go and see Slade, with the Sensational Alex Harvey Band supporting, at their Earl's Court gig. You might remember my story of the evening in a previous chapter – that was the gig that Mick and I attended with our exotic model girlfriends. I'm certain that Mel did not supply us with the models.

We also had a slightly bizarre encounter with some of the Monty Python team, who were trapped for one night only in the same godforsaken provincial Motor-Post-Lodge-House hotel, and they were making the best of it, as you do, in the bar. Graham Chapman was very drunk and a little argumentative, and we quickly realised, well before it became public knowledge, that Graham was gay. He was not a happy man that evening, and I found it rather sad, as he was obviously unhappy in spite of making millions of mazoolah, making millions of people laugh. It was the Tony Hancock thing, the sad comic, the tears of a clown and all that. Life is sometimes just not funny.

June 23rd, Saturday, Boston

We played: The Gliderdrome
We stayed at: A Moat-House I think, because the wallpaper had changed.

June 24ᵗʰ, Sunday, Croydon

We played: The Fairfield Hall
We stayed at: The Copthorne Hotel

We have all been here before...it may have been déja-vu, but the Fairfield Hall was so familiar, and the Copthorne, well there must be more than one of those too.

June 25ᵗʰ and 26ᵗʰ, Monday and Tuesday, Oxford

We played: The New Theatre
We stayed at: The Randolph Hotel

I had not been to Oxford, the town or the university, since The Tennesseans supported Humphrey Littleton at the Summer Ball in the early sixties. Oxford is another world, as distant from my world as is Tokyo. The kids at the gig were okay though, so real people do live around the place somewhere.

June 27ᵗʰ, Wednesday, Doncaster

We played: Top Rank Ballroom Doncaster
We stayed at: The Hallam Tower, Sheffield (again)

'Donny' was well known to Mick, Trev, Woody and I. It was and still is a gloomy Yorkshire railway town with a good guitar shop. We were all well used to this type of dodgy old ballroom gig in our previous incarnations as Rats and Tennesseans and the like, and were a little surprised that our tour was playing the place. The people of Doncaster however were great, genuine Northerners to a man. Okay I'm biased.

An old friend of mine, a guy who had grown up with me in Scarborough, came along with his girlfriend to visit me at our hotel after the gig in Doncaster.

Alan Hydes who is these days a well-known artist, a talented and extremely successful portrait painter, had come to the stage door to find me, and so I had invited him back to the after-the-gig party at the hotel. Alan should have been in the music business when he was younger, he looked the part; Alan had the personality, was a good looking lad, but didn't have the voice. A bit like Jess Conrad really. Now there was a man who never let the fact that he couldn't sing stop him.

Alan's girlfriend was a stunner, a leggy blonde who should have been a model if she was not one already. David Bowie's antenna picked up the pair of them the instant that they entered the hotel bar, and he came over to say hello. I had to take Alan to one side in order to warn him of my friend David's unconventional approach to romance, not to mention his potential, in extreme circumstances lately, for kidnapping.

Alan took the hint, and sensibly he and the beautiful blonde girl did not stay around too long. Though I have not spoken to Alan for years (he went to live in Majorca) I have seen him being famous on television and painting pictures of other celebrities and talking a lot. I'm certain that Alan knows my 'almost-neighbour' here in the Yorkshire Wolds, David Hockney.

June 28th, Thursday, Bridlington

We played: Bridlington Spa
We stayed at: The St. Nicholas Hotel, Scarborough

I had come full circle; I had played Bridlington Spa so many times with The Tennesseans in the sixties when we had supported the likes of Gene Vincent, The Alex Harvey Soul Band and The Kinks at the huge seafront venue. We had also played several 'all-nighters' at 'Brid Spa'. These were essentially dusk till dawn drinking marathons for the youth of the surrounding Wolds and coastal villages, for the country boys and girls who never had much to look forward to in terms of musical entertainment.

Brid was home ground for Mick, Trev and Woody too of course, especially Woody, whose home town is nearby Driffield, which is either yet another one-horse town with nothing ever happening, or a nice quiet little country market town, depending on your perspective. Bridlington itself is on the coast mid-way between Scarborough and Hull and is consequently a little on the quiet side all round. As a rock venue in the sixties and seventies, Bridlington Spa was something of an enigma, stranded out on the far-eastern Yorkshire coast but it did very well. These days I'm afraid The Spa has gone the way of many seaside venues, and they proudly advertise evenings with tribute bands as if they are the real thing. They do sometimes also catch the odd famous comedian who will have wanted to fill in a tour date between Sheffield and Sunderland, thinking it a good idea. I recently saw a seafront poster in Filey, just up the coast from Brid, advertising The Peter Kay Experience. The poster showed a podgy guy, probably from the right part of Lancashire, but it was not Peter – just some guy doing his jokes I guess, and as we know it's the way you tell 'em. Tribute Bands, Tribute Comedians, X Factor Karaoke Talent shows, what next? I worry about the state of the punters who buy it more than that of the performers, who are after all just trying to make a quid or two. It has nothing to do with creative performance – they would all rather be doing their own stuff, wouldn't they?

My uncle, Ernest Hutchinson OBE, my dad's youngest brother, retired from Town Clerkship in Castleford in the West Riding of Yorkshire to Bridlington, which is in the East Riding, and where Ernest spent his last years in raising so much money towards the restoration fund for Bridlington Priory that they put a gargoyle of him up on the outside of the Priory. I was to see it when I attended Ernest's funeral at the grand old place. The stonemasons had carved my uncle wearing his glasses, which is fair enough, it is the way I remember him too, but I must say he does look, carved for posterity high up there on a south-facing corner of the Priory, a lot like Ray Charles.

Someone at MainMan had decided that we would stay for the night of our Bridlington Spa gig in nearby Scarborough, my home town, and not for some reason in Bridlington itself. Both David Bowie and Mick Ronson had played The Penthouse in Scarborough, and they knew that at least the place had a decent nightclub in it. It is possible that no Bridlington hotel would take us of course, as we were gathering quite a lot of publicity, and it often referred to the 'near riots' and the destruction of seats at the venues.

The owner of the St. Nicholas Hotel, located on St. Nicholas Cliff opposite the Grand Hotel in Scarborough, was certainly taking no chances with us. We were informed on arrival that the hotel would not permit any shenanigans of any kind, and we were told specifically that members of Mr Bowie's tour party would not be allowed to entertain any guests in their rooms after 9pm. The St. Nicholas Hotel, where I had played a few dinner dances in my time, was a family owned business, and the double-barreled matriarch was to be on duty and on full red-alert, for the entire duration of our stay in Scarborough. The redoubtable lady positioned herself for much of the time, from late evening into the early hours, in a high-backed chair placed between the hotel entrance and the stairway to the rooms. No one could pass without scrutiny – this was worse than Tokyo! Of course we found a way around our guardian; I was on familiar ground after all. I learned later that the hotel had attempted to kick us all out, in the middle of the night in fact, when someone was caught in the act, red-handed or whatever, but at the time we knew nothing of it, and would have cared less if we had. Jamie Andrews was a match for any provincial hotelier, day or night.

Almost everyone I had ever known in Scarborough, apart from my two sons who were too young to come to gigs and my parents who were too old and anyway thankfully always stayed clear of my rock and roll business altogether, came to Bridlington Spa to see the gig. They all came to see David Bowie and the Spiders from Mars, but they also came to see the bloke that they all knew, the 12-string and rhythm guitarist John Hutchinson from Scarborough.

My ex-wife, my future wife, the Spiders from Hull's wives and ex-wives, girlfriends and ex-girlfriends, they all were there. David Bowie fever, Aladdinsanity had come to Scarborough, well Bridlington actually, but it was all too close for comfort in my home town that evening.

Bridlington Spa is a huge old ballroom with a balcony all the way around, and the sound is usually pretty good – it's not a bad place to go and watch a band. Unfortunately for me that evening, and for the several hundred people who wanted to see me in my superstar-supporting role with David Bowie, I was to be barely visible from the ballroom floor. Those that really wanted to see me in action in my green lurex spacesuit had to go up on to the balcony for a half-decent view, to make sure I was there, just in case I'd been having them on.

Pete Hunsley our stage manager regarded himself essentially as an original Spider, having been a roadie with The Rats for years before Mick Ronson had left to join up with David Bowie. Pete consequently always treated the rest of us, the sax players, Geoff

MacCormack and me as auxiliaries, just the hired help who should do as we were told. Even though the stage at the Spa is quite big, Pete had set our rostrum as far back and to the side as possible; in fact we were almost standing in the wings in Bridlington. I think Pete Hunsley would have put his auxiliary musicians behind a curtain for every gig if the decision had been his to make. Pete meant no harm, but he would, if he could have done that for Trev and Woody. The pair of them, the original rhythm section of the Spiders may well have felt that some of their limelight was always in danger of being stolen by the additional musicians, but in fact the stage lighting, for all of the 'back line' musicians, was often quite dim and a lot of audiences barely noticed us most of the time. Even Mike Garson, who was arguably the most gifted of all the musicians on the tour, sat at his piano in the gloom, with just a small lamp to read his chord sheets by.

Apart from the spotlights on David Bowie and Mick Ronson, the lighting on the rest of the stage was intentionally minimal, and friends told me that it could have been anybody up there at the rear of the stage at Bridlington Spa that night. Geoff MacCormack and I protested to Pete, in vain as usual, and then we just did as we were told; we got on with the job. Even if people could not see who was wearing it, they could certainly at least see my green lurex and satin suit on-stage at Bridlington, and the suit was to prove over the years to be a useful identifying feature for me when looking at old films and photographs of the 1973 concerts. These days if anybody is interested enough I can pick myself out in old photographs by virtue of my sparkling green suit and my sanded-down Telecaster, or the blonde 12-string Harptone guitar. I could probably even look at a photograph and define, by checking out the outfit that David was wearing and which of my two guitars I was using, the song most likely to be the one being played at the time. Okay, I've never actually done that, but I have seen a lot of photos of David and

Mick, with just a bit of my glittery suit and my guitar barely visible in the background which, by my own expert analysis, proves that I was indeed there on-stage on that particular evening. I've even seen a Mick Rock photo where I appear between Mick Ronson's legs while he does battle with David Bowie – even though I am standing several paces behind them both at the back of the stage.

Funnily enough, I was actually stopped in the street by a guy waiting outside the St. Nicholas Hotel in Scarborough on the morning after our gig in Bridlington, and the man asked me how come I could walk in and out of David Bowie's hotel without being stopped by security. I told the man that I was in fact a guest at the hotel, and, seeing as he was so interested, that I was a member of David Bowie's band. The guy became extremely angry and told me that I was a lying bastard, and that I should be locked up for pretending to be somebody else.

I left the angry chap to work it out for himself, but strangely enough, years later I was to discover that more than one person in Scarborough had, for whatever reason, pretended to be me. It even turned out that a couple of others had amazingly claimed to have played guitar with David Bowie themselves. One of these sad cases was a loser who had been a friend of my ex-wife's for a time after we had split, and the guy was eventually caught out in his lie when he and I happened to be in a café one day and his mate mentioned the Bowie connection. To save everyone's embarrassment I decided that I had to go along with the story and conceded that, oh yes after all he had maybe sat in on guitar, in London, when David and I had been rehearsing. I'm too soft sometimes; I should have ripped into the poser.

It's a fact that mistaken identity is a common problem for many musicians. In my case, I have heard that there have been, over the years, several other singer/guitarists called Hutchinson around in London, even at least one other called John. There is the James

'Hutch' Hutchinson who plays bass for Bonnie Rait, and who some of my Swedish friends had thought was me, and the great drummer Johnny Hutchinson who was with the amazing Big Three in Liverpool in the sixties also has my name. Or I have his. I even found by chance a website where the Big Three Hutch and I were somehow morphed into the same guy. It seems that this talented morphed Hutch had played drums with the Big Three in the Cavern Club in Liverpool, then taken up guitar and joined David Bowie in The Marquee Club. This morphed Hutch guy was some musician.

There was an Irish Mick Hutchinson touring Brittany when I was playing there in Saint Marine some years ago, and there is a guy still playing working men's clubs around Hull using backing tapes and annoyingly calling himself 'Hutch'. In 2013 I played a gig at Scarborough's Acoustic Gathering with The Sultans of Thwing and I was told that a young local guy had earlier walked on-stage and said, 'Hi I'm Hutch'. Nothing to do with me, there are a lot of us about. The 'John Hutch' who played country music venues around the UK and was nominated by *Country Music Round-up* for 'Top UK Country Singer' of the year, sometime way back in the darkest eighties was, I have to admit, me.

June 29th, Friday, Leeds

We played: Leeds Rolarena
We stayed at: I don't remember where the rest of the band went, but I stayed in Scarborough for a couple of days.

The Leeds Rolarena had been slotted into our itinerary to make good the cancellation at Leeds University on June 2nd. A matinee show was added for good measure, and both shows were successful and unremarkable from the band's point of view. We were all ready for a break, and we were about to get one, though none of us could have imagined the kind of break that it was to be.

July 3rd, Hammersmith, London

We played: The Hammersmith Odeon
We stayed at: The Grosvenor House Hotel

In view of our imminent short holiday, planned to be taken just before our 1973 European summer concerts were due to start, I had decided to drive to London, and then back 'home' again to Scarborough, in my little Renault 4. I was very fond of my little French car as it was my very first car, and it had been hard-earned with the proceeds from my previous year of dinner dance gigs with The Roger Dean Five. The Hammersmith Odeon would be the final date on the current tour for David Bowie and the Spiders from Mars, and so I would no longer need the band bus, trains, limousines or taxis. I took my own suitcase and my own guitar case along with me, and parked my own private transport in the Grosvenor House Hotel underground car park in Central London. I was free again for the time being, I was already outside of the tour bubble.

Tony Defries had by now on several occasions laid out for us his plans for the coming months ahead. Tony had explained that the successful UK tour that we were about to finish off in style at the Hammersmith Odeon had been merely the start of many months of well paid activity for all of us. Following the European tour, for which we strangely still did not actually have an itinerary, we were to embark upon 'USA Tour III'. Tony had told us that thirty-eight dates had been booked, opening with a concert for 18,000 people at the Toronto Maple Leaf on September 1st 1973, moving to Newhaven, Connecticut in the USA on September 7th, working westwards across the country and finishing in front of 10,000 people in San Antonio, Texas on October 31st 1973. Tony Defries predicted that there could possibly be seventy concerts across North America in all, and David himself had talked informally to one or two people about going on to play in China in 1974. I was not going to refuse to go; I would not let David and Mick down, I had nowhere else to go anyway and nothing else planned and yet somehow I found the idea of another immediate tour, and a huge tour at that, a bit hard to take. We were all quite tired of the routine, of the same old faces on the road. We had played the Aladdin Sane album to death and I thought that surely David needed some new songs – a new album in fact – before he could tour again like that. David Bowie, as Ziggy Stardust, had set the bar so high that surely the next tour would need more than Japanese costumes and flashing lights. It would need clowns and elephants, the full circus, never mind the new songs with the twin lead guitar parts that Mick and I had discussed.

In spite of any misgivings that some of us may have had about the future, the concert at Hammersmith Odeon on July 3rd 1973 saw David Bowie and the Spiders from Mars at their best. There was all kinds of publicity stuff going on, film cameras were everywhere backstage and celebrities were coming and going. The audience was sensational and we would probably have said that this final gig of the UK tour was, appropriately, the best one we had ever played.

During the short intermission, David Bowie had unusually come over to me backstage and asked that I wait for his signal before starting the intro to the final encore number, 'Rock 'n' Roll Suicide'. It seemed obvious to me that David was going to make a little speech of thanks, appropriately at the end of our last show, to his adoring fans at the Hammersmith Odeon.

As the applause rang out for our 'last' song, 'Suffragette City', David waited motionless in centre stage and I waited as I had been instructed. Some of the band were giving me nervous looks, of course wondering why I had not started the encore. When the applause eventually died down a little, David walked forward to the microphone and raised his hand, signalling for silence. People shushed at the noisy ones until there was silence and David was able to begin his speech.

"Everyone," he shouted to the crowd. "This has been one of the greatest tours of our lives, and of all the shows on this tour, this particular show will remain with us for the longest because not only is it...(pause) not only is it the last show in the tour but it's the last show we'll ever do."

With a brief 'thank you' into the microphone, David turned his back on the audience and walked towards me, nodding that I should start my intro to 'Rock 'n' Roll Suicide'.

The crowd was stunned, as were the road crew, not to mention seven of the eight-piece band on-stage. The exception, apparently (I have always thought that Geoff MacCormack surely must have known) the only one of us to whom the speech was not a surprise was Mick Ronson who had, we soon realised, already been taken to one side and told of David Bowie's 'retirement' decision. Mick had been told not to worry however, he still had a great future ahead of him as a solo star – his career success was guaranteed, because the new Mick Ronson would be managed by Tony Defries and MainMan Management. Mick had been given no choice but to go along with the deception for the last few weeks of the UK tour, and it must have been very hard on him. I know that Mick would initially have suffered greatly at the thought of betraying his long term band mates Trevor and Woody, but the germ of the idea of a solo career had been put before him some months previously and Mick had plenty of time to think it over. David had always known that he would have to ditch the band someday, that he would have to kill off Ziggy Stardust and be David Bowie again, and Mick had probably become used to the inevitability of the split.

As we came off-stage I still wasn't sure what David had said exactly, but I knew it had certainly been something about 'retiring'. Everybody in the band was looking at each other in the dressing room and trying to put together what David had just said. Mick Ronson had disappeared, and Trevor and Woody looked devastated. "He's fuckin' sacked us," said Trevor.

Indeed he had. We had been sacked on-stage at Hammersmith Odeon, and we were, all of us, in a state of shock.

It would be many years later before I was to learn the real reasons behind the sudden demise of Ziggy Stardust. I had of course seen at first hand the excessive expenses incurred on the Aladdin Sane tour of the USA in 1973, but these had apparently been nothing compared to the frenzy of spending that had been the main feature of the previous tour, the very first David Bowie and the Spiders from Mars USA tour in 1972. Rocco Laginestra, the senior RCA man who had sanctioned the underwriting of both the 1972 and 1973 tours, had by now been persuaded by shareholders with quite possibly similar Italian names to Rocco's, to be a little more careful with the company's money, and so he had refused to allow the overambitious 'USA Tour III' to go ahead as planned. Laginestra had instead proposed a much smaller tour itinerary, but Defries had refused and instead, in close collaboration with David Bowie, he devised the elaborate 'retirement' deception. This barefaced lie enabled David to call RCA's bluff and show that he as the artist had ultimate control, but also importantly the 'retirement' was a perfect way to kill off his alter ego, his Frankenstein's Monster, Ziggy Stardust. The monster was doomed anyway and so he just died sooner, rather than later. Acts like Ziggy are destined for a very short life; the candle just has to burn so brightly.

A party had been arranged as an end-of-tour celebration, and it was to be held the following evening at the prestigious and very expensive Café Royal in Oxford Street. All of the now redundant

311

band musicians and tour personnel were told that the party was to go ahead as planned and that we were all very welcome to attend. Our hotel room bookings would also be valid for another day for that purpose, just another few items on a huge final tour invoice that RCA would have to pick up.

The party could hardly be cancelled; the guest list was phenomenal, although I don't think that they all attended. For instance I didn't see Paul McCartney, Sonny Bono or Tony Curtis at the do, and I think I should have noticed if they had been there.

The full list of invited guests was impressive: Mick and Bianca Jagger, Ringo Starr, Paul McCartney, Keith Moon, Britt Ekland, Lulu, Tony Curtis, Cat Stevens, Lou Reed, Jeff Beck, Elliot Gould, Ryan O'Neil, Sonny Bono, Barbara Streisand, Peter Cook, Dudley Moore, Spike Milligan, Hywel Bennett – and one D. A. Pennebaker. Mr Pennebaker surely does not remember the D.A. – the 1960's Duck's Arse – the slick precursor to the Mullett. The famous filmmaker had been employed by Tony Defries to secretly film and record the 'farewell concert' at Hammersmith without the knowledge of the band on-stage – that is, other than David Bowie and Mick Ronson. Pennebaker had hidden microphones in the side curtains of the stage and also recorded sound directly from the mixing desk, so the sound man Robin Mayhew and his crew must have been told to keep a secret too.

Pennebaker's film turned out to be so very dark, probably due to the pathetic lighting rig, but it is still shown regularly on television – often at Christmas for some reason. I can point myself out by means of my sparkling green suit in spite of the darkness, and my name does appear among the credits at the end of the film. Though they released the concert as an album, a film, a video and a DVD, nobody has ever offered me any performance fees or royalties for the recorded Hammersmith performance. Not so far anyway – and I never say never.

I was quite happy to take up David's party invitation, I did not hold him personally responsible for the collapse of the USA tour plans, and although I was sad that it was all over, I did not feel let down or betrayed, and of course I'd had quite enough of touring.

For Trevor Bolder and Woody Woodmansey it was quite different, and although Woody decided to go to the Café Royal party, Trevor was too angry to attend. Woody would have stayed away too I'm sure, if he had known that David had already chosen his musicians for a new album, to be called 'Pin Ups', and he had decided to use another drummer instead of Woody. Mike Garson would be given the task of telling Woody that he was not wanted, but Mike had decided to wait until the day after Woody's forthcoming wedding to June, his long-time girlfriend. The wedding ceremony was to be conducted by Mike Garson himself, who as a 'minister' of the Church of Scientology was able to marry the couple before telling his friend and protégé the bad news.

I travelled to the Café Royal party in a limousine with Mick Ronson and Woody, and I supposed that I must have been using Trevor's seat in the car. As we got out of the limo we found that a red carpet was laid across the pavement and camera flashbulbs were popping as if it were a film premiere. I was still wearing blue jeans and Mick's old snakeskin-collared suede jacket, so I dived as quickly as possible into the Café Royal so as not to lower the tone of the Spiders from Mars' entrance.

As we walked in to the hotel ballroom I was delighted to see the folk singer Colin Scott, an old mate of mine, sharing a table with an older but very beautiful blonde lady, and I gratefully joined their friendly faces at their table. The place was teeming with famous people, and it was a huge relief to me that I knew at least one of the guests. Colin Scott had been a regular visitor to The Penthouse at Scarborough, he was a pal of Peter Adams the owner, and I had played support act to Colin on several occasions before he went off to live in Amsterdam. Colin was a lovely guy, he enjoyed life, and he liked to smoke in peace, so Holland will have suited him. In recent years I have played in Noord Holland from time to time, and Colin is fondly remembered there; he never grew old, he died in Amsterdam. When Colin introduced me to his partner for the evening at the grand Café Royal do, I was amazed to discover that she was the Danish Princess known to the world as Nina of 'Nina and Frederik' fame – the folk-singing stars of the early sixties who had been managed by Ken Pitt at one time.

Nina was great company, as was my old pal Colin of course, and although I rarely ever dance, I danced with the Princess that night at the Café Royal. In fact, as Nina and I danced – just the one dance mind you – David Bowie was also on the dance floor with Bianca Jagger, and so that is where I made my farewell to David. I just caught David's eye for a second, he sort of said 'alright?' and I said 'fine' and that was it. It was all over.

I drank quite a lot and enjoyed the party. My abiding memory is of a scene where I was sitting talking to a model kind of girl who I had met before somewhere, when Ringo Starr walked past us on his way to the Gentlemen's toilet doorway. Ringo paused and looked at me as though he knew me. I had drunk too much to be surprised at anything, and I just grinned back when Ringo said, "We're in the big time now eh mate?" and walked on. Ringo had played seasons at Butlins too in his time and I will always enjoy that memory.

I left London the following morning, having failed to get through to David Bowie, or anyone else, on the telephone. I did speak to Tony Defries on the phone a couple of days later, but he just said David was tied up and to try later. I never called again.

It had been a 'morning after' like no other I have experienced. Of course I did not know then why David Bowie had decided to quit, and so I had tried to find somebody who might give me the real explanation. None of the MainMan people had been available that morning however, and the sax players had just disappeared, as had Mike Garson, Geoff MacCormack, Mick Ronson and Trevor and Woody.

I had no option but to leave the hotel without any farewells to my ex band mates, or any others on the tour staff, or to my old friend David Bowie. For the few minutes that it took to check myself out of the Grosvenor House Hotel and load up my car, I felt the full weight of anti-climax. I had never been a real star musician, not a proper one anyway, but I had been a Spider from Mars for a while, albeit an auxiliary one. I had enjoyed it immensely and now it was all over.

As I drove northwards again in my little Renault 4, it occurred to me that the car, my guitar and the suitcase that I carried were my only possessions, that I was now out of work again, and that I had nowhere to live. The short speech that David had made two nights ago at Hammersmith Odeon had abruptly turned my world upside down again, but somehow I had easily accepted my latest change of fortune. My life as a travelling Spider auxiliary was finished but I could not have cared less and was surprised to find that I was as relieved as I was disappointed that this fantastic episode in my life was over. Ziggy Stardust and the Spiders from Mars were no more, which meant that I now had either left or been kicked out of, three of David Bowie's bands. Maybe that's a world record.

Who knows, I thought as I passed Watford Gap services, maybe some day I will rejoin David again. The phone will ring and he'll ask me to play with him again. Why not, some day, I thought, why not?

David Bowie UK Tour II – 1973

David Bowie – The Artist, vocals, guitar, mini-moog, percussion

Band
Mick Ronson – Musical Director, lead guitar, vocals
Trevor Bolder – bass guitar and vocals
Woody Woodmansey – drums
Mike Garson – piano, mellotron
Brian 'Bux' Wilshaw – tenor saxophone, flute
Ken Fordham – tenor, bariton, alto saxophone
John 'Hutch' Hutchinson – rhythm guitar and vocals
Geoffrey Alexander MacCormack – percussion and vocals

Crew
Robin Mayhew – sound engineer
Peter Hunsley – stage manager
Mick Hince – equipment manager
Willie Palin – equipment manager
Stuart George – personal security to Mr Bowie
Sue Fussey – wardrobe mistress, hairstylist
Bob See – lighting director
Ron Meadows – lighting operator
Stephen Hurston – lighting operator
Jamie Andrews – Road Manager
Tony Zanetta – Tour Co-ordinator (MainMan)
Barrie Bethell – Tour Manager (RCA)
Martin Pierpoint – Assistant Tour Manager (RCA)

Tour promoter Mel Bush
Photography by Sukita
Front and back cover photography by Duffy

Programme design by Splodier Group

An RCA Record Tour

Chapter Thirteen - Can You Hear Me Major Tom?

David Bowie did eventually call me, though he took his time about it, in fact it was twenty-nine years later when the call came, but it was not about another gig. It was about this book.

It was just after lunch, probably around 2pm UK time, on Monday 29th April 2002 when David called me at my home in York (that is old York, the original York, England) and he was returning the call I had made to his New York office around six weeks earlier. I had been back to Sweden for a few weeks to play some small bar gigs and to see old friends, the guys I had played with back in the sixties, and I had almost forgotten that I'd asked David's New York office if he would please call me back. I certainly didn't really expect him to call me; I thought he might be away somewhere, far too busy, or most likely that my message would not get through to him. I knew that Coco Schwab his sometime assistant might even be back on the team and it was said that part of Coco's job used to be sorting out who gets through to David and who doesn't. Coco is a nice lady however, she worked for Tony Defries at MainMan in 1973 and I met her quite often in those days.

Ken Pitt had given me David's office number in New York way back when Ken and I were still on Christmas card terms; I had kept it handy for years and not used it. I had decided long ago not to pester David with persistent attempts at making contact – or if I did call him there would have to be a good reason. I'd been thinking about writing my Bowie & Hutch story for some time, and a gap in the day job routine in 2002 gave me the opportunity to make a start – to see if I could do it, find out if I could write or not. I was kicking around in York, pretending to help my wife Susie with a trendy specialist food shop that she had opened in the so-called 'latin quarter' of the city, and I did not intend to go back to a proper job in London or Aberdeen unless, or more likely until, I really had to.

Of course I didn't finish the book in 2002, or you should have picked it up ten years ago. I didn't think I had any kind of an ending to my story back then so I filed all the notes and photos away, found a job in the oil and gas design business again, and forgot all about the book. It was not until the spring of 2011, a year or two after I had moved out of the city of York and into a small cottage in a small village in the East Yorkshire Wolds countryside (not too far from Scarborough) that I picked up my old drafts and bits and pieces and started writing again. I put the book away for a while yet again when I realised that the big publishers were never going to be interested in my small memoir and I decided that I didn't really care whether it saw the light of day or not. I didn't need the hassle; I was busy enough making music with friends in York and Scarborough and enjoying my full-time, semi-retirement holiday in the Yorkshire Wolds.

Then out of the blue in January 2014, a week or so after I had tried to let my 70th birthday slip by uncelebrated, I was contacted by the brother of a local publisher in Bridlington. Andy Hutchinson (no relation) had sent me a song by email and I had said no thanks, but then he asked how my book publication was doing and within days my book project was up and running again.

Now I'm into the final chapter, and in my 'old age' I see that there really are (because we say never say never) no endings. As far as we know there is just the big one.

Back in 2002, having finally decided to see if I could write my story and produce the book, I had realised that David Bowie would be the one person most likely to be able to put me in touch with Ray Stevenson, the photographer who had taken so many great pictures of David and me and Hermione back in the sixties, the Feathers days. I also had another good reason however, and a much more personal reason at that, to want to speak directly to David – if I could get through to him.

Only weeks before, I had been through a bad telephone experience with Ken Pitt. I had called Ken and asked if he might be able to help me to get some recognition, and consequently some payment, for the various recorded and filmed items taken individually from his 'Love You till Tuesday' film and commercially released as separate 'David Bowie' products. Though Ken had properly paid me an agreed film-release fee for 'Love You till Tuesday', it seemed that nobody had included my involvement as a performer when selling on the recordings used in Ken's film to others over the years. Nobody paid me any session fees at the time, as I was in fact a performing artist, a member of David's trio Feathers on those recordings, not a session musician.

Albums, singles, videos and DVDs, which include my performances on more than one 'Love You till Tuesday' track, have been sold around the world for more than forty years without any performer royalty payments coming my way. Various releases of 'The Original Version of Space Oddity' might have sold millions, who knows? It has David Bowie's name on the label, but anyone can hear that it's my voice on there with David. It's my voice that starts the song and it's really not as good a voice as David Bowie's – is it? The fact is that David Bowie wrote the song for two people, for Bowie and Hutch to sing, and on this 'Original Version' I sang the 'Ground Control' part and David sang the 'Major Tom' part.

Anyway Ken didn't want to know; he refused to listen and became very angry. Ken let rip down the phone at me with an angry tirade about it having been my decision to pack in the music business in 1968 and that it had been my choice to go back to a career as a draughtsman. Ken said I should just be grateful for the memories of the old days and not go stirring up trouble for myself and why was I so bitter about it all? Well, I have often over the years felt plenty of frustration and anger about the business side of 'the music business'. Getting properly paid has always been a problem (it is no different for musicians today) but I have never been bitter; the ingredients for that would have to be a lot more complicated I imagine, and anyway my life has had many more ups than downs, I have made my own choices and been happy with them.

So I had two good reasons to want to speak to David Bowie in person if possible, even if only briefly on the telephone. Firstly, I thought that probably David would be able to put me in touch with Ray Stevenson. The photographer had been a good friend of David's and mine, and he had taken several wonderful pictures of Feathers in the old days. I thought they would be great for this book, and I wanted to ask Ray if he might let me use some of them.

Secondly, I very much wanted David to know that my book, this book, would not be full of any regrets or bitterness or sour grapes from me over his long and successful career – much of it achieved in spite of not having had much assistance from me – and that I have only fond memories and total admiration for his creativity and his longevity as a performer. I knew that David himself would not expect me to be bitter about the past, after all we had spent time together in 1973 and I think he knows that I am reasonably well adjusted, if that is the word, with regard to my outlook on life. I was concerned however that Ken Pitt might call David and express his own interpretation of the facts of our telephone fall out. I wanted David to know that I planned to write a memoir and truthfully tell of what happened in the old days, it had all been great fun and I would give my point of view and my recollections – even if not everybody (even David Bowie himself) agreed with me. In spite of the passing of so many years I still regarded David Bowie as an old friend, albeit a distant and well out of touch friend, and I wanted him to know that I would not set out to be controversial just in order to sell my book.

The phone rang and the voice said, "Hello Hutch, it's David Bowie." I sat down on the stairs with a bump. Quite a surprise I can tell you, and god knows what I said to David, though eventually I was able to explain why I had wanted to talk to him. David was just the same, friendly and laid back, and he sounded interested in my book idea. He gave me Ray Stevenson's number, telling me that Ray was in fact living in Spain. David also told me that Ray's brother Nils Stevenson, the young guy who had managed the Sex Pistols for a time, had tragically died very recently. After a quite brief but friendly telephone conversation during which I was able to assure him that I was whatever is the opposite of 'bitter' ('sweet' is not really the word) about our old days, David and I wished each other well and said goodbye. That telephone conversation on 29th April 2002 was the first time that David Bowie and I had spoken since he killed Ziggy Stardust off in 1973, and so far we have not actually spoken to each other again since that call. We did try, just once since then, to arrange a meeting while David was playing the UK on his 'A Reality' tour in November 2003 – and we have basically kept in touch, as we do sometimes exchange emails, albeit quite brief ones. Sadly these days I have to accept that mostly I belong in David's past, just as he belongs in mine. I do live in hope that we will meet again mind you – stranger things have happened in my life.

Okay, back from the future; it was autumn 1973, the Spiders from Mars were no more, and I was back in the North of England and out of work. I had though written a few songs whilst on the road with David, and the people I played them to seemed to think they were pretty good. My songs had titles like 'Nashville Moon', 'Baby's in Brooklyn' and 'Ladies of the Road' and they were of course about my recent life experiences. I also had my solo versions of 'Life is a Circus', 'Love Song' and 'Let me sleep beside you' from the Feathers days, and a good bag of folk-blues standards and Americana that I had gathered over the years, and so I played solo acoustic gigs around the north-east of England and shamelessly traded off my 'ex-Bowie guitarist' status. I still do that, I'm still shameless, if it gets me a gig I will always pull the 'Vintage ex-Bowie Guitarist' story out of the bag. Some vintage it is too, it has been 41 years now since the fall of Ziggy Stardust in 1973.

By the mid 1970s I had graduated northwards from Scarborough and I found myself living in the west end of Newcastle-upon-Tyne. I played Newcastle City Hall a couple of times as support to the famous Geordie band Lindisfarne, and also I played for a while in their singer Ray Jackson's offshoot band Harcourt's Heroes around the Newcastle area. The band, co-led by the redoubtable Charlie Harcourt, the ex-Lindisfarne II and Junco Partners veteran guitarist, was my introduction to the world of Working Men's Clubs and it was an eye opener. It was money for old rope I thought, but the trouble was that the punters were not interested in originality and they only wanted old rope ('covers') – and Newcastle Brown and Federation Bitter and Bingo.

I had formed my own band too for a while, we were based back in Scarborough and I called it Hutch & Its Easy. It turned out to be not so easy after all – there were to be two or three versions of the band and my ex-Bowie drummer chum John Cambridge played with me in all of them. It was a decent band I think and we were okay locally, we even did Tyne Tees Television – a live show called Geordie Scene – but apparently the band had little potential on a national level. One version of the band included talented friends Dave Magson on vocals and congas and Greg Holt on piano and they came with me to Basin Street Studios in London where we did some demos of a few of my own songs for Island Records who had expressed an interest. Afterwards the American A&R guy just told me, "Come back in a week or two Hutch and we'll do it again with some decent session guys." It was my own fault, I had given away lead guitar duties in 'Its Easy' to Ian Hawkins, a mate who was a very good guitarist but a bit of a widdler at the time, and I knew I should have played lead myself and kept hold of the 'feel' of my original songs. There were some other little mistakes though, like not rehearsing the band – not even once – before the studio sessions. I never called Island Records back, I'd lost interest in my own songs by then, and any get up and go that I might have had for Hutch & Its Easy had got up and gone.

By the later seventies I had acquired a manager in the form of Barry Mackay who had initially come down to Scarborough to open a record shop in the town. Barry was a Newcastle rich kid who was operating quite successfully at the time as world famous Geordie folk-rock band Lindisfarne's manager and so I thought he might advance my career prospects too. It turned out that Barry's efforts did not make me a star, and of course this was not entirely his fault. Any singer-songwriter has to get his own act together, give total commitment to his songs and his performance skills, and he cannot just rely on a bit of good luck and a good manager to get him ahead in the game. Looking back now, I don't think I was really trying hard enough, whether Barry was or not.

I had become attached to Newcastle, and even more so to a lovely girl who was originally from Scarborough, and who would eventually become my new wife, my lifetime partner – for more than three decades now anyway – and so far so good. Susie was working for an insurance company in Newcastle city centre and so we moved in together – or rather I moved into her downstairs flat just off the West Road. I was playing a few gigs and more or less getting by when one evening I saw a local singer-songwriter called Pete Scott on regional teatime TV. Pete's lead guitarist immediately impressed me; the guy was effortlessly playing some amazing country licks on a Telecaster which seemed to have a Clarence White B-Bender on it. By the way, a Telecaster B-Bender is a bolt-on device that replicates a pedal-steel guitar effect by raising and lowering the B string by a semi-tone when operated by the player pulling the guitar-strap against his shoulder. Gene Parsons (no relation of Gram Parsons) who played drums with a later edition of The Byrds and who had a machine shop in his garage, had come up with the design and the prototype of the B-Bender at the request of the late Clarence White, the already phenomenal bluegrass guitarist. The B-Bender made Clarence's incredible Telecaster playing even more incredible. Even Jimi Hendrix had to ask Clarence, "Man, how do you *do* that??"

When I enquired, Barry Mackay knew immediately who the chicken-pickin' Geordie was, and Barry put me in touch with him. Jimmy Hornsby was and still is something of a legend amongst Geordie guitarists, and with good reason. Jimmy plays country like he was born to it, he plays as if he had been born and raised in Nashville Tennessee, not in some obscure village in Tyne and Wear. Albert Lee is the famous one, but in my view Jimmy Hornsby is his match any day. I had always harboured a liking for good country stuff, I had grown up singing the Everly Brothers songs that their daddy had taught 'em, and old Elvis country songs and so on, so Jimmy Hornsby and I hit it off from the start.

I had a support gig coming up, it had been booked some months earlier, and it was for me to play solo at the Newcastle City Hall as the opening act, support to another Lindisfarne offshoot band called Alan Hull and The Radiators. Alan was of course Lindisfarne's creative genius, a great singer and songwriter, and he also was managed by Barry Mackay. The gig was in just a couple of days time, but Jimmy Hornsby and I decided we would play it together, and Jimmy said he would bring along a bass player who 'would busk it no problem'. I would meet the bass player at a quickly arranged rehearsal to be held the following day at an old cinema at the bottom of the West Road, which was possibly owned at the time by Barry Mackay's dad. Alan 'Bumper' Brown arrived on his motorcycle; he just rode up the cinema steps and into the cinema where he parked the bike in the stalls. Bumper was Jimmy's best mate, and he was a great character. The Geordie stories about Bumper's musical career that I like best, although I have no idea if they are really true or not, are:

That Bumper successfully auditioned in Newcastle for a guy called Bryan Ferry who was forming a new band which was to be called Roxy Music. After receiving Bryan's hospitality in the bar, and then an invitation to join the band, a temporarily financially embarrassed (totally skint) Bumper just climbed out of the toilet window and went home.

That when asked by two young Geordies, the Knopfler brothers Mark and David, if he might consider joining their new band – to be called Dire Straits – Bumper listened to their music then decided to decline the offer because he thought that they 'sounded like the bloody Ventures'. Bumper did have a point.

The City Hall support slot went more or less without a hitch, and although I almost forgot both Jimmy and Bumper's names on-stage when I tried to introduce and thank them (we'd only just met), the under-rehearsed set was well received by the audience. The bass parts were…unusual. Bumper's bass guitar lines swooped (that's the best, maybe the only description I can give) around and beneath Jim Hornsby's country licks, and both complemented my songs of love and loss on the road in the USA. Whatever Bumper was smoking required an ashtray on stage and so he improvised by using one of his boots. I didn't see the boot ashtray business happening, I was the frontman, but behind me Bumper kept at least some of the crowd entertained, just in case the music was not entirely to their taste. Northsound Radio recorded the gig for local broadcast, I still have a cassette copy somewhere, it is one of the things I always find when I move house and it still makes me smile when I hear it.

The 'money for old rope' trick was to suck Jimmy Hornsby and me into playing the Working Men's Clubs around the North East. We had started to develop a repertoire of hip country material by playing in a pub or two as a duo, and somehow without really trying too hard we went from strength to strength in the country music direction. I had come up with the name American Echoes as a joke, but also to demonstrate to whoever might be interested that I understood that the roots of American country music were in fact English, Irish and Scots folk music. Early American music was just traditional tunes and songs that had gone westward across the Atlantic with the early settlers on their wooden ships, and then eventually echoed back here as 'Country Music'. I always thought it was funny that many punters in the UK don't really get that basic fact. It was transatlantic musical evolution, that's all.

The American Echoes, Jim and me, added a bass player (obviously not Bumper Brown – just too risky) and a drummer, we entered and won a local country music contest that was a promotion by Marlborough Cigarettes, and went forward to The Final at Wembley. It was not actually on the famous pitch, it was just a 'talent contest' in a big hall somewhere around the stadium. We didn't win and we had not expected to. At all our gigs, all around the United Kingdom country music circuit, we were to remain conspicuous by our lack of a band uniform, also by our choice of good songs and by our ability to play. We were unusually more of a rock and roll band than grab-a-granny dance band. We played Rodney Crowell and Guy Clark songs, we got drunk now and then and we wore jeans and pointy cowboy boots. We wanted to be The Flying Burrito Brothers, however this was England and we were just the New Riders of the Foggy Tyne. The audiences at the Country and Western venues all over the UK would mostly asked for Marty

Robbins, Johnny Cash and Don Williams songs – you get the picture. I was told several times by experts wearing cowboy outfits that my band was not actually playing Country Music and, on one occasion at least, that we were certainly playing some sort of Rhythm and Blues.

Some people liked us though, I think we were perceived as 'New Country' even though we played Hank Williams and the like, so we recorded sessions at BBC Maida Vale studios for BBC Radio 2's 'Country Club' and we put out a single – initially on Blueport Records, then nationally on the Mercury Records label. It was an up-tempo Gram Parsons cover called 'Ooh Las Vegas' which had always gone down well at gigs, mostly due to Jimmy Hornsby's blistering solo. One of my own jangly compositions called 'Can't Believe It' was on the B-side. Amazingly, (at the time) family favourite DJ Dave Lee Travis, who had been on a Country Music Crusade for a couple of weeks, picked our record up when Blueport boss Mike Maurice called in to the BBC to plug it in person. Mike was a mild eccentric who liked a smoke in those days and he obviously got his foot in the door and did the business for us at the BBC. Dave Lee (the hairy cornflake?) Travis made it his 'record of the week' – it was the end of August 1979, the week that D.A. Pennebaker premiered his film of Ziggy Stardust's farewell gig at Hammersmith, 'Bowie 73' (the film that I didn't get paid for).

Our intensive BBC airplay came just one week before The Charlie Daniels Band made millions with 'The Devil Went Down To Georgia'. Our good old boy Dave Lee Travis had picked it (yet another up-tempo country record) as his following record of the week. Incidentally, the week prior to our record, Albert Lee's 'Country Boy' had been Dave's selection; the DJ was on a country music crusade alright, it's just a shame that we were not third up.

Hutch & It's Easy, Scarborough © Brian Cooke

Page 16 — New Musical Express 15th September, 1979

American Echoes: l to r: Martin Duffy, Jim Hornsby, John Hutchinson, John Cader.

American Echoes: Country Boys From Way Out North-East

Home, Home On The Tyne

IF THERE'S anything harder than finding an empty cab in Kensington High Street on a Saturday afternoon it's getting a single released by an independent record label onto the Radio 1 playlist.

It's the vicious circle we know too well; no playlist — no hit/no hit — no playlist. Breaking ground with English country and western music is even harder than that.

But the single most difficult task facing such hopefuls and said small label must surely be to impress Tony Parsons so much that he makes it his single of the week. Sheeit — It's all happened for American Echoes from the deep north, down Newcastle way. Do—wee!

Their single 'Las Vegas' was originally released by Newcastle's Blueport label on blue vinyl before Mike Maurice clinched a leasing deal with Phonogram, who released it on plain old black on their Mercury label. Mike, who takes part in Echoe's management, singlehandedly persuaded Tony Blackburn's producer Paul Williams to get it onto the playlist via a live session specially recorded at Maida Vale Studios for Blackburn's use.

Dave Lee Travis liked the single so much he made it his single of the week (what an honour! — Thrills Ed) while on TV Nationwide also filmed the band live in Newcastle, but only aired it in the region. A lot of positive reaction.

For anyone (and I must assume that means the vast majority of you) who hasn't seen the band, American Echoes are a four piece fronted by guitarist/singer/songwriter John 'Hutch' Hutchinson who was once part of Bowie's entourage and appeared with ol' red eye on the fabled Ready Steady Go. They possess a driving rhythm section in John Calder (bass) and Martin Duffy (drums), venturing slightly into the rock territory with emphatic ease. The shining light of the band must be seasoned guitarist Jim Hornsby who adds so much colour to the basic sound with his master of country picking, banjo, dobro and pedal steel. They may not be spring chicken pickers, but there's not an ounce of fat on this band.

Although the standard of Hutch's songs is high the single is a Gram Parsons/Rik Grech song, which they perform with not inconsiderable verve. As they do play country music, their problems are not the same as the problems of heavy metal or new wave bands. Record companies seem to take a dim view of English c&w, whilst churning out the American stuff on cheap labels with titles like 'Your All Time Top Country Favourites'. And most of the other bands seem content to play cabaret (my god, I mean have you seen Poacher?) or to back up third rate balding American artistes as a pick up band. No way no how for Echoes. They're masters of their craft doin' what comes natural, and doing it particularly well, especially from their audience's point of view.

The final question, is, given that they have a lot going for them, will the single chart? For American Echoes from sunny Newcastle, Opportunity Knocks?

DAN TANNA

THRILLS

Echoes NME

329

Country Music Awards 1982

Both the *Melody Maker* and the *New Musical Express* were able to take the piss out of the American Echoes of course, as we would have expected, and they created half page features about us with witty headlines like 'Home Home on the Tyne', 'Country Boys From Way Out North-East' and the like. Still we had some good photos in the papers.

American Echoes were musically just too hip for the mighty Mercury Records, for their United Kingdom office anyway. They just didn't get it, they didn't see the potential, and in my opinion they especially missed the promotional possibilities that a UK country band like us (one that could play) might have in the USA at that time. In spite of Mercury Records signing us up in haste one weekend and rush-releasing our single to coincide with the BBC's Dave Lee Travis 'Record of the Week', not to mention Radio Luxembourg's 'Powerplay' airplay, the record disappeared without a trace. Many punters around the country told me that our record was not in the shops in their area, and they had been told, 'We've never heard of it'. Some kind of management would have helped us; Barry Mackay had lost interest and so we had none, we were on our own, driving around the back roads of the United Kingdom in an old van, looking for our country music club employment for the evening.

These bizarre gatherings, these Country & Western nights, were to be found in all sorts of venues, including cricket clubs, rugby clubs, the back rooms of pubs, village halls, working men's clubs and, out of season, in otherwise deserted holiday camps. We built up a following, we went round and round the UK, and then we toured as backing band with a talented lady fiddle player from Nashville called Tokyo Matsu. Her publicity photograph had shown a very attractive young Japanese girl and we had been told what a great player she was. When Matsu (as she wanted to be called) arrived in the UK for rehearsals we realised that her promo photograph had been taken many years earlier, when she was 24, not 42. Still she was a great performer and we got along fine. Many of the London gigs with Matsu were in large ballrooms in the inner suburbs, filled to capacity with proper dancers – the forerunners of the rather less elegant 'Line Dancing' craze I would say – and the promoter for these ballroom evenings was one Bernie Clapton, who turned out to be an uncle of the famous guitarist Eric.

In 1980 American Echoes memorably played at the first (and the only) Portsmouth International Country Music Festival, held on the huge unused old Portsmouth Airfield, having been asked to be the backing band to a new American singer, a girl from Nashville called Terry Hollowell. Terry was a pretty, slightly chubby girl with a decent voice and she was married to a successful Nashville record producer called Jeff Walker (not the Jerry Jeff by the way) who was managing and promoting his wife in the UK. Others on the remarkable bill for the three-day event included Kenny Rogers, Glen Campbell, Billy Joe Spears, Tom T Hall, and er, George Jones I think, anyway loads of other big acts – you just think of one, and he or she was bound to have been there. Certainly Hank Williams Jnr. was there because we became chums with his band in the hotel bar, drinking late and on into the early hours, and we all exchanged phone numbers with promises to keep in touch and to go to Nashville. I remember well that Hank Jnr. himself couldn't get served fast enough at the bar and so he went to bed early, in a huff. The guys in Hank's band were real people though; they were just musicians like us, and bloody good ones. We never kept in touch of course.

The festival site was like a mini Woodstock, the sound desk was half a mile back from the stage and the backstage area was fenced off like Guantanamo Bay. Large American 4x4s raced around the place on important business. All alone, right in the middle of the huge backstage compound there was a small caravan, and this turned out to be the Festival Site Office, the place where the Festival Accountant was stationed. He was the guy who would be paying us, paying all the acts in fact, after the gig – so we were told when we enquired about payment, as was our custom upon arrival at any venue. The standard procedure for the big country stars, the common practice with all visiting American acts, was that 50% of their fee would be paid into their USA accounts before they even left home, with the balance becoming payable on completion of their performance. Of course American Echoes were not big country stars, but we were old hands at this game, and upon arrival we were dismayed to see very well that the festival audience, on that day at least, did not quite reach back as far as the mixing desk. The festival had just not pulled the expected audience numbers, and we knew that somebody was probably going to lose their cowboy shirt.

In fact a whole group of promoters were about to lose a lot more than their shirts, as these huge stars from the USA were very expensive commodities. On the other hand American Echoes were a mere UK backing band, and we were not at all expensive. We had no 50% up-front contract clause and as usual had only a few quid between us, and we needed the three hundred quid (or whatever it was on the day) in order to get to the next gig at the next town hall or rugby club. Martin Duffy, our drummer was of Manchester Irish parentage and of Licensed Trade upbringing and Martin would always go for 'The Bit' on the band's behalf. 'The Bit' meant 'our fee' – for all who don't speak Irish Mancunian.

Martin Duffy stopped the accountant in mid-signature. "We're not taking a cheque mate, it's strictly cash with us," said Duffy. The man was about to argue the point when Duffy informed him that we had noticed that the whole event was a financial disaster, but that some of the Americans had perhaps not noticed. Did he want us to let the whole compound know that the 50% fee balance cheques he was issuing with a smile to the American acts were certainly going to bounce? Duffy then told the accountant that in two minutes, if the cash was not in his hand by then, he would drive our old Transit van 'right through this fuckin' caravan'. The man paid us and we left. We did of course have a lot of sympathy with the promoters, they had tried hard and it was a magnificent effort, but it had failed on a grand scale. The great British public was just not ready for country music on that kind of scale and to this day, in that respect, things have not changed very much. The Country to Country Festival, promoted with Nashville money at the O2 Arena in March 2013 and again in 2014 is, as I write, the latest shot at selling the brand, but I would not put money on it, even with Bob Harris on board. Country Music is the music of the American People after all, and its cowboy-hat culture is an uncomfortable business for us British – although the Irish and the Scots do seem to have more of an affinity with it than the English.

I left American Echoes not long afterwards. I told the band that we were just a bunch of middle-aged pissheads going round in circles in an old van and I'd had enough. It had been great fun mind you and the guys, Jimmy and Martin, and Kiwi Johnny Calder on bass, were great players and had been great company. Still, we were certainly middle-aged pissheads, to a man.

I played solo gigs for a while, around the pubs and clubs and festivals in the UK, and I even did solo radio and television, as 'John Hutch'. Bizarrely I was nominated by the monthly paper *Country Music Round-Up* for 'top UK country vocalist' but I came third (or it might even have been second, I can't remember for sure) behind the winner, the famous Aussie crooner Frank Ifield.

Both Frank and another pop music 'legend', the bonny Clodagh Rodgers, had opportunistically become 'country' overnight to see if there was any money in it, and somehow I once found myself hosting an open-air country gig on the pitch at Norwich football ground with the pair of them as bill toppers. The things we'll do for money. There wasn't much money in 'UK Country' though, as both Frank and Clodagh will have discovered quickly enough. I was certainly ready for a change myself, and I was more than ready to hang up my cowboy boots if I could find another straight job again. Our daughter Hayley had been born in Hexham, Northumberland and Susie and I were struggling along in our pretty little rented cottage in Haydon Bridge on the North Tyne River with no real prospects of making enough money to get ahead.

As I had been more or less suitably apprenticed, qualified, trained and experienced as an engineering design draughtsman I looked for a job in the new UK boom industry of Oil & Gas, and Aberdeen, Scotland was now the centre of the North Sea Black-Gold Rush. It was 1982, Aberdeen was buzzing and people were coming in from all corners of the UK to fill the job vacancies. Through the job centre in Scarborough I found a job in Aberdeen as a draughtsman and so I put the guitar away for a while. My career had changed again; change was nothing new to me, so I just never looked back. My previous lives as a Spider from Mars and then as John Hutch the UK Country and Western Star were gone – as if they had never happened.

David Bowie on the other hand was, as I would have expected of him, still going strong in 1982. He had never for an instant intended to 'retire' or even take any kind of rest or break after the Hammersmith gig. In spite of reportedly experiencing a minor heart problem in November 1976 (the military hospital in Berlin, his home city at the time, later issued a statement saying that David had simply 'overdone things and was suffering from too much drink').

David had, since killing off Ziggy and his band in 1973, finally divorced Angie, toured Europe, Japan, and Australia, and the USA several times. He had produced the albums 'Pin Ups', 'Diamond Dogs', 'David Live', 'Young Americans', 'Station to Station',

'ChangesoneBowie', 'Low', 'Heroes', 'Stage', 'Lodger', 'Scary Monsters' and 'ChangestwoBowie'. A phenomenal catalogue, but do you know I didn't buy even one of those albums. I can't explain why, I don't understand it myself but I suppose I had deleted David from memory.

I found a small flat for Susie, Hayley and I in a small town called Ellon, some twenty miles north of Aberdeen, and my old car lasted just long enough to get us up to Scotland, unloaded and parked outside our new home – then it died. I had taken out a mortgage using a surprise windfall – some sort of government sponsored, worker relocation grant – as a deposit, and I commuted by bus to Aberdeen where I quickly learned the ropes in the oil business.

The most important thing I learnt was that I should as quickly as possible become a 'Contractor' – that is to work for myself and hire out to the highest bidder. So before too long I left the full-time employment of 'Charlie' YT Chan, a Chinese engineer from Sarawak who had pretty much cornered the market for 'Drillers' Consoles' (a control station a bit like a recording studio mixing desk) in Aberdeen. I was grateful to Charlie; he had given me my fresh start back in engineering and a way into the oil game. I bought an 'off the shelf' limited company and went to work for various oil service companies – these are engineering design houses doing all necessary upgrades and technical modifications to offshore installations on behalf of the big oil companies. The 'Contractor' arrangement is an American hire and fire model, and it suits the oil and gas business. It suited me too, as I was more or less my own boss.

I soon started to make some decent money and we moved out into the Aberdeenshire countryside, to a village called Methlick, where we bought 'North Arnybogs Croft' – a small place but with great potential as it had several outbuildings and eight acres of our very own fields around it. I made offshore survey trips, and even flew over my own croft in the helicopter on its way from Dyce Airport to the offshore platforms once or twice, and I enjoyed the banter in the design offices. I enjoyed being offshore a little less so – the banter out there was not so good. The resident offshore guys generally were a dour bunch of technicians, and I was relieved that my offshore survey trips were usually of just a couple of days duration. I made some good friends in the many jobs I had in Aberdeen though, and I have kept in touch as best I can, and have even worked with some of them since, in both London and Azerbaijan. Contractors in Aberdeen would move around a lot between oil service companies, and if another company offered an improved hourly rate, you changed jobs, with just a seven day period of notice needed. I was amazed and delighted to find that contractors were somehow more like musicians in that respect than 'staff' engineering people were. Contractors were independent and consequently rather free-spirited by comparison. I would never work 'staff' ever again.

One weekend Paul Graves, an enthusiastic lad from Manchester who I had worked with for a while, took me to a local 'festival', it was a so-called 'Music Marathon' being held at a pub called The Northern Lights in the small village of Hatton of Fintray – a few miles outside of Aberdeen, not far from Inverurie. This wonderful event was in fact a drinking marathon too, and when I sat in with guitarist, singer and radio music producer Kenny Mutch (a Scotsman) and bass player Paddy Byrne (an Irishman) that evening I enjoyed myself so much that I agreed on the spot to join their band Special Branch. The three of us quickly became and remained the best of friends and we were to play at the Northern Lights every Saturday for several years, it could have possibly been five or six years but I'm not really sure. We played Country, Scottish and Irish music, we drank quite a lot of whisky and the Englishman, the Irishman and the Scotsman that were Special Branch had a laugh I can tell you. The years flew by, the money flew into the bank and I rarely if ever thought about David Bowie and the world of pop music. Those old days were a distant memory; I had a new lease of life in Scotland.

My family were better off too, Susie was making cakes with the Women's Institute, our daughter Hayley was attending a small village school called Cairnorrie Juniors for whom she played centre-half in the otherwise all-boys football team, and as a family we took holidays in the West of Scotland and walked in the hills with our little dog Hamish.

A mixture of traditional Scottish and contemporary American acoustic music (my collection, The Byrds and the rest) engulfed Hayley during her formative years in Scotland. I formed an additional acoustic band and I called us The Ythan Pythons (the Ythan is the river that flows through Methlick, through Ellon and to the sea) and we would play a wide range of music: traditional Scottish, Country, Bluegrass and original material. The Pythons had fiddle (Ewan Cameron), guitar (me), 5-string banjo (Alan Smart) and bass (Cathleen Smart), and these days my daughter says that the rich musical climate that surrounded our life in Aberdeenshire is what inspired her and influenced her to become a singer and songwriter herself. Hayley just picked up one of my guitars one day and began to figure out her own chords, she didn't ask for or really need my help too much. Just hearing me playing guitar around the house, the record collection at home, the few gigs that she came along to and the band rehearsals that she experienced apparently did make a lasting impression on my daughter from an early age.

I never wanted to leave Scotland, and especially I did not want to leave North Arnybogs Croft, but the time came around, as it does for all of us, when our parents, both Susie's and mine, were approaching the end of their lives. We decided we had to move back to Yorkshire in order to keep an eye on the old folks, so we sold the croft and bought a large terraced house in the small but vibrant tourist city of York, as it was far enough away but not *too* far away from Scarborough where our parents and also my two sons and their families lived. I commuted weekly from York to Aberdeen for a while, sometimes by plane from Leeds Bradford Airport but more often by train even though it was a long journey (six hours minimum) each Monday morning and Friday evening. It was not the same as living in Scotland of course, it seemed that part of my life was finished forever, and so eventually I took jobs nearer home, at first in the York and Hull areas, and then in London and eventually out in Baku in Azerbaijan.

Azerbaijan was a country that I had not heard much of, and it was one that many people had never even heard of, but which because of its huge oil and gas reserves has been strategically and economically one of the most important places in the world to western governments since well before the First World War. Azerbaijan is ruled by a presidential dynasty, and the family are enriched by oil contracts with the western government backed oil multinationals. The country has an Islamic majority with widespread poverty right alongside their oil-rich elite of mostly Russian descent, they have ongoing trouble with the neighbours including Georgia, Russia, Turkey and Iran, and the whole area is another ticking bomb.

Baku was a real buzz though and it made me some good money as I had a good contract with accommodation and flights home included. The strenuous leave-cycle of six weeks out in Baku and two weeks back at home took its toll on my marriage with Susie a little, but we stuck with it for the money that I made and we survived it.

In order to keep my guitar hands in good form whilst away from home I would jam with a local Azeri band in Baku and I eventually formed a 'jazz-blues' trio to play in a little ex-pat's jazz bar on a

Saturday night. A Scottish workmate was leaving Azerbaijan for good and had given me an almost playable Korean Stratocaster copy which, as was apparently the custom in Baku, I would just plug straight into the PA system wherever I played. Guitar Combos were like hens' teeth in Baku, just one guy in the city had a Fender Twin but he wanted a fortune per night to hire it out.

One long hot afternoon in Baku in 2006, out of total boredom, I emailed David Bowie from my desk, just to say 'hello I'm in Azerbaijan whaddya think of that?' Eileen, the lady in David's office, had given me the email address when I had last called her, and though the message was not about anything very much I knew that David would be interested in where life had taken me.

David's response was along the lines of 'Hutch! What on earth are you doing out there?' I told him that I'd found a place on the planet where most of the local population don't know who David Bowie is. In fact there had been just one local Azeri who had asked me 'Isn't he a big film star or something?' David was at his PC or laptop, at home in New York possibly, or anywhere else in the world for that matter, and we exchanged a few one-liners. David was interested in what I'd been doing and he seemed pleased that I had made contact again. That was it, it was short and sweet but it was at least some contact between Bowie & Hutch again, and I was glad I'd tried the email address. David's life, both professional and personal, was only too well documented of course, so I had not tried to do wives and families and personal stuff. I didn't read *The Sun* newspaper or buy Bowie albums anyway.

The bass player in my Baku band, Emil, was of Russian descent and he played jazz on a Fender 5-string Jazz Bass, and our drummer Gena was an ethnic Azeri. Neither of them had played rock and roll at all, or blues very much, as Azerbaijan, being for so many years a far corner of the USSR, had experienced no 'Sixties' for rock musicians to grow up in. The Russians, who had run the place until the recent break-up of the USSR, had not allowed pop music to be broadcast or played during 'The Sixties'. They had though, bizarrely allowed the Azeri musicians since the days of Benny Goodman to retain and develop a 'jazz' culture of their own alongside the indigenous Turkic traditional music. Jazz is everywhere in Baku, although hidden just beneath the surface. What I mean by the 'surface' is the traditional eastern 'Turkic' music that is heard everywhere, played expertly on some strange stringed instruments by both Azeri and Turkish virtuosos for the locals, and then there are the few aspiring local Azeri pop covers bands, together with the 'disco' type establishments that are intended to capture the ex-patriot oil workers.

Azeris and oil workers alike are quite happy with that arrangement, but those of the local population, both Russians and Azeris who are into jazz, do really know their stuff. One evening I attended a concert by the brilliant US jazz guitarist Al Di Miola, held at the white and gold wedding-cake palace in the centre of Baku, and it was sold out, even with tickets at $100 – a fortune to most Azeris. Al's gig had no air-conditioning, the seats were gold-painted hard-back dining chairs, it was hot as hell, you heard one tune you'd heard them all, I needed a pee and I was gasping for a cold drink. The concert staff had not permitted bottles of water to be taken into the concert and so I just got up and left before the interval and walked home – sod the hundred dollars. Incidentally I remember that evening particularly well because I was followed home by two rough looking Azeris, and I had to shake them off by ducking into a doorway down an alley, as we have all seen done in the spy movies. Baku was a dangerous place in which to walk home alone at night.

Ghengis, the grizzled old guy who every day drove our minibus to the rig construction yard, turned out to have been a professional jazz flute player in his younger days, and his dad had been a big star in the old USSR, a clarinettist who had been known as Azerbaijan's

341

answer to Benny Goodman – and Ghengis's daughter was now a jazz flautist too. Ghengis and I got along just fine and he taught me some bits of Russian and played me jazz tapes on the way to work and back. There were of course protests from the rest of the guys, who all preferred anything but jazz on the cassette machine, but they protested in vain, it was Ghengis's bus.

My new Baku band had some style, musically there were no rules and really no reference points and I had heard nothing quite like us before. Emil the jazz bassist was playing flat-five substitutions and fast runs, and Gena the drummer was playing a fusion of traditional Azeri beats and jazz-blues behind whatever I played. I particularly remember enjoying an impromptu 'Me and Bobby McGee' that a lady had requested – it was to her a Janis Joplin blues song, and Emil and Gena had never heard of it anyway. The ex-pats in the bar, my fellow contractors, didn't mind as it did sound a bit like rock and roll sometimes, and the few local guitar players that were around seemed to be impressed enough, and to have accepted that I was trying to play 'jazz' of some kind.

When I left my last job in Baku in August 2006 I gave my inherited white Korean Stratocaster copy to Emil the bass player and asked him if he would keep it for me, for a couple of years at least, just in case hell froze over and I (or the engineer who gave me the guitar) came back.

I was glad to leave the place, I had both loved it and hated it, but mostly I had become scared stiff of walking home alone after dark. I often had to walk around at night anyway as I lived alone in a supposedly luxurious city centre apartment. Taxis home were dangerous too, the drivers were crazy and potential muggers themselves (taxi muggings were commonplace) and I had no car. It was bad enough in daytime; everybody on the street was scuffling, begging, stealing and struggling to get by. Two of my mates had been very badly beaten up, in separate incidents, while I was there, and they could easily have been killed for the $100 or so that they carried. One of them nearly lost an eye, never mind his camera and his Rolex. I'd had enough of Baku, I had learned to always keep my options open, but I had no intention of ever going back.

In spite of having had to deal with the rough side of life in Baku, I have never regretted for a minute the time that I spent on the two oil platforms that I helped (in a very small way) to design for the Azerbaijan oil industry. I always have it in mind that those two platforms have, ever since I saw them launched from the beach (the construction yard) in Baku, been pumping millions of gallons of oil – taken from beneath the seabed of the Caspian Sea – down a huge-diameter pipeline from Baku through the mountains of Georgia and on to the Black Sea coast in Turkey where western tankers collect and then deliver to UK oil terminals like Milford Haven. My schematic drawings are in use to this day, every day, for maintenance, reference or for changes in that operation. The drawings are never discarded, just continually modified and kept up to date. That's how we put petrol in our cars in the western world – it is not a trivial occupation.

A couple of weeks after my return from Baku my daughter Hayley and I went to London where we had been booked by producer and promoter Tom Wilcox to play as a 'double header' at the Whitechapel Galleries in the East End. Tom had booked me because he had lots of David Bowie related contacts and he knew that there would be enough interest in the first 'Hutch' gig in London for many years to fill his little venue, which was located in the café part of the world famous art gallery itself. Tom booked Hayley to accompany me because she had begun to make a name for herself, she was getting lots of airplay and the Bowie fans in London would be interested in checking her out.

I had been taking time out between jobs in Baku and somehow I had fitted in a few recording sessions and two support tours around the UK with Hayley during 2005 and 2006. The first tour had been with Nick Harper, a great guitarist, songwriter and performer, who will be forever cursed with being known as 'Roy Harper's son'. Hayley would not have any of that, right from the start she refused to mention me in her press releases and when interviewed and asked about her dad and his David Bowie connection, she would simply say 'you should ask my dad about that'.

I had in fact met both Nick and Roy Harper a year or so before, when they toured together and made a Radio York promotional appearance. I was on the show too, playing a solo acoustic gig live for Doctor Rock, real name Charlie White, an ex-pat Irishman who had been Little Richard's biographer, who day-lighted as a chiropodist in Scarborough, and who is an old pal of mine. The good Doctor had apparently asked Roy if he wanted to jam live with me, but Roy had declined. Nick however had complimented me on my playing; they had been listening to me on the car radio on their way into York.

My second UK tour with Hayley was in support of the talented and musically rebellious Jackie Leven, the late Scottish singer-songwriter and ex Doll by Doll guitarist who had always had something of a cult following rather than a broad popularity. Jackie was a very unusual guitarist in that he played with a unique self-invented open tuning. He told me he had just picked up a guitar and taught himself how to play by listening to the radio; Jackie didn't have anybody to ask how it should be tuned so he had just tuned it to an open chord of his own devising. Jackie was a very talented chap, if a little dour – as Scots can be – and he must be greatly missed by those bright few devotees (including I understand our ex-Prime Minister Gordon Brown, along with writer Ian Rankin and other Edinburgh luminaries) that 'got it'.

By 2005 my daughter Hayley Hutchinson had released her first album. Called 'Independently Blue' it had been put out by Gut

Records, a reputedly good independent national label, and at the BBC Terry Wogan and his producer, the late and much missed Paul Walters, had very soon heard and immediately liked the album. Terry decided to play a bouncy track called 'Here's the Love' on his popular BBC Radio 2 morning show *Wake up to Wogan* and it received really good feedback from his listening public. The song was in fact one of the few bouncy songs that Hayley had written, as most of her debut album was much more introspective and kind of 'folky'. The album received great reviews, both in the music press and online, and the single release of 'Here's the Love' became a BBC Radio 2 'record of the week' – just as my 'Ooh Las Vegas' had been...some twenty-six years earlier. 'Here's the Love' was play-listed by the BBC and so received huge airplay as all the top presenters played it regularly, on both BBC's Radio 1 and Radio 2.

Because of all the airplay and consequent media attention Hayley had taken on a manager, perhaps – in retrospect – a little hastily, as the guy's musical ideas soon turned out to be rather at odds with Hayley's own musical ambitions. This artist/manager relationship inevitably took a turn for the worse during a visit to the 'South by Southwest Festival' in Austin Texas USA in March 2006. Hayley had played her gig successfully, with a good response, albeit from a quite small audience in a not-very-important venue. A day or two after the gig however, during a sort-some-things-out chat in the hotel coffee bar, Hayley's manager had quit, on the spot, and had walked out. Fortunately my wife Susie had also made the trip to the USA to keep Hayley company – and it was a good thing she had or my daughter would have found herself abandoned and all alone in Austin. It was just another part of the ongoing, long and hard learning curve in the music business. The fact is that the music is the fun part and the 'business' is the pits. In spite of the manager's surprise walkout both Hayley and Susie made the best of it and they both enjoyed their Austin experience, rubbing shoulders with Lyle

Lovatt in a restaurant one evening and catching Norah Jones playing live outdoors. I was in Baku at the time, earning the money that would pay for the Texas adventure.

Well before the girls made the Texas trip, off and on during September and October 2005 and slotted in between my regular trips to Baku, I was to finance and play on some studio work with Hayley. My daughter had decided she wanted to make some recordings of several new songs at The Cluny Studios in Newcastle-upon-Tyne, and she wanted me to contribute some more of my jangly guitar work to her new tracks. I had previously called Jimmy Hornsby, my old country pickin' mate from the American Echoes days, and he had suggested the studio. Jimmy, who lives in Newcastle of course, had worked regularly with the engineer at The Cluny – a guy who also played very good keyboards. In fact Jimmy Hornsby was to provide Hayley with a complete ready-made studio band. Jimmy himself was happy to not only play guitar, banjo, mellobar and dobro, but also to help Hayley to produce the 'alt-country' style album that she was looking for.

The first sessions were great fun, but then three headstrong bandleaders in one studio proved to be at least one too many for Jimmy Hornsby's liking. Jimmy told Hayley that it couldn't work, and so after contributing some guitar parts and harmony vocals on a few songs, I had no choice but to leave Jimmy and Hayley to it for a couple of weeks. The result was certainly some excellent stuff, but without my involvement in the studio some of it had gone just too 'Country and Western' for my taste, and I thought that probably would be the case for most UK record labels too. You have to remember I had been there, seen it and done it already with American Echoes. So I was unfortunately proven to be right, the major labels would not touch the album, though Hayley herself was happy with the results and went ahead and released six of her favourite tracks on her own label, as an 'e.p.' titled 'Held to

346

Ransom', and she sold it from her website. The title was a swipe at her ex-manager, the one that had bailed out in Austin, and who had at first refused to release the recorded 'masters' to Hayley. Girls will be girls.

The first album, 'Independently Blue', had been a home-grown affair, and Hayley had made good use of the local musicians and the 'Studio 7' on hand in York. Fraser Smith, who played with top band Shed 7 in those days, had both produced and played keyboards, and many of Hayley's friends, the York based members of Shed 7 and The Seahorses included, had contributed. I played on it too, in spite of some disapproval from the odd local musician who didn't like 'dads' being around. I was not everybody's favourite in York – but that was mostly just because I could still do the business in my old age just as well as the younger guys.

The result of the Studio 7 sessions was a stunning debut album I thought, and the press and media reviews were to agree with me – if not even more so. Before the single – initially the album was released on Hayley's own label – became BBC play-listed then re-released nationally by Gut Records, I had decided to see what David Bowie thought of the album, and having first phoned the New York number and spoken to the always pleasant Eileen, I posted him a copy. Over the years I had called David's office maybe half a dozen times and Eileen always took my calls. She would deal with my inquiries in a non-patronising and friendly manner, and I think that David Bowie picked a good one there. David responded to me by email a few days later and he generously said that the album 'is lovely' and that my daughter is 'a very talented girl Hutch'. I had wanted David to hear my daughter's voice, to hear that talent does run in families, you know the usual proud parent thing. I had also wanted him to hear that I am playing guitar better than ever too (just in case – you know – he might need a guitarist) so I sent him my own e.p. 'Life is a Beach' which features six of my own songs.

David was complimentary about my CD, and about my guitar playing too, and I was really happy about that; we all need a pat on the head sometimes, especially from someone whose opinion we respect.

'You'll do for me David' I thought, you liked Hayley's voice and her songs and you are a good judge, and I believed right then that Hayley's album would do well for her. And it did, it was critically acclaimed, with great reviews, and it gave my daughter a good start in the music business. Of course there was still a long way to go, from those starting blocks to wherever the finish line might prove to be.

It's been a long way to go to gigs too, most of the time. It should be remembered by all punters living south of Watford that for any band from The North, a gig in London, no matter how prestigious it may be, requires a lot of time and effort. A departure before lunchtime is essential before a five hour (even more for the Scots) drive to London precedes a difficult search for the venue (with or without the blessing of Sat-nav) around the one-way systems of our capital city, getting the 'gear' in and setting it up, sound checking then finding somewhere to eat that doesn't cost the entire gig fee. The actual performance, when it eventually comes around, demands that the performer must suspend any thoughts of having to reverse the whole procedure at the end of the evening. That is when the musicians must take the gear down, carry it out and pack it away in the van, then drive northwards through the endless succession of joined-up city high streets, round the ring roads and up through the entry gates of the M1 escape road. Then we drive north again for five hours minimum. We usually get to bed as the folks south of Watford are thinking about breakfast. Of course we love it. I won't do it anymore these days but I do feel better for mentioning it, it's just a northern musician thing.

The Whitechapel gig on August 25th 2006 (by the way Susie drove us home when the gig finished that night too) went very well indeed, we had a great time and some friends from York, an up and coming young band called Boss Caine, were in town and so they popped in to see Hayley. We had two other acts opening for us, one was a really good young singer-guitarist (whose name I'm ashamed to say I can't remember) and the other was Roger Glover's talented daughter (the Deep Purple Roger) with her band, then I played a solo set to start the second half, then I brought Hayley on. As I had played quite recently on both Hayley's debut album and her new e.p. I remained on-stage and played jangly bits on my little Taylor 412 behind the rhythm guitar open chords that she played on her big Gibson J200. On Hayley's songs I would usually just put a capo on my acoustic, play different inversions and see what happened – pretty much as David Rawlins does with Gillian Welch really. Something usually did happen, and Hayley always seemed to be happy with my guitar contributions on her recordings, on both her demos and her commercial releases.

Being on-stage with my daughter however has always been a quite different kettle of fish. Hayley has, quite understandably perhaps, never really been happy about having her old dad on stage with her, even if he happens to be an 'ex-Bowie veteran' who can still play a bit. I would tour with her in the early days simply because she needed transport around the UK, and if I was at the gig anyway I was not going to just sit in the audience when my guitar parts could add so much to her sound. That's what I thought anyway. I think Hayley introduced me only once on-stage (as in telling the audience 'this is my dad' I mean) and that was when as part of the Middlesbrough Festival we played Middlesbrough Empire, appropriately on Fathers Day in 2005. I got a very loud cheer from the audience on that single occasion and I will always remember it. My mum sang on that stage too, when she was a girl.

Most of the time when on tour with Hayley I would just sit at the back of the stage and try not to overplay or engage with the audience too much. Being a proper side-man is a real talent, and I don't have it. Jimmy Hornsby knows how to do it, he keeps his head down and just grins now and then, whereas – I'm reliably informed by both my wife and my daughter – I tend to make myself be noticed in one way or another, and in their view it's just not on when it's Hayley's gig. In fact, since we played the Whitechapel gig on August 25th 2006 together, so far anyway, Hayley hasn't asked me to play on-stage with her again. I have more recently played on a new album track for my talented daughter, and so I am more than content with that contribution these days, now that even I think that I might, just possibly, be getting too old to tour.

Don't get me wrong, Hayley and I have always loved each other to bits, but we did fall out – just once or twice – while we were travelling together on the Nick Harper and Jackie Leven tours in 2005 and 2006. We would exchange a few harsh words and it would almost always be about me deliberately getting us hopelessly lost whilst trying to find very small venues in very big cities without the benefit of satellite navigation. I have to admit that in those circumstances I did, under stress and many years ago at that, tend to bang the steering wheel a bit and swear quite a lot. And okay, I would never have let my dad on stage with me, ever, no matter how well he played guitar, had he played guitar.

My son Jesse and I incidentally have a slightly different musical relationship. I think we play great music together, but there is certainly an element of duelling banjos going on when we do. Jesse is a great guitar player himself, and these days, around Scarborough where he mostly plays his gigs, he has taken over the role of 'fastest picker in town'. I wonder if in due course either of my grandsons, Harry or Zak Hutchinson, will displace their old man too.

Although my eldest son Christian (he was the little blond lad in the old photos with David and me) still has one of my very old and very battered guitars, fortunately neither he nor my lovely granddaughters Mia and Amy seem to be particularly inclined towards the rock and roll business.

Tom Wilcox had invited Maggie Ronson, Mick's sister, to the Whitechapel Galleries gig as Tom is a good friend of Maggie's, and it was great to meet up with her again. I had met her a few times, several years before when we were touring in 1973, but I had not really spoken much with her then; she was young and pretty and most probably Mick would have endeavoured to keep her away from his band mates. Maggie is a lovely lady (she is a lot like Mick in a way) and she had brought with her a friend, a lady who had organised the Mick Ronson Tribute Concerts following Mick's tragic early death from cancer of the liver. I know that Mick told John Cambridge that he believed that excessive drinking had been the cause of his cancer. Not long afterwards I was to meet Freddie Lundberg, a keyboards player in Gothenburg who had been a member of the Swedish band Leather Nun for whom Mick had been producing an album – in spite of his illness. Freddie told me that Mick had bravely fought his cancer and that when he became tired he would just lie down and sleep for a while in the Stockholm studio, then just wake up, grab a cup of coffee and continue the session.

I took my opportunity at the Whitechapel gig to explain to Maggie Ronson and the tribute concerts organiser lady that I had been very disappointed to have been deliberately excluded from Mick's tribute gigs, both the one in London and the one in Hull. I told Maggie and her friend that Mick had been one of my best mates, even though we only toured together for a short time, and that I should have been there. I couldn't know exactly what went wrong with my invitation, so I just put it down to Trevor and Woody's indifference and perhaps to Kevin Cann's determination to promote his friend and fading protégé Bill Nelson. Bill had been successful with Be-Bop Deluxe and Red Flag, and was said to be a great guitarist. Kevin Cann had written an excellent and very successful 'David Bowie Anthology' and he seemed to have some current connection with David, something to do with publishing I thought.

Some time later Kevin Cann came to my house in York to talk to me, to get the story from the horse's mouth – as some Bowie biographers like to do. Kevin is a decent sort, a quiet type, a nice guy but a hard as nails journalist underneath I think. We got along very well, we have kept in touch and we are email friends, and very occasionally we Skype. Kevin and I still don't talk about the time Bill Nelson took to the stage as my substitute in the Spiders from Mars line-up at the Mick Ronson tribute concerts. When I was in York, Bill apparently lived just a few miles away from me in his home town of Selby; I never met him, but I did once notice the unmistakable Bill in the street in York one day, he was wearing a very brave bright green overcoat. I guess Bill Nelson could have been a mate of Mick's too, I don't know, but in any case good luck to him, I can't bear any grudge against Bill. Or against anybody else for that matter, it is just water under the bridge and all that.

David Bowie himself had told me that negativity was a waste of energy. I had asked David during our brief 2002 phone conversation if he wanted me to send him a copy of the recently broadcast Equinox television special on 'Bowie's Millions' that I had taken part in. I had told David that Angie's contribution had been full of bitterness, though it had been quite entertaining in a Joan Rivers sort of way. David had said 'no, thanks Hutch, don't bother'. David has had a million times more of that stuff thrown at him during his life than I could have put up with, and he knows how to deal with it.

After the Whitechapel gig Maggie Ronson called me over and introduced me to another old mate of her brother's. It was none other than Glen Matlock, and the former Sex Pistol had come down to see the gig and to say hello. Glen is a decent chap, a nice bloke, and not at all what I might have expected from a member of that notorious bunch he'd played with. I told Glen that I'd missed the Sex Pistols gig in Scarborough at The Penthouse years before, and he told me a funny story about him and Johnny Rotten being refused entry into every pub in the town that evening. I had forgotten the old small-town stuff; the pubs had A-board signs outside, not advertising 'karaoke nite' or 'pub quiz' as they do these days, but proclaiming 'No Bedrollers'. People used to carry their own bags and sleep on the beach – they must have been long hot summers in the old days. I had really appreciated Glen coming down, somehow my connection with my pal Mick Ronson had been re-established, and I felt that I had at least paid my respects to Mick's sister Maggie. Tom Wilcox and Maggie both said let's keep in touch, let's get together again. Of course we should, but the weeks, months and years fly by these days and we all have far too many things going on most of the time.

In 2011 I had another email out of the blue from Tom Wilcox, very kindly inviting me to accompany him and Maggie Ronson to a Roxy Music concert in London, a grand reunion event indeed. I was excited by the prospect, and even though Roxy were never really my kind of band I thought that, well, it would be great to see the bright lights of London again, and Tom and Maggie too. Then I thought of the energy that would be required of me in getting myself up and out of my cottage in the middle of nowhere across the Yorkshire Wolds to the train station in York then down via Kings Cross and via taxi to some glitzy venue located in the depths of the big city. And where would I sleep, and eat, and what would it cost? And hell, it would be a two day bloody excursion. So I had to decline

353

Tom's invitation and it crossed my mind that I might have just finished with the music business – maybe London is just too far away these days.

While I had spent many long and tiring (though lucrative) days over the past several years producing schematic design drawings and documentation which enable the recovery (or plunder as some would have it) of the earth's oil and gas resources, David Bowie had been keeping busy too. He always has kept busy, even in the old days he never stopped working, never stopped creating and promoting his art and his ideas, not to mention the business of making money. I would have said that David is probably not the type to take up golf or fishing, although I did hear once that he had a boat in the south of France. Maybe he scuba dives or water-skis, or maybe he just sunbathes and drinks gin and tonic on his boat on the Mediterranean. Okay I don't believe that either.

In 2003 David Bowie announced a new worldwide concert tour. It was to start on October 7th 2003 at The Forum in Copenhagen; it would run throughout Europe, North America, Asia, New Zealand and Australia, then back into Europe where it would finish on July 23rd 2004 at the Vieilles Charrues Festival in France. David had the previous year made a mini-tour and a highly acclaimed album called Heathen with a new band which included my old chum, the amazing pianist Mike Garson. The Heathen tour band had been: Sterling Campbell (drums), Gail Anne Dorsey (bass), Mike Garson (keyboards), Gerry Leonard (guitar), Earl Slick (guitar) and Catherine Russell (backing keyboards and backing vocals). David and this band had subsequently made a new album, he called it 'Reality', and the forthcoming tour would promote it around the world.

The rehearsed tour repertoire was comprised of over fifty of David's songs, it included songs from every era in his career, and the set-list was to change nightly. David even took along a stylophone and played Space Oddity – what a shame I didn't get through in time, I could have done a guest spot, sung my part and played 12-string couldn't I? Okay maybe not, but in any case, based on my own experience a very big set-list is a very good idea for a very long tour. Overall the tour was to be a huge undertaking, there were one hundred and thirty-five concerts planned, designed and contracted for. The band prepared to tour for nine months and to play to more than one million people. It was a marathon by any standards, and comparable in magnitude to some of the big oil jobs that I had been working on. It was to be called 'A Reality Tour' and had obviously been conceived with the intent of making a lot of money. The 'Reality' was most likely that David had decided that he needed that money. Every business has its ups and downs, and the Bowie brand can be no different in that respect.

In New York, David had his responsibilities; there was another mouth to feed in the house. David's wife, the beautiful Somali model Iman, had presented David with a daughter, Alexandria Zahra Jones (subsequently nicknamed Lexi), at 5.06am on 15th August 2000. So David had to work, just like me, well maybe not just like me exactly, but he probably needed the money so he planned the album and the tour. Reality bites, even for multi-millionaires sometimes.

By March 2004, the US finance experts Moore Investors Services were to announce that in their judgement some $55m (£30.5m) worth of 'David Bowie Bonds' were at that time just one level above 'junk', fairly obviously the lowest rating for bonds (incidentally the Bowie Bonds did later recover). In 1997 David Bowie, the corporate entity, had been the first major star to sell bonds to fans, awarding them a share in his future royalties. The bonds had not initially performed as well as the financiers and the accountants who attempt to rule the world (and often fail) had hoped, but in any case they had committed David to repay his new creditors out of his future income, along with a fixed annual return.

Not long before the starting date for the 'Reality Tour', October 7th 2003 at The Forum in Copenhagen, David Bowie was recording in a Copenhagen studio and by coincidence I was in that city playing some very small venues, gigs I had booked for myself through email contacts in Denmark – as I had previously done quite successfully in Sweden. I was playing some small café 'singer-songwriter' gigs run by some lovely people who would make me a guest in their homes for a few days, and it was Michael, one of my hosts, who told me that my 'famous ex-employer' was in town. I tried to get a message through to David via his New York office, but I received no response. I believed that Eileen in the office would pass the message on to David; I had thought it worth a try that's all, why not? I didn't really expect him to pop down to my café gig and watch my set – he was in Copenhagen to work too after all. It was sad though, there was no response, David and I were living in different worlds.

'A Reality Tour' had blazed its way through a dozen countries by the time it got to the MEN Arena in Manchester, England on 17th November 2003. The band had played twenty-three concerts already, although they had to cancel one gig just five days earlier in Toulouse when David had been unwell. He had recovered and typically rejoined the tour after just one day off.

I had decided that I would try just once more to meet with David, if possible, during his short time in the UK. I had not seen the incredible tour itinerary and so I had no idea of just how busy his schedule would be on the 'Reality' tour. If I had known I might have decided to try some other time. As it was, David responded to my email enquiry in personal and friendly fashion just as before, and he told me that he had arranged for three VIP tickets and backstage passes, one each for my wife, daughter and me, to be available at the ticket office at the MEN gig in Manchester. I was delighted of course, but had protested to David that the last thing I wanted was a backstage meeting, the horrible five minutes allocation that old friends should not be subjected to. David had explained that time was very tight on this tour and the backstage thing was the only thing we could do. He wrote 'don't worry Hutch, it'll be fine'. I agreed to the arrangement, I had to because of course I wanted to see David again, but also I really wanted my wife and daughter to meet David, if only briefly. I thought if they talked to him they might better understand my history, my long-distance friendship and my ongoing long-distance correspondence with David Bowie the superstar.

So it was then on 17th November 2003 that Susie, Hayley and I drove the M62 westwards across the high Pennines to Manchester, and we collected our tickets at the desk at the MEN Arena as David had instructed. We had raised side-stalls seats quite near the front, and during the gig I was convinced that David had picked me out in the VIP seats; I was certain that he could have spotted me when the big lights dimmed from time to time. It was strange to be so near yet so far from my famous old pal. As usual I wanted to be on-stage, a part of the show, not sitting in the stalls watching it. The girls enjoyed the gig though, and I guess that I too was impressed with the stage design, the slick professionalism of the band and with David's energetic performance skills. It seemed to me that his MEN audience were responding well to David's efforts on-stage, but then David surprised everyone by asking, "What's up? I expected a better response to my first gig back in England!!" Perhaps the European audiences had been less reserved than we Brits are naturally inclined to be – anyway David's ticking off did the trick and the rest of the concert, certainly in the stalls where we were seated, became a much livelier affair.

There had been an interval, during which a group of people with several security guys around them had walked quickly through the hall and into the backstage area. One of them had been Debbie Harry; she was touring the UK too.

At the end of the concert we waited in our seats, as we had been previously instructed when we collected our tickets, for the arena to become almost empty, and a security guy who must have been given our seat numbers came along and asked us to follow him backstage. We were escorted through the concrete labyrinth to a large room that was obviously some sort of sports team changing room; the arena is also a sports venue and the room had showers in the back and lots of clothes hooks along the walls. There were a dozen or so other people in the huge changing room, and they turned out to be some other audience members who had been admitted on special passes. I spoke to one group of guys and they said Mike Garson had given them passes, and they hoped he was coming out to meet them. One of the group said that he had been a driver for some of the musicians, including Mike, on a previous tour. Sure enough Mike came into the allocated meeting area, and after he had spoken to his group of guests I surprised the hell out of him and said 'hello'. Mike Garson is a very decent chap, and he was at his charming very best in talking to my wife and daughter. To me, Mike just kept saying, "Hutch, wow man, thirty years? Wow man." He was genuinely surprised; I suppose from Mike's perspective I had just disappeared without trace after the 1973 tour. Maybe I shouldn't have, maybe I should have kept in touch with Mike Garson after all.

When I told Mike that I had arranged to meet with David, I asked what he thought and Mike confirmed what I had already realised, he said, "No man, David won't be coming out now." So Debbie Harry and her party drank the rider. Fair enough, perhaps Debbie is a 'current' good friend of David's and I suppose I am a very old friend from a previous era. It was still not easy for me to take at the time though, and I had to hide my disappointment from my family and instead just express my anger at being mucked about. You know, 'I'm never doing this shit again' and all that. David had told me that I should just contact his tour manager and that the guy would know what to do. I had asked around backstage for the tour manager without success and so Susie and Hayley and I all just said goodbye to Mike Garson and we set off back to York. On the way back through the backstage labyrinth we passed David's support band, The Dandy Warhols, as they walked through. They were very skinny Americans and Hayley was very impressed, especially when the Dandys had a good look at her as we walked by. She's just like her dad and in more ways then one; her mum is always saying that.

Hayley continues to surprise me, she still makes albums, with The Sorry Kisses – that is Hayley with her now husband Sam Forrest, who also plays with a noisy band called Nine Black Alps – and some resulting Sorry Kisses tracks have been played on US TV shows like *Grey's Anatomy* and on hip Californian radio. 6 Radio DJ Mark Riley is a fan (they have played live on his show) as are, I believe, both the hard to please whispering Bob Harris and the even harder to please Sir Terry Wogan.

I emailed David the following day and told him that I was disappointed not to have got to meet with him at Manchester MEN as we had planned. In fact I probably said 'I told you that would happen, backstage meetings are just not on mate'. I was possibly being a little unfair, David had tried, done what he could to set our meeting up, but there is an inevitable though distasteful pecking order where backstage access is concerned and he was after all only twenty-four dates into the one hundred and thirty-five concerts booked for the tour. He was a little busy.

David remained busy, although he did have to cancel four dates in America and one in Toronto due to others in his band going down with a 'band illness', quite possibly the same one that David had. One gig in Miami had also been cancelled due to a fatal accident, when a lighting technician had tragically fallen to his death just before the show was due to start.

After playing more than one hundred gigs in a row, on 23rd of June 2004 the tour had reached the T-Mobile Arena in Prague in the Czech Republic. The concert was briefly interrupted when David left the stage believing he was suffering from a pulled muscle or a trapped nerve in his left shoulder. A few days earlier, on 18th June in Oslo in Norway, bizarrely David had been struck in his left eye by a lollipop which had been thrown by an idiot in the audience. The thing had lodged in his eye socket and David had just pulled it out and carried on with the show. I had myself seen David grit his teeth on-stage and carry on in spite of anything and everything – whether it be a bad fever, a common cold or a twisted ankle – many years earlier with both the Buzz in 1966 and with the Spiders from Mars in 1973.

David carried on at the T-Mobile Arena in Prague too, as he always would, despite the acute pain in his shoulder, but in the middle of his performance he had no choice but to leave the stage again. This time a doctor was summoned, the concert was abandoned and David was rushed to hospital. He was diagnosed as having an acutely blocked artery that urgently required something called an angioplasty procedure, which as I understand it means that a small tube called a 'stent' has to be fitted in order to widen the blocked artery. David received the best medical care, the Czech surgeons operated in good time, and of course David survived, but it must have been scary for him. No one can play one hundred and ten or so concerts and be in the very best physical condition, so it might have been a close call. David Bowie was fifty-seven years old at the time of his heart trouble, exactly the same age, to within a few weeks in fact, at which his father John Jones had died, some thirty-five years earlier in Beckenham.

I heard about David's illness and immediately emailed him my best wishes for a speedy recovery, I was genuinely shocked at the news, I was concerned and David will have known that. I may be his very distant friend, from the very old days, but what difference does that make when it comes down to life and death? A few weeks later an email titled 'heartbreak' arrived, it was from David himself, saying thanks for my message and that he was now well on the road to recovery.

David will have had more time to be at home with his family, and to just be himself since his illness in 2004, but he will also have kept himself creatively occupied even if he has not been appearing in public very often. In May 2007 David played at an outdoor concert at the High-Line, a public park that had been created on top of a disused elevated railway line in New York. David had accepted an invitation to curate the very first High-Line Festival, and he had selected the performers for it himself, as he had done previously in 2002 for London's Meltdown Festival. Prior to the High-Line appearance, David had made just one brief stage appearance since 2004, and that had been with the band Arcade Fire at a fashion show in New York in 2006.

In 2007 David met the actress Scarlett Johansson at a party in New York, and having been asked by the lovely lady – he couldn't say no, could he? – David contributed his vocals to two tracks on Scarlett's 2008 debut album which was apparently a collection of songs written by the wonderful Tom Waits. It was called 'Anywhere I Lay My Head'. A collectors item no doubt.

As for me, it was during 2007 and 2008 that I began to cut down the time I would spend earning my living in the oil business. I had decided that I would take longer breaks between contract jobs and so put more time into making music instead. It was a plan that I hoped would ease me into semi-retirement, where consequently I would have to live on less money and accept the life changes that would bring. I also decided to take plenty of time over it, but I would look for an affordable place in the country to semi-retire to. It could have been anywhere really, but initially my favourite areas for the move were the Yorkshire Dales, the North Yorkshire Moors – or the Yorkshire Wolds. I also love western France, and western Sweden too, but they were both too impractical for this granddad to consider.

With some help from Bert Slappendal (my good friend and fanatical Dutch collector of all things Bowie) I found an energetic part-time manager called Jan Deken who agreed to book me into several small acoustic venues around the small and picturesque rural towns of Noord Holland. Music was Jan's hobby really; for his day job he had a vital role in the maintenance of emergency and extreme weather equipment at Schiphol Airport. In return for Jan's efforts on my behalf, as well as paying him due commission as my agent, on some bigger gigs I would play guitar for the talented Dutch jazz singer Rini Oudhuis, who was Jan's partner at the time. On these gigs I would borrow Rini's excellent Dutch musicians, bassist Micheal Peet and drummer Sebastian Mazereuw, who would play with me on my own set of jazz-blues originals before Rini came on. The guys were great players, and although they always played far too bloody loud for my taste, we had some good gigs together.

I had kept in touch with a Danish guitarist who I had met at a Django Reinhardt festival in Samois sur Seine in France in 1995. Karsten Knudsen had, like me, seen a TV program about the festival and had made the journey in his car, in which he then slept on the campsite for the three-day event. There were no hotels in the small village, only some very expensive ones in nearby Fontainebleau, so Susie and I had used a tent for a couple of sleepless nights.

Camping? – never again. Karsten like me had been bitten by the Gypsy Jazz Guitar bug and we both decided that we could play this old jazz stuff on a few tunes if we ever found some gigs together. We eventually found a gig in Copenhagen that would book us as a 'double header', it was a good place that I had played before, a kind of arts and social centre called the Beboarhus. It turned out that Karsten was famous in his home country, as he was one third of a kind of Danish music and comedy Goodies type group called De Nattergale (the Nightingale). They were very popular and they had their own television series.

I had told Karsten about the 'Bowie Stuff' at the campsite in France, but I only discovered how famous Karsten was when we arrived in Copenhagen. After dropping off our gear at the gig we went for a walk around the famous city centre hippy island of Christiana. It is all gone now of course, reclaimed as Danish territory, but for a while it had become a separate Hippy State. It was a too-late version of sixties California where people could build their own homes with turf roofs and no planning permission needed, and ride unusual home-made bicycles – and smoke dope freely. As Karsten and I walked through the streets of Copenhagen and on to the island of Christiana I began to notice that people were turning their heads and looking at us, nudging each other and muttering what must have been roughly translated 'Look it's him out of De Nattergale'. Proof of my new partner's fame was confirmed when we reached the street market on Christiana. The row of market stalls were selling dope and dope smoking equipment, out in the open without fear of a bust. I was informed by a stallholder that when the police occasionally did plan a raid on the market, the residents of Christiana were always informed in good time. The same stallholder, when he realised that I was with the famous Karsten, generously offered me my pick of his wares at no charge. When I told him thanks but I had quit smoking he passed me a bag of Special Chocolate Brownies.

The Beboarhus gig was a strange one, I played my usual set, then Karsten and I played some tunes together, then he told deadpan jokes in Danish. You can imagine the scene, what could I do but sit straight-faced, while the Danes rolled about in hysterics. We never did another one, Karsten is a nice guy and a good guitarist but I can't do comedy in English – never mind in Danish.

In Amsterdam in 2007 I visited a 'Bowie Fest', an all-day event held in a gloomy little city centre nightclub. I had been invited to attend the event by the lovely (although Bowie obsessed, obviously) people who both produced *The Voyeur* Bowie fanzine and ran the website for the Holland based International David Bowie Fan club, and so I had agreed to 'just call in for five minutes' in the afternoon before going on to my own solo gig in the evening at the wonderful De Harmonie café in Edam. De Harmonie is one of the best, most atmospheric little acoustic music venues that I have ever played in.

After being photographed with almost everyone who was there in the darkness of the Amsterdam nightclub afternoon, I ended up agreeing to do an impromptu half-hour solo spot for the Bowie fans, and by popular request my 'set' was destined to include quite terrible versions of two of the songs I had played with David in our Feathers days, namely 'Life is a Circus' and 'Love Song'. I know they were really terrible because they surfaced on YouTube the following day... I had not even thought about the danger of that possibility when I attempted to remember the old songs, and I fooled around on-stage even though I had faced a battery of mobile phones and camcorders. Okay call me old-fashioned, but I am still living and learning.

By the time that summer of 2009 came around, I had realised that I had probably done enough trips to Holland playing small venues, sleeping on floors and barely breaking even. It had been great fun, but the Dutch tours had been holidays really, just breaks from the reality of my day job. I had worked as a draughtsman on a 'Monday to Thursday night in crap digs' basis in London since leaving my last contract in Scotland in 2001, but I had also been away for several months, with very short home leave, on two different projects in Baku, Azerbaijan. I had seen enough B&Bs and hotel rooms, enough 'Dog Boxes' as they are known in the contractors' world – both at home and abroad – to last a lifetime.

I had made a few trips back to my old home town of Gothenburg, Sweden too, but the gigs I had played there, some solo and some with friends, had dwindled down to a couple of very small cafés. One of them, a great little café called KOM, turned out to have a 'pass-the-hat' arrangement at the end of the evening instead of an agreed fee, and that gig, although it was a lovely place to play, was probably where I realised that the old days were over, and that probably not too many people in Gothenburg would care if they never heard me play again. My musician friends in Sweden, Denmark and Holland were apparently all experiencing the same kind of apathy too; their own local live music support was gradually diminishing as the gigs were closing down. The times were changing, and good musicians were going to have to specialise and find their own niche market to perform in. Those with less talent could just form tribute bands and make money.

I had developed a particularly good musical rapport with Henrik Nagy, a great young guitar player from Gothenburg. 'Henke' is the nephew of my old mate Jan-Ake 'Lillen' Ahlkvist, the leader of The Apaches when I played with them in Sweden in the sixties, and Henke eventually came to England and we played a few gigs. Also I went back to Sweden where we played in a leafy Gothenburg park for their Blues Society, then the following evening we crossed the spectacular Oresund Bridge to Denmark and played a late-night dive in Copenhagen.

If ever Henke and I get around to setting up some gigs in Gothenburg again we will just give the local media the old 'ex-Apaches and ex-David Bowie veteran returns to Sweden' ultimate farewell tour story – a swansong perhaps. As I said, I have no shame.

In reality I had not, by the end of summer of 2009 spoken face to face with David Bowie since 1973 – amazingly thirty-six years had drifted by while real life went on. I had not spoken with David on the telephone either, since 2002, and although our email contact was still intact, it was always brief and often quite cryptic – as emails can be. I never thought about 'the old days' very much but the 'Bowie Stuff' is a part of my past and so it was and always will be a part of me. If I meet new people they eventually, inevitably, have to know about the 'Bowie Stuff', it's only natural.

There had been quite enough of my own stuff to be getting on with during 2009 mind you; I had folded up my contracting business, done final accounts and Susie and I had sold our house in York and bought a little cottage up in the Yorkshire Wolds. I believed that I might have found my place, the little place where every day would seem like a holiday. We were now in a quiet little village, I was going to have the old garage rebuilt and I would sort out the garden. I had finished with the oil business, I had no gigs in the diary and so far nobody in the village knew about my 'Bowie Stuff'.

It came as a surprise then, as you can imagine, when Kevin Cann phoned me to say that David had asked him to act as intermediary with me over the impending re-release of the 'David Bowie' album on the EMI label. The album would be a special edition for his fans and it was to have a 'disc 2' which would include two 'demos' recorded in the sixties by David and myself. The tracks were to be 'Space Oddity', a mix that I had never heard before, and 'An Occasional Dream', a song that I did remember well, because it

366

shows that David can 'really sing'. The track received a fair slice of Scott Walker vibrato style voice control from me too; as I tried my best to 'really sing' as David does naturally.

I have no idea how David Bowie came to have ownership of these tracks, but that business was none of my business, and so I agreed to sign a contract with David and with EMI for their release. I have the document with both our signatures, David's and mine – and signing it felt very remote, very cold, not how it should have been really.

The album has a sleeve that includes a great old Ken Pitt photo of David and me with guitars and my eldest son Christian – he was just one year old at the time – taken round at David's flat in Clareville Grove in November 1968. The CD sleeve, written by Kevin Cann, also has a paragraph which briefly but succinctly outlines my own contribution to David Bowie's output back in those days. Kevin's paragraph, together with David's instruction that 'We have to make sure that Hutch gets paid for this release' mean more to me than whatever the royalty payments might amount to.

Ever since that EMI re-release of the 'David Bowie' album in 2009 (the one where I sing on two bonus tracks) I had been absolutely sure that David would have been keeping himself busy in New York, and as ever he would be creative, though now it would be at his own pace. David had been keeping a very low profile, to such an extent that he might have appeared to have retired from the music business altogether, but my guess had always been that he would have a new album cooking, a new project in mind. An internet whisper even appeared to confirm my suspicion; it hinted that guitarist Robert Fripp was in the frame to play on the projected album. I believed that the project would be totally under David's control, no record label or manager would have any say in its content or progress, David would take his time and do it his way. In his shoes, that's what I would want to do.

I had been right. The new album 'The Next Day' was announced on 8th January 2013, David Bowie's sixty-sixth birthday (four days after my sixty-ninth), and then released on 8th March 2013 on his own label ISO Records under licence to Columbia Records. Robert Fripp had not taken any part after all, possibly because somebody had leaked the story of the secret recording sessions which had taken place sporadically over a two year period. David had as I predicted, worked at his own speed. The album caused quite a stir and it earned David his first number one album in the UK since 'Black Tie White Noise' in 1993.

A year or so later David Bowie was to create an even bigger stir when the success of this album earned him (for the second time in his career) the 'Top Male' award at the Brit Awards in London on February 19th 2014. It had been thirty years since David previously won the award, and at the age of 67 he gives us old boys hope eh?

In the spring of 2013, not long after his album release, a big 'David Bowie Is' exhibition opened at the Victoria and Albert Museum in London. It was apparently a collection of stage outfits and the like and I was not remotely interested. In any case nobody would have wanted me at the exhibition, even if there had been an 'old ex-guitarists sparkly stage suits' section.

I did though get another call from my old chum Tom Wilcox, saying that Mick's sister Maggie Ronson wanted to talk to me about taking part in a Mick Ronson Tribute that she was producing at the ICA in Pall Mall, London on Saturday 27th April 2013 – in fact it would be during the time of the Bowie V&A exhibition, but with no connection to it. Maggie called me and we chatted a couple of times, it sounded like a very interesting project and so I said thank you for asking me, and yes, as long as I had a train ticket and a hotel (no more driving north in the early hours) I would be there.

It was an enjoyable trip to the big city again. My cabbie kept me entertained with a story about Ronnie Wood (who had apparently been a previous fare that day) as we traversed the streets I used to know so well, and I was fascinated watching, like an out of town voyeur, the current lease holders of London going about their lives on the crowded West End streets. My hotel (it had faded somewhat since the days) turned out to be the one The Beatles and Brian Epstein used when they first came to London – so my taxi driver told me.

Maggie Ronson did a really wonderful production job on her brother's tribute evening, she is a talented lady and she surprised me with her own on-stage performance – I had known that she was a proper (trained) singer, but I had never heard her sing before. She had put together some wonderful musicians for her band, there were guests like my old mate Glen Matlock (he handed me a Vocalzone lozenge for my croaky voice, saying 'it's okay they ain't drugs mate') who talked about Mick and sang a bit, Ian Hunter's daughter Tracy who sang together with another rock chick who I recognised and was very nice though I never got her name. The finale of the show was particularly poignant; with a backdrop of clips and stills of Mick, they played his incredible instrumental version of 'Sweet Dreams of You'. That track shows perfectly what a wonderful player Mick Ronson was, and it made me remember what a good friend he had been to me during the Ziggy tours. The effect of the finale was to bring a tear to my eyes and I was choked for a good few minutes after the lights went up at the end.

My own part in the tribute was to perform one of my own songs and then Space Oddity as a duet with Mick's daughter Lisa Ronson who had come over from the USA for the event. Lisa was lovely, so much like Mick and very professional – we barely had time to run through the song together before we went on, but it went amazingly well and we went down a storm. We had taken a chance, blagged it and got away with it. I also met Lisa's mum again, the lovely Suzi

Ronson (formerly Suzi Fussey, David's 1973 wardrobe girl) and Mick's brother David Ronson for the first time.

I had somewhat foolishly said to Tom Wilcox that I didn't think coming all the way down to London to play just two songs was a great idea, so Tom arranged for me to play a little gig in the bar after the theatre show was finished. Of course that was my mistake, the little PA was rubbish, the ICA bar and foyer has a large echo, it is not a venue and I should not have done it. It was not all that bad though, as Bennie Marshall the singer and harmonica player from Mick's old Hull band The Rats joined me and we just played some blues together. Lisa and I casually reprised our 'Space Oddity' in the bar too, but best of all Geoff MacCormack turned up, sat right in front and watched the set!

I had not seen Geoff since the farewell party at the Café Royal in 1973 but it seemed like only yesterday. He still dresses immaculately and has not gained much weight, and as he said, we both still have our hair. We did not have much time, but it was great to see Geoff again, and we promised to stay in touch – as you do. Geoff told me that he would be seeing David Bowie in a week or two in New York, on Geoff's way back from a holiday in Cuba (these guys live in a different world, or planet even, to me) so I asked that he pass on my best wishes to David.

That's as close as I'll get these days I thought to myself and yet it seems to me that David and I are not out of touch altogether, and I really hope that our long-distance and very old friendship will survive my ramblings in this little book. I suppose that it is just remotely possible that David and I might yet manage to organise some sort of reunion one day. Our meeting, if there ever is to be one, will remain private. David, I promise.

I believe that David and I (just as with Geoff MacCormack and I) would find very little real difference in each other (okay I have put on a few pounds). David like me will have mellowed with age – we all do – and we will both certainly be looking back over our lives as he approaches (already entered in my case) the eighth decade. We may well I think be both enjoying life as older guys too, in fact David recently said, "I think the last ten years have slowly become the most rewarding period of my life," and that, "I like where I'm at and I'm very comfortable. I like being who I am, who I'm with and what I'm doing. I seem to have found equilibrium in my life." So these days David sounds just like me talking – doesn't he?

You might remember that during 'Ashes to Ashes' he 'Got a letter from the Action Man – I'm so happy, hope you're happy too'?? Well I think David was possibly talking about a poorly timed message from me at a stage in his life when he wasn't so happy. Am I the Action Man? – I could be – but only David knows.

It was way back in the sixties, when David was well into Buddhism, that he asked me, "Hutch, do you want a young death or an old death?" I think it must be a standard Buddhist question – anyway it appears that it will turn out to be the 'old' option, for both of us.

I well remember saying to David, during our last phone conversation in 2002, "You know David, apart from those who notice my guitar playing or like my songs, most people that I meet seem to find that the most interesting thing about me is you." David could not disagree, he knows how it is, and both of us know that it doesn't matter very much. Life is a Circus.

These days the seasons are important again, the winters in the Yorkshire Wolds are not always easy; we can be cut off in our village quite quickly when the snow drifts across the narrow access roads, and our little 4x4 has proved to be essential during two recent hard winters up here. Village life has suited me very well for the past few years, the small community welcomed us in from the start and I even became a Parish Councillor. I can only hope that my perspective as a well worn and well travelled outsider can be of some benefit to the village.

I have a continually evolving acoustic band of friends called The Sultans of Thwing who play the local country pubs, the occasional Gypsy Jazz jam in York and at a few Scarborough gigs like the Jazz Club with a repertoire of some of my own songs, some old blues and old standard jazz tunes that I play on a Cordoba Gitano 'grande-bouche' gypsy guitar or my favourite guitar, a little Taylor 412 acoustic.

My little band came together piece by piece after I offered to play an Acoustic Jam evening at the local pub. We put up posters advertising a Blues, Roots and Jazz Acoustic Jam and the Bridlington paper proclaimed that musicians could 'Jam with a Star' if they turned up. Some came along thinking that it was a pub talent show, some thought it an open mic opportunity, or a new folk club, or whatever. The result has been that we have a regular turnout of excellent players from the surrounding towns and villages, and from that pool of players I can put together several variations of line-up for The Sultans of Thwing (The Wolds' Most Famous Band) for the odd 'proper' gig.

Christopher Lea (from Transylvania) our bass player is like me an experienced pro-level player, and Gypsy Jon Horton the resonator slide and rhythm guitarist is an art teacher and wildlife painter from Kilham whose natural feel for music makes up for any lack of years on the road. Our 'players pool' also includes Spanish Paul, a retired music educator who plays gypsy jazz violin in the Grappelli style just as well as he plays the blues, Johnny (the jazz pistol) Watton and Dave Clarke-Fyffe the retired bus driver who plays great harmonica. Other talents up here in the middle of nowhere are Gary from Foxholes (the fastest picker in the east) and Sal Martinez and Dodgy Jim and Mick from Toronto and Brian the washboard player and – well you get the idea.

After spending most of a lifetime always wanting to be somewhere else, I sometimes feel that I might have found a place to grow old in. On other days I think I might easily move back to the city again and find some little bars to play jazz in – and within walking distance of home. I realise that old survivors like me and David Bowie can easily sound a little smug about slowing down and growing older, but believe me we both know that things can, and probably will, still change yet again in the blink of an eye. We have to be glad that we are still here and that we are still making some good music. We keep on dancing while we can.

I have no 'bucket list', my remaining ambition is simply to be the best jazz guitarist that I can be – and to have people notice and enjoy my playing. My daughter Hayley thinks I should make an album, and I think that if Bowie has just made his twenty-fourth studio album then perhaps it is time that Hutch made one – albeit his first and probably only one.

It is more than unlikely that David Bowie will call me up to play on his next album – there are just so many great guitar players available for David to choose from – and yet I still can dream.

The best, most workable plan is that David just calls me next time he is on this side of the Atlantic and we meet for a cup of coffee, even if I have to catch a train to London again to buy the coffees – and promise to keep the secret.

Can you hear me Major Tom?

Jazz Gypsy © Russell Watkins 2014

Acknowledgements

My thanks to Susan Hutchinson (no relation) of Lodge Books for her edit and for her time and patience.
To Susan's brother Andy Hutchinson for his enthusiasm in picking it up and putting it out.
To Marc Riley and Doctor Rock and to my daughter Hayley Forrest for her valuable help in finishing it off.
To my old friends Brian Cook, Hans Siden and Ray Stevenson, and to Masayoshi Sukita, Clive Arrowsmith and Russell Watkins for allowing me to use their fabulous photographs in this book. My respects to the families and friends of the late Brian Duffy and Leee Black Childers.

Some of the Bowie books I have interviewed for and read and consulted and enjoyed:

David Bowie: The Pitt Report by Kenneth Pitt
Published 1983 by Design Music Ltd. ISBN: 0 9508816 0 0

David Bowie: A Chronology by Kevin Cann
Published 1983 by Hutchinson Publishing Group ISBN: 0 09 153831 9

Alias David Bowie by Peter & Leni Gillman
Published 1986 by Hodder & Stoughton ISBN: 0 340 40290 3

Bowie: Loving the Alien by Christopher Sandford
Published 1996 by Little Brown and Company ISBN: 0 7515 1924 3

David Bowie: Living on the Brink by George Tremlett
Published 1997 by Arrow Books Limited ISBN: 0 09 995840 6

David Bowie: A Biography by Marc Spitz
Published 2009 by Aurum Press Limited ISBN: 978 1 84513 551 5

Starman: David Bowie by Paul Trynka
Published 2010 by Sphere (Little Brown and Co.) ISBN: 978 1 84744 238 3

David Bowie: Any Day Now – the London Years: 1947-1974 by Kevin Cann
Published 2010 by Adelita Ltd ISBN: 978 0 9552017 7 6

Index